Praise for *SOA for the Business Developer*

"Stands out from the crowd, complementing the 100+ books now available on SOA. The clarity of descriptions, the naming of pitfalls and how to deal with them, and finally its comprehensiveness make this book a great advisor for everybody involved in implementing SOA."
Norbert Bieberstein lead author of *Service-Oriented Architecture Compass*

"*SOA for the Business Developer* offers a comprehensive yet very approachable introduction to service-oriented architecture. Drawing from their considerable practical experience, the authors provide numerous examples that illustrate best practices in applying SOA to an enterprise. This book will help you untangle the technologies that underlie SOA — XML, WSDL, SOAP, XPath, BPEL, SCA, SDO, and WS splat — so that you can meaningfully begin your journey in the use of services."
Grady Booch, IBM Fellow and co-creator of the Unified Modeling Language

"Business and IT managers alike have been searching for a book that provides a straight-forward and easier-to-understand explanation of service-oriented architecture and its benefits. *SOA for the Business Developer* is such a book, and should be on the must-read list for every business and IT manager."
Bob Thomas, publisher of *Align Journal*

"Covers services and their recursive composition into more complex services at a profound technical level, incorporating all relevant WS-* standards in their most current form, including WS-BPEL 2.0 and SCA. A big plus of the book is that the authors worked with technical experts from the various domains, ensuring utmost consistency with the official standard specifications, and, even more important, ensuring consistency with the specifications' intents."
Matthias Kloppmann, IBM Distinguished Engineer, Business Process Technology

"SOA is ultimately supposed to simplify and improve how we construct IT solutions — the devil, of course, is in the details. And, at a time when those details are still being worked out by the IT industry, the challenge of understanding how they all fit together can be quite daunting. In this book, Ben Margolis does us all a great service by bringing together the many different technical threads that make up the complex fabric of SOA, and weaving them into a coherent pattern that ordinary mortals can hope to understand and, more importantly, practically apply to their own situations."
Michael Guttman, Object Management Group authority on Model Driven Architecture (MDA), co-author of *Real-Life MDA*

"*SOA for the Business Developer* gives programmers and managers a friendly and rapid introduction to service-oriented architecture, with practical examples."
Frank Cohen, author of *FastSOA*

T0191321

SOA for the
Business Developer

SOA

for the Business Developer

Concepts, BPEL, and SCA

Ben Margolis
with Joseph Sharpe

MC PRESS
MC Press Online, LP
Lewisville, TX 75077

SOA for the Business Developer: Concepts, BPEL, and SCA
Ben Margolis with Joseph Sharpe

First Edition

First Printing—April 2007

Every attempt has been made to provide correct information. However, the publisher and the author do not guarantee the accuracy of the book and do not assume responsibility for information included in or omitted from it.

The following are trademarks of International Business Machines Corporation in the United States, other countries, or both: DB2, Lotus, Tivoli, WebSphere, Rational, IBM, and the IBM logo. All other product names are trademarked or copyrighted by their respective manufacturers.

Java and all Java-based trademarks are trademarks of Sun Microsystems, Inc., in the United States, other countries, or both.

MC Press offers excellent discounts on this book when ordered in quantity for bulk purchases or special sales, which may include custom covers and content particular to your business, training goals, marketing focus, and branding interest.

For information regarding permissions or special orders, please contact:
    MC Press
    Corporate Offices
    125 N. Woodland Trail
    Lewisville, TX 75077 USA

For information regarding sales and/or customer service, please contact:
    MC Press
    P.O. Box 4300
    Big Sandy, TX 75755-4300 USA

ISBN: 1-58347-065-4

To my parents, who expected excellence.

Acknowledgements

Our thanks to the many people who worked on this book — in particular, to Ralph Earle, whose technical edits helped set the tone; to Bob Cancilla, whose extensive scenario gave a practical focus; and to Orly Margolis, whose illustrations and day-to-day assistance contributed much.

We thank these core experts by subject area:

- BPEL: Dieter Koenig, Simon D. Moser, and Thomas Schulze

- SCA: Michael Beisiegel, Daniel Berg, David Booz, Jean-Sebastien Delfino, Mike Edwards, Simon Nash, and Devang Parikh

- SDO: Stephen Brodsky, Frank Budinsky, Brent H. Daniel, Kelvin Goodson, Fuhwei Lwo, Shawn Moe, Daniel Murphy, Edward Slattery, Kevin Williams, and Geoffrey Winn

- Web services: Daniel R. Bruce, Russell Butek, Christopher B. Ferris, Heiko Ludwig, Marcia L. Stockton, Andre Tost, and Greg Truty

- XML and XPath: Anders Berglund, Scott Boag, David Marston, and Henry Zongaro

Tim W. Wilson's insight into computer languages accounts for the book's deep foray into BPEL 2.0, Jeri Petersen's reviews were thorough as ever, and Hayden Lindsey's support and guidance were essential. Special thanks go to Susan LaFera, with a smile for Valentin Baciu, Grady Booch, Mike J. Brown, Wendy Butt, Jim Colson, Francisco Curbera, Leigh Davidson, Klaus Deinhart, Steve Graham, Matt Heitz, Sridhar Iyengar, Sam Kaipa, Rania Khalaf, Stephen J. Kinder, Henry Koch, Grant J. Larsen, Matthew Oberlin, Bob Schloss, Robert Will, Tara Woodman, and Jim Zhang; and for the folks at MC Press, especially copyeditor Katie Tipton.

Contents

Preface

Service-oriented architecture (SOA) is a way of organizing software. If your company's development projects adhere to the principles of SOA, the outcome is an inventory of modular units called *services*, which allow for a quick response to change.

That's it, more or less. So why read the book?

We tell the story as simply as possible to keep you from the heartbreak of *MEGO* (*My Eyes Glaze Over*). We assume that you have an elementary knowledge of software, but we give you a fast explanation of any phrase that might leave you uncertain. At the same time, we offer examples and illustrations, giving a practical meaning to abstract ideas.

The book can make you feel comfortable as you start to work with service-oriented products, but there's more. The level of detail will enable you to get the most out of technical articles and even to explore the publicly available specifications that describe the technology in depth.

Clarity and Imagination

In November 2006, the magazine *Network Computing* published a survey of its readers and found that *SOA* is the "technology buzzword they most despise." Respondents said that their primary concerns were threefold: a lack of familiarity ("What does that stand for again?"); a sense of being overwhelmed (SOA "gives me a headache"); and a perception that the technology "is useful but still too complex and expensive." We personally know of software professionals who dismiss the excitement about services. The perception of some people is that SOA is a marketing ploy or is, at most, a small variation on older technologies.

In truth, SOA includes ideas that have been around for decades. Information hiding, for example, has long meant that a developer can access an existing unit of logic without needing to learn details that are internal to that logic. Even developers in the 1960s wrote modular code, adding building blocks to an inventory of software.

Our reading, however, is that SOA is both genuine and a genuine advance, bringing the older ideas into the world of networked computers. Even if some people are dismissive or choose to wait for tools that simplify service development at less initial expense, we believe that the needs of business will force the adoption of the newer technology. The way of the future is to deploy accessible and more-or-less independent services on varied platforms.

Two characteristics can hasten the transition to SOA. The first is clarity. This book offers technical detail not only because developers need it to fulfill their jobs but because non-developers can interpret situations better if they understand how the technology works.

A second desired characteristic is imagination. Any company can fulfill the promise of the technology to a degree; but the fulfillment is greatest if at least some developers extend their expertise from programming to the details of what the business does and then to the details of what the business might do in the future. To provide insight into the kind of imagination required, this book offers a business scenario.

A Note to the General Reader

We'd like to address the reader who is stretching to understand software of any kind.

We hear a whisper from behind us. "Please! You can't expect someone who lacks a background in software to understand the details of SOA!" The objection is duly noted, and now we have a story to tell.

We gave an early copy of this book to a professor of neuroscience, a man whose work clarifies how multiple genes affect brain function. After reading and pondering, the man asked, "What do you mean by 'run time'?" He spoke with us and soon came to his own conclusion: "Run time is the duration during which a unit of software (for example, an email program) is available for use."

We want to encourage readers who are unfamiliar with even the most basic concepts of software. SOA is not neuroscience. You can pick up a lot of the fundamentals quickly, and this book (with a little research) can introduce you to an important if hidden aspect of modern business.

Let's turn now to the specific technologies covered.

Technologies

SOA relies on one of the unifying ideas in modern data processing: *Extensible Markup Language (XML)*, a set of widely accepted rules for organizing data in a text format. We provide an overview of XML and include details that will deepen your understanding of the following technologies, all covered in this book:

- *Web Services Description Language (WSDL):* WSDL is an XML-based format for describing how to access a *Web service*, which is a service that itself uses XML for data exchange. Increasingly, WSDL is used to describe services of any kind.

- *SOAP* (which stands for . . . SOAP, though it was once called Simple Object Access Protocol): SOAP is the most widely used format for transmitting data to and from a Web service.

- *XML Path Language (XPath):* XPath is a language used to derive data from XML source such as SOAP data. The language is useful for working with a variety of technologies, including several described in this book. We offer a tutorial introduction. The material is probably sufficient for your work in XPath 1.0 and is intended to make your investigation of XPath 2.0 far easier.

- *Business Process Execution Language (BPEL):* BPEL 2.0 is a language that coordinates services and whose preceding version is already in numerous products. We give you a comprehensive description of BPEL 2.0, including a quick-reference guide.

- *Service Component Architecture (SCA):* SCA is a proposed standard for composing and deploying SOA software that can include but is not limited to Web services. SCA is slated to become the basis of commercial products from several vendors in 2007.

- *Service Data Objects (SDO):* SDO is a proposed standard for representing data in a single way, even if the data comes from different types of data sources. SDO is likely to accompany SCA into the limelight.

- *WS-*:* This abbreviation (sometimes called *WS splat*) refers to a group of Web-services specifications being developed to handle runtime quality-of-service issues such as reliability (is the transmitted data guaranteed to arrive?); security (will the data be protected from unauthorized viewing and change?); and transaction control (will the data be saved only after a business interaction is complete?). We give a brief and clear description of more than a dozen of these specifications.

CHAPTER 1

Introduction

Service-Oriented Architecture (SOA) is a way of organizing software so that companies can respond quickly to the changing requirements of the market-place. The technology is based on *services*, which are customized units of software that run in a network.

A service

- handles a business process such as calculating an insurance quote or distributing email, or handles a relatively technical task such as accessing a database, or provides business data and the technical details needed to construct a graphical interface

- can access another service and, with the appropriate runtime technology, can access a traditional program and respond to different kinds of requesters — for example, to Web applications

- is relatively independent of other software so that changes to a requester require few or no changes to the service, while changes to the internal logic of a service require few or no changes to the requester

The relative independence of the service and other software is called *loose coupling*. The flexibility offered by loose coupling protects your company from excessive costs when business or technical requirements change.

A service can handle interactions within your company, as well as between your company and its suppliers, partners, and customers. The location of service requesters can extend worldwide, depending on security issues and on the runtime software used to access a particular service.

In most cases, the requesting code has no details on the service location. Like the requester, the service can be almost anywhere. The location is set when the service is deployed. At run time, a requester or network may be able to redirect a request to a service at a different location.

SOA implies a style of development, with concern for the business as a whole and with an increased focus on modularity and reuse. SOA isn't only for new code, though. Migration of existing applications is especially appropriate in the following cases:

- The applications are monolithic, combining the logic of user interface, business processing, and data access, with update of one kind of logic requiring your company to test multiple kinds of behavior.

- The applications are hard to understand — first, because the logic is monolithic, but second, because logic was repeatedly patched rather than rewritten as requirements changed. Updates take extra time as developers try to decipher the logic, and as the complexity grows, additional errors accompany updates.

- The application inventory has duplicate logic. Requests for change are unnecessarily disruptive, requiring changes in several places.

From the point of view of a business developer, a change to SOA is a change in emphasis, and many aspects of the job are unaffected. Consider the task of function invocation, for example. When you invoke a function, you aren't concerned with the internal logic of the invoked code or with how the function receives arguments or returns a value. Similarly, when you code a service request, you care only about the syntax for requesting the service. At best, service requests are as easy as function invocations.

Open Standards

In many industries, companies adhere to standards that allow for greater prosperity than would be possible if each company followed its own proprietary rules. Standards in housing construction, for example, ensure that manufacturers of pipes can benefit from economies of scale in pursuit of a larger market than would be available in the absence of industry-wide standards.

The primary benefit of SOA standards is that they make services *interoperable*, which means that services can communicate with one another, even if each implementation is written in a different computer language or is accessed by way of a different *transport protocol* (software that oversees the runtime transmission of data).

Standards also ensure that an SOA runtime product can support Quality of Service features, as described in Chapter 2.

SOA standards are *open* in the sense that any software manufacturer has the right to use those standards when developing an SOA-related product. In addition, the process of creating and revising the standards is based on a political process that is more or less democratic. Any interested party has the right to participate in all meetings that lead to decisions about a standard.

Each company that works on an open standard seeks a text that matches the company's marketplace strengths. The competition among those companies is one reason for the long delay in making a standard final.

Several major organizations oversee development of open standards for SOA:

- Open Grid Forum (*http://www.ogf.org*)
- Organization for the Advancement of Structured Information Standards (OASIS; *http://www.oasis-open.org*)
- Web Services Interoperability Organization (WS-I; *http://www.ws-i.org*)
- World Wide Web Consortium (W3C; *http://www.w3.org*)

Later chapters give you practical insight into standards that are in effect or under consideration, and Appendix A describes several others.

Open standards are distinct from *open source*, which is source code that you can learn from and use in your own projects, with certain legal restrictions. Open-source implementations of Service Component Architecture (SCA) and Service

Data Objects (SDO), for example, are being developed in the Tuscany incubator project of the Apache Software Foundation. For details and code, see the following Web sites: *http://incubator.apache.org/tuscany* and *http://www.apache.org*.

Structure of a Service-Oriented Application

A *service-oriented application* is an application composed largely of services. Often, the invoked services are in a hierarchy, as Figure 1.1 illustrates.

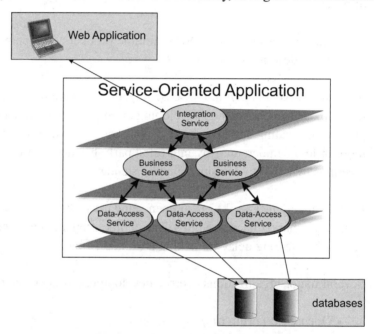

Figure 1.1: Service-oriented application

The topmost level contains one or more *integration services*, each of which controls a flow of activities such as processing an applicant's request for insurance coverage. Each integration service invokes one or more business services.

The second level is composed of services that each fulfill a relatively low-level business task. For example, an integration service might invoke such *business services* to verify the details provided by an insurance-policy applicant. If the business services return values that are judged to mean "issue a policy," the integration service invokes yet another business service, which calculates a quote and returns the quote to the software (for example, a Web application) that invoked the service-oriented application.

The third level consists of *data-access services*, each of which handles the relatively technical task of reading from and writing to data-storage areas such as databases and message queues. A data-access service is most often invoked from the business layer.

Great complexity is possible. Some integration services, for example, provide different operations to different requesters, and some invoke other integration services and are said to be *composed* of those services. Many applications, however, fulfill the three-level model described here.

Web and Binary-Exchange Services

This book also classifies services by the format of the data exchanged between a service and its requesters. A *Web service* exchanges data in a format based on Extensible Markup Language (XML). The W3C Web site suggests that the use of XML for data transfer is the only defining characteristic of a Web service. In many cases, the following description also applies:

- Details on the data are described in Web Services Description Language (WSDL).

- The format of the transmitted data is Simple Object Access Protocol (SOAP).

- The transport protocol is Hypertext Transfer Protocol (HTTP), the primary mechanism for exchanging program data over the Internet or a corporate intranet.

In contrast to a Web service, a *binary-exchange service* exchanges data in a format associated with a particular computer language or a specific vendor. Although a service written with Enterprise Generation Language (EGL) can be deployed as a Web service, for example, the logic also can be deployed as a service that exchanges binary data.

The use of binary-exchange services provides several benefits:

- allows a faster runtime response than is possible with Web services

- avoids the need to maintain WSDL definitions and related files

- avoids the need to learn the Web-service technologies

The cost, however, is reduced accessibility. A binary-exchange service is directly accessible only to software that transmits data in the binary format expected by the service.

Business Implications

SOA has several important implications for business. First, to the extent that loose coupling is in effect, changes made to the service logic won't force significant changes to requesters of that software. When each component is a relatively stand-alone unit, your company can respond to business or technological changes more quickly and with less expense and confusion. At best, a service can even be re-deployed to another machine without changing logic or recompiling the code. A further implication is that your company can develop services for different platforms and with different implementation languages, letting the organization use the best available technologies.

In general, a company's ability to respond quickly and well to change is known as *agility*. The main promise of service-oriented architecture is that a well-crafted SOA will increase agility over time.

SOA also has an important effect on how people work together. Aside from the most technical services, a well-written service is *coarse-grained*, meaning that the area of concern is broad enough so business people can understand the purpose of the service even if they know little about software. To the extent that a collection of coarse-grained services handles your company's business procedures, the firm's business analysts and software professionals can share information knowledgeably, can include end users in early deliberations about the purpose and scope of each service, and can understand all the implications of changing a business procedure. Ease of human communication is an important benefit of SOA and suggests that the architecture will become the primary organizing principle for business processing.

Last, well-designed services are more likely to be reusable. Your company benefits from reuse in at least two ways: first, by avoiding the expense of developing new software, and second, by increasing the reliability of the software inventory over time. The firm can do less extensive testing if an existing service is placed in a new application, in comparison to the testing required to deploy software that was written from scratch.

Criteria for SOA Implementation

A company is most likely to develop an SOA if the firm anticipates substantial change, has problems with existing applications or application access, and is willing to make the initial investment in analysis and planning.

A company is most likely to embrace an SOA based on Web services if it wants its software to be accessed by partners and customers — specifically, partners and customers that lack the binary-exchange solutions the company might otherwise favor. A Web service implementation is also the approach of choice for companies that want to depend less on particular software vendors.

Migration of Existing Applications

A company can develop an SOA to increase the rationality of its existing applications. A migration can be costly, though, in part because the design team must complete an analysis that reflects a concern for the business as a whole. A business-wide focus means that the team is better able to isolate services for use in multiple applications, including applications that are likely to arise in response to future requirements. The need is for knowledge and vision, so that interaction with business people can reduce the amount of duplicate logic in a company's software and can increase the ease of future updates.

Although planning for service development is essential, the actual development can occur in stages, with the cost of work spread over time and over several projects. As a start, a company might convert code that has strategic value, is accessed by different systems, or is likely to change in any case.

An incremental migration lets the company learn from experience. Decision-makers may begin a migration to an SOA that's based on Web services, for example, and then turn to a binary-exchange solution. The company is likely to benefit from whatever design was accomplished in the initial phase. It can even benefit from completed Web services because in most cases, code that depends on binary-exchange technology can access Web services.

Reasons to Reject Web Services

A company may require that its software respond more quickly than is possible with Web services. In this case, the company can use a binary-exchange technology and still gain the benefits of SOA. For example, if COBOL programs access one another, a firm may want to avoid the runtime overhead that comes from converting data into XML and back to native COBOL.

Similarly, if a subsystem requires hardware or software from specific vendors, a company may consider using binary-exchange services that continue the firm's reliance on these vendors. A cost of this strategy is that the company is vulnerable to the vendors' pricing and customer response.

Last, a company may avoid developing Web or binary-exchange services to replace software that isn't expected to require a lot of change. This consideration applies when applications have fulfilled their mission for years and an appropriate statement is, "If it ain't broke, don't fix it."

Presentation Services

An important variation on the themes addressed in this book is the *presentation service*, which provides business data along with a stream of technical detail for constructing a graphical interface. The interface in turn lets the user interact with the data and access remote services and other software.

Different kinds of presentation services are in use. Although a comprehensive review is outside our scope, let us introduce a kind of presentation service that is widely used.

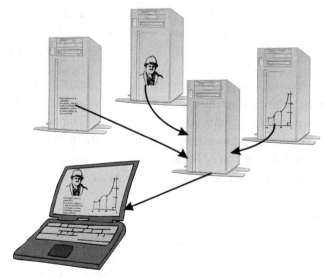

Figure 1.2: Portal technology

As Figure 1.2 illustrates, a *portal* is software that resides on a server and coordinates different interfaces, each affecting a different area of a Web page. From the perspective of a user, the output of a portal can provide a variety of news, business interaction, and entertainment, although an employee who accesses a company's internal portal is working primarily with applications that support the company's business.

Each application is controlled by a *portlet*, which is a unit of software that contributes sections of markup language such as Hypertext Markup Language (HTML). The portal collects those sections and submits them to devices such as Web browsers and personal digital assistants.

Portal technology empowers the user, who can select a subset of applications and may be able to customize the runtime behavior of individual portlets. Portals can even retain user preferences so that the experience is individualized as soon as a user logs on.

Traditionally, the portlets resided on the same server as the portal. In a natural extension of the technology, the portal requests data from a set of remote portlets, each of which acts as a presentation service. The standard that guides the interaction between portals and remote portlets is Web Services for Remote Portlets, as referenced in Appendix A.

SOA Runtime Products

Software vendors are now creating SOA runtime products that oversee a network of services. The general direction of that work is to allow a programmer, business analyst, or network coordinator to change product-configuration settings that affect (for example) the following issues:

- how security is handled
- which of several identical services at different locations is accessed by a requester
- whether a set of services is invoked in response to a requester's invocation of a single service
- what log information is collected

An SOA runtime product might allow the configuration of *intermediaries*, which are processing centers that do administrative or technical tasks during the transmission of data between a requester and a service. An intermediary might reroute messages in response to network traffic or business priorities; might reformat messages because the requester uses a transport protocol different from the one used by the service; or might provide security — for example, by authenticating requesters or by shielding the service from a flood of messages.

In the future, a subset of runtime products will incorporate guidelines from Service Component Architecture, an emerging open standard that permits flexibility at development, configuration, and run time.

CHAPTER 2

Services

In this chapter we continue our SOA overview with a focus on services. A service includes the following aspects:

- a service implementation
- elementary access details
- a contract

A *service implementation* is the core business logic, which might be written in Java, COBOL, Enterprise Generation Language (EGL), or any other programming language.

Elementary access details include the *location*, which is an address where the service implementation resides, and the *binding*, which identifies the transport protocol (such as HTTP or Java Message Service) that formats a message at the start of transmission and unformats it at the end of transmission. Formatting occurs when the invocation message originates at the requester; in that case, unformatting occurs when the message arrives at the service location. Formatting also occurs if the service issues a response; in that case, unformatting occurs when the response arrives at the requester.

A *contract* describes the service's intended behavior and is independent of the implementation details. The contract includes two elements: a service interface and a Quality of Service.

The service interface provides a description of the data that can pass between a requester and a service, along with details on each operation the service provides. The interface includes information on the messages and answers the questions, "What is the format of a message (for example, two strings followed by an integer)?" and "What are the restrictions on content?" The interface also includes details on the message exchange patterns, which indicate how the requester and service interact. "Does the service always respond to the requester?" "Can the service do a task without reporting back?"

Some aspects of the service's behavior are implicit in the service interface. For example, a service might provide a stock quote but return an error message if the submitted stock symbol is invalid.

An interface is an aspect not only of a service but also of a high-level design for the service. The interface precedes the implementation in most cases, and the service implementation (or sometimes the service as a whole) is said to *implement* the interface.

The service's *Quality of Service (QoS)* is a description of interaction rules that go beyond those implied by either the elementary access details or the service interface. For example, the service might require that the invocation message include authorization details that prove the user's right to use the service. You'll learn more about QoS later in the chapter.

One note about the service contract: Rather than "contract," we could have used the phrase "proposed contract" because a requester and service may undertake a negotiation, possibly at run time, to determine certain details of the interaction. We expect this kind of negotiation to become more prevalent as time goes by. For further details, see the description of the WS-Agreement specification in Appendix A.

Last, the terms "service" and "service implementation" are often used interchangeably. The second term is most appropriate when the focus is on the details of the business logic.

Loose Coupling

As you learned in Chapter 1, an important characteristic of an SOA is *loose coupling*, which means that one unit of software is largely independent of another. This independence implies that changes to one unit of software cause less turmoil and cost to an organization than when the software is more interdependent. It also means you can substitute one unit of software for an already-deployed unit relatively easily. The value of loose coupling is greatest when technical changes are expected over time.

The following questions identify some of the ways in which a service might be loosely coupled with other software.

How easily can the logic inside a service be revised without changing how the service is invoked?

The logic and programming language of a service implementation should be independent of the service contract. You can change the service internals for greater efficiency without changing the requester in any way.

How protected is the requester from disruption in the face of increased service capabilities?

An SOA runtime product may support either of two kinds of service interface:

- *Remote procedure call (RPC):* In this case, the requester submits a set of arguments to a particular service operation as if invoking a local function. The service uses each argument as a discrete unit in accordance with the meaning and type of the related parameter.

- *Document:* In this case, the requester submits a string of arbitrary length, and the service reviews that string to determine what operations to perform.

The RPC and Document categories overlap, as when an RPC invocation submits a single string to a service that in turn dispatches the message to one of several subroutines. The point, however, is that if the contract between requester and service features a long string (rather than a set of typed arguments) and if a later version of the service adds new functionality, the service interface is unaffected.

Requester updates (as needed to use the new service functionality) are likely to be needed only over time rather than in urgent response to a change in the service.

How easily can a service be incorporated into a larger process without changing the service implementation?

A change to a runtime security mechanism, for example, shouldn't require the code for a service to be rewritten or recompiled. The looseness of coupling in this case may depend on the power of an SOA runtime product because that product allows more decisions to occur at configuration time.

To what extent is a requester dependent on service availability?

If an SOA runtime product maintains message queues on each side of a remote transmission, the product can guarantee message delivery between requester and service, in which case network failures will tend to have less of an effect. The benefit is greatest if the requester isn't waiting for a response.

Can the requester continue running in the absence of a response?

If the requester can invoke a service and continue running, the requester is less dependent on service availability.

Is the service dependent on state information?

A specific requester might invoke the same service repeatedly to fulfill a single task (to update a checking account, for example), and the service might need to retain *state information* (such as a checking-account number) between each invocation. In general, state information is the set of values that are needed for the service to maintain a conversation with a specific requester.

If a service needs to retain state information, the SOA runtime product won't be able to direct processing to an identical service at a second location, as might be necessary in response to network traffic. If the SOA runtime product can redirect the state information as well, the restriction does not apply.

Service Registry

A requester must be able to reference a service's access and proposed contract details, which are often available in an online registry. Such a registry often conforms to the rules of Universal Description, Discovery, and Integration (UDDI), as described in Chapter 5.

A company can create its own registry for internal use and can create additional public registries, often in concert with other companies in the same industry. In addition, the company SAP AG operates a public UDDI registry.

In theory, the requester can retrieve the registered information at run time; however, this kind of programmatic retrieval is rare in practice. In most cases, the registered information is retrieved earlier. The registered information may be available to the requester at development time, as reflected in the requester's code or in the requester's call to a library that contains the details. The library may be written either before or after the requester is developed.

Alternatively, the registered information may be available to a network administrator or other professional who configures and then deploys the requester. This availability gives an organization greater flexibility because the selection of a service can occur relatively late.

Chapter 9 describes configuration-time opportunities that are available when you're working with Service Component Architecture.

Service Level Agreements

A *Service Level Agreement (SLA)* is a document that gives human readers the information necessary to decide how and whether to invoke a particular service from other software. The presence and use of an SLA varies by SOA vendor and corporate user. If present, the SLA

- includes elementary-access and proposed-contract details in most cases

- may be written by software designers to help negotiate what functionality is to be included in a given service

- may communicate plans to potential service users and other interested parties

- may be the basis of a legal document that indicates what level of reliability the service offers (for example, how many hours per week the service is available)

- may be used as an input to an automated process that creates invocation details for use when developing a requester

Message Exchange Patterns

A service supports one or more *message exchange patterns (MEPs)*, or kinds of interaction between requester and service. At this writing, only two elementary MEPs are widely used.

Figure 2.1: One-way pattern

Figure 2.1 depicts a *one-way* pattern (sometimes called *in-only* or *fire-and-forget*), in which the requester invokes the service with a request (an input message) but does not receive a response.

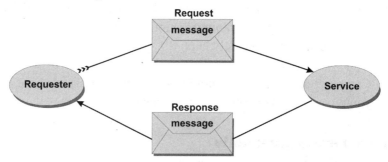

Figure 2.2: Request-response pattern

Figure 2.2 depicts a *request-response* pattern (sometimes called *in-out*), in which the requester invokes the service with a request and receives a response.

Two other elementary MEPs are uncommon but will be supported over time.

Figure 2.3: Notification pattern

In a *notification* pattern (sometimes called *out-only*), the service submits a message in the absence of an ongoing conversation, as when a service sends news to a subscriber. Figure 2.3 illustrates this pattern.

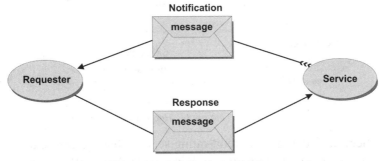

Figure 2.4: Solicit-response pattern

Figure 2.4 depicts a *solicit-response* pattern (sometimes called *out-in*), in which the service submits a notification to a requester and receives a response.

The following advanced features are available for the first two MEPs and will be available for the others in the future:

- A message in the returning direction can be optional.

- A service or requester can submit a *fault message*, which is data sent in response to a runtime error.

Synchronous and Asynchronous Communication

The request-response pattern and the solicit-response pattern represent *synchronous* communication, which means that the initiator of the message suspends processing until the initiator receives a response. In contrast, the one-way and notification patterns represent *asynchronous* communication, which means that the initiator of the message continues running the next coded statement, without suspending processing.

Callbacks

Assume that Service01 invokes Service02. To complete the interaction, Service02 may issue a *callback*, which is an invocation of an operation that can be provided by Service01. The invoked operation is called a *callback operation*, as shown in Figure 2.5.

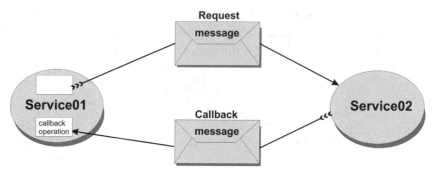

Figure 2.5: Request and callback

Service02 could be a credit-rating service that can respond to a request for customer details only after an hour, while Service01 is a service that requests credit details. Service01 shouldn't wait for the details, because the wait would use memory and other resources. Instead, the overall business process can ensure that Service02 invokes a callback operation in Service01.

A callback doesn't necessarily involve asynchronous processing, although the two ideas often come together. Consider the following variations:

- Service01 requests a credit report and receives a confirmation of the request, then waits for the report as before.

- Service01 allows Service02 to issue synchronous callbacks that request additional details.

From a business point of view, a callback operation is like any other. Service01 can have multiple operations, and the callback operations in Service01 are those invoked by services that previously received requests from Service01.

Quality of Service

A service interface defines the interaction between a service and a requester in a narrow sense, but the interaction can have many additional characteristics. In some contexts, Quality of Service refers only to reliability guarantees, such as the percentage of time a service is promised to be available. In our view, however, QoS refers to all runtime processing aspects that go beyond the service interface.

QoS also includes advanced aspects of runtime processing:

- reliability guarantees
- security mechanisms
- service coordination, including transaction control
- runtime update of address, binding, and message content

A particular service may be offered with different QoS characteristics, as when a company charges a different fee in exchange for a different level of reliability.

In describing the QoS issues, we hope to give you a sense of the flexibility and power of an advanced SOA runtime product.

Reliability Guarantees

Reliability guarantees may be described in a Service Level Agreement. The guarantees can be affected by the quality of the network hardware, and most are quantitative. For example:

- During what percentage of time will the service be available, or during what hours?
- What is the expected *throughput* — the number of messages to which the service will respond in a given duration?
- What is the expected *latency period* — the waiting time between a service request and response?
- What is the probability of a successful response within the latency period?
- Is message receipt assured, even if the network fails?

Security Mechanisms

Security mechanisms are often affected by features of the SOA runtime:

- *Authentication:* How does the SOA runtime ensure that a message is from a specified requester?

- *Authorization:* How does the SOA runtime ensure that a specified requester is allowed to access a specified service?

- *Confidentiality:* How does the SOA runtime ensure that the content of a message isn't viewed during transmission?

- *Integrity:* How does the SOA runtime verify that a given message was unchanged during transmission and was delivered with all data in the appropriate order?

- *Non-repudiation:* How does the SOA runtime verify the integrity of a given message and ensure that the message came from the specified requester? Non-repudiation proves (for example) that a party to a transaction made a promise, as in an online purchase.

- *Protection from denial-of-service attacks:* How does the SOA runtime prevent a flood of messages from reaching a given service?

Service Coordination

Service coordination concerns how services work together to fulfill a business process. Coordination takes one of two forms: orchestration or choreography.

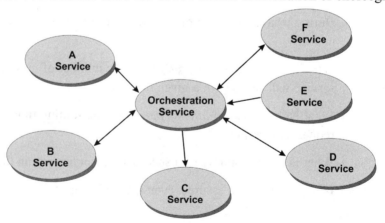

Figure 2.6: Orchestration

As Figure 2.6 illustrates, *orchestration* refers to a form of processing in which one service acts as a controlling hub in relation to other services, which act as spokes. The hub might receive a message from one spoke and make decisions based on that message, as by changing the format or content of the data and invoking some other spoke.

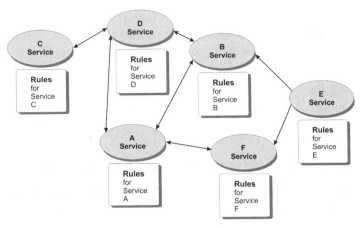

Figure 2.7: Choreography

As Figure 2.7 shows, *choreography* refers to a more decentralized form of processing, where multiple services interact without submitting messages to a hub. This sort of processing is based on rules known to each service and may be enabled by establishing a local configuration file for each service.

Often, orchestration is said to coordinate services in the same company, while choreography is said to guide the interactions of trading partners. Usage of the terms is inconsistent, and some analysts employ them interchangeably.

An important subset of service coordination is transaction control, which primarily concerns how services handle the update of databases. In general, a service may *commit* changes (ensuring that changes are permanent) or *rollback* changes (returning the database to a previous level of update). Among the QoS issues:

- Is the service allowed to revise database changes that were made (but not committed) by the requester and possibly by other services?

- Is the service prohibited from issuing a commit or rollback? A prohibition is likely if the requester is responsible for committing changes made by the service.

- Does the service depend on a *compensating service?* A compensating service is one that will be invoked only if necessary to make up for a runtime change (in this case, a database change) that is later found to be undesirable. As invoked by a coordinating service, for example, Service01 commits a database change (to indicate that a purchase was completed); days later, the coordinating service receives a cancellation and invokes a compensating service to reverse the effect of the committed change.

Last, the term *coordination* sometimes refers specifically to a kind of orchestration that is detailed in the WS-Coordination specification, as described in Appendix A.

Runtime Update of Message Content or Destination

Some QoS issues are especially meaningful in the context of a network that handles a variety of services, computer types, and data-traffic patterns. Among the issues:

- Can the flow of traffic be changed at run time? The change usually has one of two purposes: to provide faster access to higher-priority services or to equally distribute the data being directed to services that provide the same functionality but reside at different locations.

    The process of altering data traffic to conform more closely to a performance ideal is called *load balancing*. This process might occur in response to a configuration setting or to an operator's intervention.

- Can a message be reformatted at run time — for example, to allow transmission to a computer that uses a different transport protocol? If so, a configuration setting may be involved.

- Can a service be configured to send messages to a destination other than the requester — for example, to print a runtime error or to invoke an additional service in some cases but not others? If so, either a configuration setting or details in the message itself can cause the change.

Endpoints, State, and Correlation

The language of SOA is a bit messy, with the same terms having different meanings in different contexts and in different minds. This section tells the relatively absolute truth.

An *endpoint* is a location: the addressing details that are necessary and sufficient to access or provide a service at run time. If service A is on both machine 1 and machine 2, you can speak of two endpoints, and in this case, endpoint is synonymous with service location.

The endpoint is a step removed from the implementation. The operating system

- receives inbound data at the endpoint and presents that data to the implementation code. The implementation is said to be *listening* at the endpoint.

- accepts outbound data at the endpoint and transmits that data to a service at another endpoint.

From the point of view of a network administrator, a *service instance* is an implementation that is listening at a particular endpoint. If service A is on machines 1 and 2, two service instances are available. When a request arrives at run time, the service instance dispatches the request to a *thread of execution*, which is an operating-system facility that runs the service. If two requests arrive at the same time, each request is given its own thread.

Most services (specifically, most service implementations) are *stateless*, which means that the runtime code never relies on data from a previous invocation. A stock-quote service, for example, receives a trading symbol and returns a quote, and the data used in one invocation is independent of the data used in the next.

A *stateful* service, in contrast, sometimes needs access to values that were assigned in a previous invocation of the same or another service. The need arises because the service participates in a multi-step *conversation*, which is a sequence of invocations that constitute a relationship between the service and a requester.

In the usual situation, a requester's invocation initiates the conversation, and subsequent requests from the same requester are valid only if they arrive in a specific sequence. The service has a technology-specific way to ensure that each request is directed to the appropriate conversation rather than to a conversation occurring at the same time between the service and a different requester.

A conversation can be based on a persistent connection, but two other options are far more likely, especially in services that run for days or months. In one option, an SOA runtime product uses the input message or a system value to direct the message to the appropriate conversation. In a second option, the service implementation itself uses the input message. In either case, *state* is a processing status — the sequential position of the last received message in the sequence of messages that are expected on the service's side of the conversation.

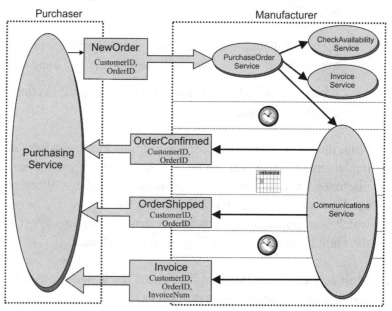

Figure 2.8: Conversation over time

Figure 2.8 illustrates a service conversation over time. As shown, a purchasing service establishes a conversation with a manufacturing service and expects a sequence of messages (confirmed, shipped, invoiced) for a specific order. When the endpoint of the purchasing service receives the confirmed message, for example, the service implementation ensures that

- the message applies to the appropriate conversation
- the state of the purchasing service changes so that at the next receipt of data from the requester, only a shipped message is considered valid

When a business analyst talks about "directing a message to the correct service instance," the meaning is really to direct a message to the appropriate conversation. We'll accept this point of view, using the term *service instance* (or *process instance*) to mean the runtime logic that handles a conversation with a specific requester.

To ensure that a message is directed appropriately, you often need to include specific IDs in the message — for example, a customer ID, an order ID, an invoice number, or some combination of identifiers. Those identifiers also *correlate* the processing done by the instance of one service (for example, the service that sends a purchase order) with the processing done by instances of other services (to confirm an order, send a shipment notification, and so on).

We say more about correlation in the chapters on Business Processing Execution Language (BPEL).

Highlight Insurance

To illustrate an SOA implementation from a business point of view, this chapter introduces Highlight Insurance, Inc., a fictitious enterprise that sells car insurance. We review the company's concerns, along with the changes that will be needed to support the company's expansion. We then consider how to design software whose structure reflects the business process.

We talk only about sales, not about the insurance claims that follow accidents and hail storms. From the customer's point of view, a sales interaction with the company has two main steps.

First, the customer submits a *quote request*, providing data that the company uses to determine whether to issue a *quote* (a price for a given policy, for a given customer). If the company decides to issue a quote, the two parties may interact repeatedly to find a suitable combination of price and coverage.

In the second step, the customer submits a *policy request*, furnishing the data needed to ask for the coverage specified in an earlier quote. The policy request includes a deposit, and on receipt of that fee, Highlight uses industry sources to determine the customer's credit worthiness and to verify details that were provided by the customer. Those details include, for example, the traffic-violation history of each driver on the requested policy.

An industry-standard phrase for a quote request is *insurance application*, but in this book, we use the word *application* only when referring to software.

Introducing the Company

In the United States, an insurance company must be licensed in each state where the company does business. Highlight Insurance has been profitable in the western states for years, but it doesn't sell insurance policies directly to consumers. Instead, the firm contracts with *independent agencies*, which are companies that are licensed to sell the firm's policies in a given state. The relationship between agency and insurer is similar to the relationship of retailer and manufacturer. Several agencies sell policies for the insurer. Each agency, however, sells policies for several insurers.

The executives at Highlight Insurance are conservative about their business. ("We protect our customers," says one, "and ourselves.") They avoid direct sales to avoid the expense of setting up a direct-sales program and to give the agencies an incentive to keep selling. The background here is that agencies need to compete with other agencies, but none of them wants the expense of marketing an insurance policy that a consumer can buy directly (and less expensively) from the insurer.

As Highlight Insurance considers a plan for expansion, the executives are aware of two related issues: legal requirements differ in different states, and legal requirements are changeable. State legislatures and insurance departments make political and regulatory decisions on varying schedules, sometimes with little warning.

Highlight is gaining approval to do business in additional states, where the firm will sell directly to consumers. The intent is to create an advertising campaign that directs automobile owners to a Web site. Some executives want to include a talking animal in the TV spots, but few take the idea seriously.

Analyzing a Business Process

As you begin analyzing a business process that significantly affects the enterprise, you have several tasks that sometimes overlap. You must collect information about the business, including details on the current process and on the reasons for change. You must negotiate with personnel who have a stake in the process. Last, you must recommend solutions that make sense for the long term. Regardless of how you complete these tasks, the human element is crucial. A workable methodology

- involves a senior business executive

  - to help identify which personnel are of interest

  - to ensure that those personnel are made available

- includes a relatively short period of one-on-one information gathering, as you

  - conduct interviews

  - read documents

  - divide the areas of interest into different business areas and, within business areas, into different technology areas (for example, software on a mainframe as compared to software on Linux)

- identifies the most obvious *service points*, which are

  - the business tasks that can be mirrored by integration and business services

  - the technical tasks that can be implemented by relatively low-level services

- seeks ways to bring the company's application portfolio into an SOA. In particular, you may leave at least some of the existing applications in place and create technology-specific software *adapters*, which allow for data exchange between your newly written services and a traditional application such as a COBOL program that runs on a mainframe.

- emphasizes use of *facilitated sessions*, which are meetings in which you direct a conversation to define the current process (often described differently by different people) and to define the future direction and time frame.

- includes times when you refine plans and develop ways to communicate them

- concludes with the company's approving designs for a set of services (some of which are of general value to the business and will be usable in applications yet to be designed) and for a set of service-oriented applications that address the company's near-term needs.

Your task may be to pull together the processes of different parts of the company or of several companies. In that circumstance, rather than working with one manager who gives final approval, you'll be working with multiple managers who will make individual decisions about what is required. In addition, you're all but assured of handling data that, although similar in meaning, is defined differently by different groups. For example, the customer address used by a marketing group may include multiple contacts, yet an accounting group requires only one legal contact. Similarly, different groups in an airline may refer to cities differently, as when some systems store an airport code and others a city name, which itself may vary (in the early 1990s, the names Leningrad and Saint Petersburg were both in use).

The differences in data can be more subtle. At an airline, for example, different groups may define the meaning of *flight* differently (the fact of boarding, or the fact that a plane leaves the gate, or the duration from departure to arrival). Your task will include interviewing people from the different groups to define the differences and to work out ways to mediate the differences.

Describing the Sales Process at Highlight

An analysis of the Highlight Insurance sales process reveals the details outlined in Figure 3.1.

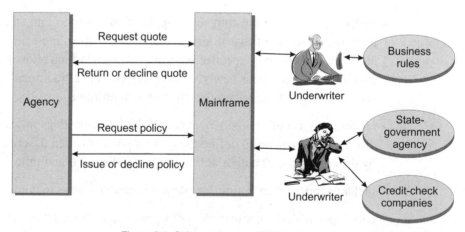

Figure 3.1: Sales process at Highlight Insurance

Here's the short story: Highlight's in-house underwriters make judgments about the risk involved in adding or keeping a customer. A set of business rules specify which underwriter handles which quote requests. When an agency requests a policy on behalf of a customer, an underwriter verifies the submitted details by writing to credit-check companies and state-government agencies such as the Department of Motor Vehicles (DMV).

Identifying Problems with the Current Process

Highlight's current process has several problems. First, it's too labor-intensive. The company's expansion will only increase the workload, and executives don't want to hire additional personnel to make up for inadequate technology.

The process is also inflexible and slow. Agents often want to see how a small change in coverage affects a quote, and they want an answer before the customer loses interest.

Another issue is that Highlight's current process doesn't handle direct sales. The company's Web site could let potential customers print request forms for subsequent faxing, but that solution is insufficient because it requires the customer to do work not required at the Web sites of other insurance companies. Aside from the issue of direct sales, the company has a competitive need to upgrade. Other insurance companies let agents submit online requests and receive quick feedback.

The process also has technical problems that are magnified by the complexity of software update, which includes coding (with technical code preparation on the mainframe), plus various kinds of testing, plus fixes and retesting as needed. After the code is correct, developers promote it from a test environment to a production environment, where the promoted code is tested yet again to ensure that users gain access to the correct version.

The main technical problems are twofold. First, existing applications combine different kinds of logic (user interface, business processing, and data access) and are hard to understand. As described earlier, the effect is additional testing, coding time, and errors. Second, the logic that handles different state requirements isn't separated from the rest. The merging of changeable code with more stable code means that the stable code is usually touched during updates. The effect is to require tests that would be unnecessary if the two kinds of code were kept separate.

Technical problems have business implications. The excessive effort needed to update and test software increases Highlight's expense and slows its response to change, especially in two situations: when the company gains approval to do business in a previously unsupported state and when requirements change in a state already supported.

Communicating the Assumptions in Writing

As you collect requirements, and even as you build a new business process, make the assumptions explicit and present them to technical and business personnel alike, in writing. Your goals are

- to specify the purpose of each application

- to identify which parts of the software inventory can remain in use

- to clarify which departments and personnel have which responsibilities during the project

- to address issues that may lead to conflict

- to help decision-makers reach agreement

- to have a record that can be useful when people later ask what the rationale was for a given decision

If you fail to identify assumptions, you're likely to present a solution that needs rework.

Assumptions can concern a variety of issues, including

- standards of measurement, with decisions such as:

  - Monetary values are in dollars.

  - Timestamps reflect Coordinated Universal Time.

- scope of effort, with decisions such as:

  - Fee collection is outside of scope.

  - Underwriters are responsible for setting rejection criteria.

- quality of service, with decisions such as:

  - Service A must be available 99 percent of the time.

  - The application must be able to support 1,000 requesters concurrently.

After you list assumptions, you'll discover that some don't apply to your project at all. That's normal. You'd do well to consider many issues even if you later ignore a few.

Isolating Services

As you begin to define a service-oriented application:

- Review the overall requirements, as well as those of each service.

- Identify which of the company's systems offer the functionality of interest.

- Consider accessing traditional application by way of adapters, so you can embrace a service orientation with less expense.

- Create a context diagram as a visual summary of the project's boundaries and relationships.

Figure 3.2 shows a context diagram for the Highlight Insurance project.

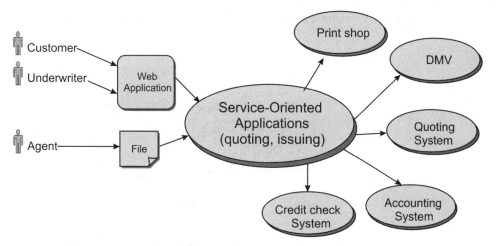

Figure 3.2: Context diagram for the Highlight Insurance project

At the center of any context diagram is the functionality being developed. The center represents a functional boundary. By defining such a boundary, you define the responsibility of the development group and of the *surrounding groups*, which are organizations that control the software that will interact with the new applications.

At Highlight Insurance, the new applications support customers, underwriters, and agents. The development group that handles the new service-oriented applications:

- needs the technical manager of each of the surrounding groups to help plan software interfaces.

- needs access to a customer's previous quote.

- needs services that determine whether to issue a new quote and whether underwriter intervention is required.

- needs services to send confirmation email as well as to print confirmation letters for subsequent mailing

- needs to inform the accounting department of purchased policies, to allow billing.

- needs to give the underwriter a way to verify credit checks and DMV information.

Creating the Quote Application

Figure 3.3 illustrates the new quote process at Highlight Insurance.

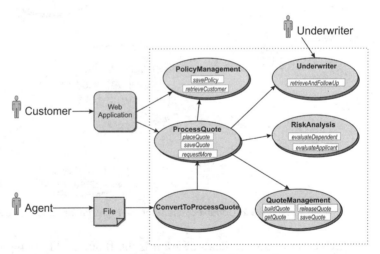

Figure 3.3: Software for issuing a quote

The steps to create a quote application are as follows:

1. *Receipt of quote request:* Highlight Insurance receives quote requests from customers who access the company Web site and from agents who transmit files on behalf of customers. In each case, someone outside Highlight Insurance is handling data entry that previously was handled in part by company clerks. The orchestration service ProcessQuote handles each

quote request, whether it originates with a customer or an agent. An agent transmission, however, requires that data first be restructured from ACORD (an industry-standard XML format) to the simpler format that Highlight Insurance uses for internal processing.

As SOA takes hold, each developer has access not only to applications that fulfill complex tasks but to individual services that provide simple convenience and are used to improve a customer's experience. If an existing Highlight Insurance customer interacts with the Web application, for example, the application can use details from the policy-management system to pre-populate the online forms. A service saves the customer from having to retype information that is already known to the company.

2. *Data storage:* The ProcessQuote service stores a quote request for 24 hours to let the applicant compare the quote with other options and to request evaluation by a company underwriter.

3. *Analysis and quote:* The RiskAnalysis service does analytic tasks that were handled by an underwriter. The interaction with RiskAnalysis

   ♦ uses company guidelines to determine the worthiness of the quote request

   ♦ indicates whether to issue or reject the quote request and returns details to ProcessQuote

   If a quote is being issued, ProcessQuote interacts with QuoteManagement, which uses the details from RiskAnalysis to calculate and store a quote. ProcessQuote either returns the quote or returns a rejection code as well as a justification.

4. *Communication and negotiation:* The interaction between the Web application and ProcessQuote is synchronous. On receiving an answer from Highlight Insurance, the customer has several options:

   ♦ to resubmit the request with updated data

   ♦ to request that a corporate underwriter review the issue

   ♦ to purchase a policy that reflects an approved quote

   ♦ to ignore the quote

If the customer doesn't purchase a policy within a day of receiving a quote, ProcessQuote calls the releaseQuote operation of the QuoteManagement service, flagging the quote for later removal from the mainframe database and notifying the applicant by email.

Creating the Policy Application

Figure 3.4 illustrates the new process for issuing a policy at Highlight Insurance.

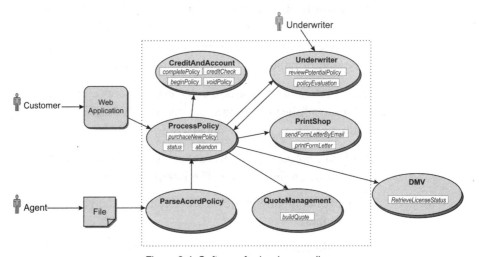

Figure 3.4: Software for issuing a policy

Unlike a quote process, a policy issuance can take several days. The steps involved are as follows.

1. *Receipt of policy request:* Highlight Insurance receives policy requests from different sources. The company Web site is the primary source, and from there, both agents and customers can submit policy requests. Requests also come from agents who transmit files on behalf of customers. A stored quote is a prerequisite to a customer's requesting a policy.

2. *Data storage:* The following cases apply:

    ♦ After providing credit-card details at the Web site, the customer's (or agent's) click invokes the ProcessPolicy service. That service then invokes a data-access service to get details on the quote being accepted, invokes other services described in this list, and returns control to the Web application, which reports that the purchase is in progress.

- If an agent submits a file, the service ParseAcordPolicy reformats the input and invokes the ProcessPolicy service. With SOA, the file transmission is viewed as a service invocation and results in the same behavior from ProcessPolicy, which requires no change to accommodate the different interaction pattern.

- The ProcessPolicy service provides an operation that lets a customer or agent query the status of a policy request. To support that operation, ProcessPolicy stores the current process status while moving toward issuing a new policy.

In general terms, ProcessPolicy indicates whether to issue a policy, to reject the policy request, or to contact an underwriter for intervention and for possible user (or agency) contact. ProcessPolicy issues a rejection immediately, for example, if the customer did not request the policy in the timeframe specified (and in that case, the customer must submit a new quote request, usually by modifying and resubmitting a previously saved one). Communication with the applicant is by email or postal service.

3. *Verifications:* ProcessPolicy verifies details, and policy issuance usually becomes more likely at each step:

- Services provided by the accounting and finance group handle credit checks.

- If credit checks result in approval, ProcessPolicy invoke services provided by the DMV to verify license and vehicle status.

Whenever possible, Highlight Insurance runs checks at the same time to speed a response to the customer.

The service handles some situations (a failed credit check, for example) but defers to underwriters in others, as when the question arises, "Did a customer provide data mistakenly or to defraud the company?" For example:

- A submitted vehicle identification number (VIN) refers to a car of a different make and model than specified by the customer.

- A submitted VIN refers to a car owned by a driver other than one mentioned on the policy.

4. *Decision:* If policy issuance is appropriate, the QuoteManagement service calculates a quote based on a variety of risk factors. In this way, the same calculation occurs for both quote request and policy request.

You may ask, "Why repeat the calculation?" Although Highlight Insurance retains a customer's trust by honoring a previous quote, the quote may no longer be appropriate. The verification process may have found new information, for example, or government regulators may have required a lower valuation since the quote request. Highlight's designers decided that a re-invocation of QuoteManagement in all cases was the best way to ensure that the price reflected the company's intent.

Highlight Insurance has a two-step process for final approval. The CreditAndAccount service creates the policy, which then is evaluated by an underwriter.

From the perspective of the ProcessPolicy service, the underwriter (a person) is a kind of service. The WS-BPEL4People specification proposes a formal mechanism to describe the interaction between automated processes and persons, as described at the following Web site: *http://www.ibm.com/developerworks/webservices/library/specification/ ws-bpel4people*.

5. *Communication:* If the underwriter decides that the policy is valid, ProcessPolicy invokes the CreditAndAccount service to begin a policy billing cycle and issues an email and the legal paperwork by invoking the PrintShop service. If the policy is not valid, ProcessPolicy invokes the voidPolicy operation of CreditAndAccount and informs the customer (or agent) that a policy is not being issued.

6. *Cancel purchase:* Highlight Insurance lets the applicant cancel the purchase even after the company has fulfilled some or all steps in the multi-day process of issuing a policy. The application provides a *compensation* action, as explained in Chapter 2. In this case, the user's cancellation request causes a new invocation of CreditAndAccount, which voids the new policy, and invokes the PrintShop service to inform the customer about the changed status. If Highlight already sent the paperwork for a new policy, the company sends legal cancellation documents.

CHAPTER 4

XML

We've described the general characteristics of SOA and now approach the practical details. At the core of SOA is *Extensible Markup Language (XML)*, a set of widely accepted rules for organizing data in a text format. In particular, each message exchanged with a Web service is in a format that conforms to those rules.

XML is described at the Web site of the World Wide Web Consortium (W3C), the standard's sponsoring organization. To give you a sense of what XML provides, we occasionally quote from the W3C recommendation *Extensible Markup Language (XML) 1.0 (Fourth Edition)*, which is available at *http://www.w3.org/TR*.

We omit many complexities that are described in the specification, as well as on the Web and in textbooks. A user interface will stand between you and those documents anyway, so your development work may not require you to access XML documents a lot.

But don't be fooled. The user interface lets you work quickly and reduces the tedium of many tasks, but it doesn't separate you completely from the underlying technology. If you understand SOA at the level of the XML-based files, you can

- respond to error conditions with greater skill

- understand the implications of user-interface settings that pertain to XML

- review or even change the XML files directly ("Oh, that's what's happening!")

- avoid dependence on tools provided by a particular vendor

Excellence often requires you to know details that are below the surface, and in any case, broccoli is good for you.

Introduction to XML

Listing 4.1 shows an example of an XML document that holds details on a request for insurance coverage.

```xml
<?xml version="1.0" encoding="ISO-8859-1"?>
<!- policy request ->
<Insured CustomerID="5">
    <CarPolicy PolicyType="Auto">
        <Vehicle Category="Sedan">
            <Make>Honda</Make>
            <Model>Accord</Model>
        </Vehicle>
        <Vehicle Category="Sport">
            <Make>Ford</Make>
            <Model>Mustang</Model>
        </Vehicle>
    </CarPolicy>
    <CarPolicy PolicyType="Antique">
        <Vehicle Category="Sport">
            <Make>Triumph</Make>
            <Model>Spitfire</Model>
        </Vehicle>
    </CarPolicy>
</Insured>
```

Listing 4.1: Sample XML document

When you create an XML document, you use a *vocabulary*, which is a set of terms that are organized in a way that reflects the data used in your business. Each tag name (such as Vehicle) is a reserved word only in the narrow context of your application, company, or industry.

Data that conforms to an XML format is handled by an *XML processor*, also called an *XML engine*. The processor is software that

- is invoked by other software

- identifies units of information in the XML-formatted input

- provides that information for some purpose such as

  - to display the data, as occurs when you launch an XML file with a recent browser

  - to convert the data to another format, as occurs when an SOA runtime product invokes a SOAP engine

  - to construct a runtime service implementation, as occurs when you invoke a Business Process Execution Language (BPEL) engine

XML benefits the business developer in several ways:

- XML allows development of specialized vocabularies that reduce the cost of business-to-business interaction. Widely used vocabularies include ACORD (for the insurance industry) and IFX (for the financial-services industry).

- You can process data with ease because of the many software products that support XML. A product might provide text searches and editing capability or might transform text from one XML vocabulary into another.

- XML provides mechanisms for validating the data, including technologies such as Document Type Definition (DTD), XML Schema Definition (XSD), RELAX NG, and Schematron. This book focuses on XSD because in many cases an SOA runtime product uses that technology to validate transmitted data.

- An XML document is clear to the human reader. The content is simple text rather than a stream of binary characters and is relatively *self-documenting*, showing data values as well as relationships. In our example, a customer is requesting two policies, and each policy includes details on specific cars.

XML As Used in SOA

XML makes possible the implementations that were anticipated during the years when SOA was just a subject for academic review:

- As you develop a service

  - you're likely to use XML to describe the service interface

- you may use XML to create the logic itself (as you'll see in Chapter 7, when we describe BPEL)

- in relation to Web services, you may access the transmitted data using technologies such as XPath, which require knowledge of the XML-based message format

- After you develop a service, you may use XML to store the service contract in a registry.

- At configuration time, you may use XML to configure the service, even to the extent of assigning different values to variables inside the service implementation. That degree of configurability is shown in Chapter 9, when we describe Service Component Architecture.

- At Web-service run time, the transmitted data is simply text in an XML format, and XML engines convert the data at the transmission endpoints, as Figure 4.1 illustrates.

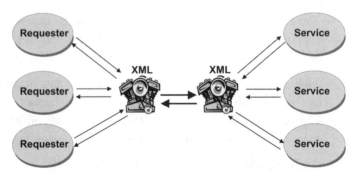

Figure 4.1: XML engines at Web-service run time

At a transmitting endpoint, an XML processor converts a message into the format required for transmission. At the receiving endpoint, another XML processor converts the message from the transmission medium into the local format.

In the absence of a universal format like that provided by XML, an SOA runtime product would need to act in one of two ways to support Web services. The product could handle data conversions as needed to transform data from each endpoint-specific format directly to every other one. With this approach, the addition of a new kind of endpoint would require significant updates to the runtime product. Alternatively, the product would restrict the computer languages used in the participating endpoints.

XML has a cost. Use of text rather than a binary format slows processing and requires more disk space. An SOA runtime product can reduce the cost of transmission by compressing each XML-based message, but time is required for data conversion in any case.

Structure of an XML Document

Let's look again at the XML document shown earlier (Listing 4.1).

Our document is composed of a set of tagged constructs, with each tag bounded by angle brackets (< and >). The first construct is called the *XML declaration*. This line identifies the XML version, specifies an *encoding* (a subject far afield from most business development), and includes an initial and final question mark (?).

```
<?xml version="1.0" encoding="ISO-8859-1"?>
```

If the XML declaration is missing, the document must conform to XML 1.0. For details on encoding, see the Web site *http://skew.org/xml/tutorial.*

Our document also includes a *comment*, which is text that an XML processor can ignore and whose purpose is usually to clarify (to a human reader) some aspect of the file. A comment is characterized by specific initial and final characters, as shown here.

```
<!- policy request ->
```

Most important (as noted in the XML specification), the document includes "one or more elements" that represent the data of interest. In most cases, an element is "delimited by start-tags and end-tags"; as shown here, the end-tag precedes the element name with a virgule, or forward slash (/).

```
<Insured>
...
</Insured>
```

Each XML document must have a root element (such as Insured), which includes a set of other elements in a tree structure. Figure 4.2 shows the tree structure for the document under review.

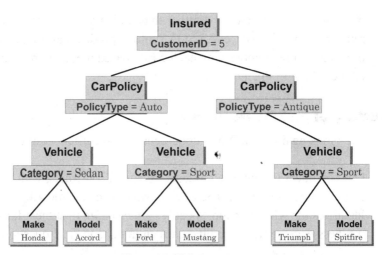

Figure 4.2: XML tree structure

An important characteristic of XML is that each superior, or *parent*, element includes its immediately subordinate, or *child*, elements completely. For example, a parent element cannot include a start-tag of a child element without including the corresponding end-tag. Child elements can themselves have children, and we use the phrase *descendants* to refer to all elements that are within the start and end tags of a parent element, at any level of nesting.

Most elements include *content*: child elements, a literal value (as is in the Make element — <Make>Honda</Make>), or both, as in the following example of *mixed content*:

```
<Vehicle>Cool!
   <Make>Triumph</Make>
   <Model>Spitfire</Model>
</Vehicle>
```

An element also can include *attributes*, which are name-value pairs that provide additional information associated with the element. You specify attributes in the start-tag of the element. Each attribute is composed of a name, an equal sign (=), and a single- or double-quoted string. To separate one attribute from the next, you use white space (carriage returns, spaces, or tabs). Here's an example of an element with two attributes.

```
<Insured CustomerID="5" Status="In Review">
```

Although attributes are part of the element, they are not considered content. This distinction has a practical effect when you work with XPath, as described in Chapter 6.

Note that each identifier in the XML document is case-sensitive. An element named vehicle is distinct from one named VEHICLE.

You can organize your data in various ways, specifying elements in some cases and attributes in others. Within the Insured element, for example, we might add an Options element to describe the insurance coverage in effect when a car is disabled:

```
<Options>
    <TemporaryRental MaximumDays="10"/>
    <Towing/>
</Options>
```

The TemporaryRental element tells whether the insurance company pays for a customer's vehicle rental; the MaximumDays attribute indicates the maximum number of days that are covered; and the Towing element indicates whether the insurance company pays for use of a towing service.

An element (such as TemporaryRental) with no content is said to be *empty*. It can have a start and end tag or (as shown) can have a single tag with an ending virgule.

A lack of content in an element can mean that the data is elsewhere. A value for the Towing element might be assigned as a default in the XML Schema definition (as described later) or in the software that accesses the XML processor.

Later in this book, we mention *processing instructions (PIs)*, which are XML statements that are used by the XML processor or by the software that invokes the processor. Here's an example.

```
<? HandleThis how="somehow" ?>
```

The PI includes a question mark within each angle bracket and specifies a *PI target*, which is a name that identifies the instruction. The PI's content is the set of parameters and related values. In this example, the PI target is HandleThis, the parameter is how, and the value of the parameter is *somehow*.

Last, you may want the XML processor to ignore characters that are otherwise meaningful in a technical sense. For example, content that appears to be an element start-tag (such as *<You&Me>*) might be a string to be printed. To hide such content, place it in a character-data (*CDATA*) section, as shown here.

```
<![CDATA[<You&Me>]]>
```

Namespaces

We now explain *namespaces*, which are identifiers that place element and attribute names in categories. If you're reading only to get a sense of SOA, you can skim this section, but you may have reasons to read straight through:

- Knowledge of namespaces can help you avoid feeling intimidated by the seemingly complex data at the top of most XML documents.

- A developer needs to know the subject at least occasionally.

- The material on XML Schema is best understood by someone with prior knowledge of namespaces.

- Later chapters in this book refer to namespaces.

Purpose of Namespaces

Namespaces are categories for ensuring that names in an XML document are unique in that document. With namespaces, a developer can combine different XML vocabularies without fear that identical names in different vocabularies will be handled in the same way. An XML processor, for example, might use a namespace to distinguish the rules for validating a name that is used multiple times for different purposes. Similarly, code that you write to review a complex XML-based message might need to identify the namespace associated with a name.

Before we tell you how to specify a namespace, consider an example that includes two instances of the element name Title. One instance refers to a book, and one refers to a person.

```
<TitleTypes>
  <Title xmlns="BookTitleNamespace">
    <Name>Oliver Twist</Name>
  </Title>
  <Title>Duke of Windsor</Title>
</TitleTypes>
```

If an element name is in a namespace, the XML processor interprets the name in a way that includes the namespace identifier. We might express the first instance of the name Title as follows:

```
{BookTitleNamespace}Title
```

An element or attribute name can be outside any namespace, as is true of the second instance of Title. In the absence of a namespace, the XML processor interprets the name without referring to a namespace identifier. We might express that second instance simply as Title.

The implication of a namespace depends solely on the software that processes a given XML document. An XML processor might use a namespace identifier to determine which of several versions of an XML vocabulary is being used or to determine which XML Schema validates a given element.

Namespace Identifiers

A namespace is usually a character string that is formatted as if to refer to a Web-based resource such as a Web site or file. But a namespace may be any Universal Resource Identifier (URI) — that is, any unique value that conforms to the URI rules defined by the Internet Engineering Task Force (IETF). Here are some examples of namespace URIs:

```
http://www.w3.org/2001/XMLSchema
f81d4fae-7jan-11d0-a765-00a0c91e6bf6
ISBN:0452010624
```

Later, we show how to declare a namespace.

One kind of URI is a Uniform Resource Locator (URL), which can be used as a namespace identifier. The specific URL may refer to a Web site that describes the purpose of the namespace or of the XML document. In most cases, however, the

XML processor does *not* access a Web site, and the URI often does not refer to a Web site at all.

The namespace URI is just an identifier, with no meaning other than to place a set of names in a category. Often, your organization's Internet domain name (such as *www.w3.org*) is appropriately included to ensure uniqueness.

Namespace Qualification and Declarations

An XML-based name is said to be *namespace-qualified* if the XML associates the name with a namespace. A name that is not associated with a namespace is not in a default namespace; instead, the XML processor interprets the name as being outside any namespace.

A name can be namespace-qualified in either of two ways. Each way requires you to first declare a namespace by using the identifier xmlns, which is an abbreviation for *XML namespace*.

You declare a *non-default namespace* by following xmlns with a colon (:) and a second identifier of your choice (for instance, target), as in the following start-tag.

```
<Insured
xmlns:target="http://www.IBM.com/HighlightInsurance">
```

Later in the XML document, you can use that second identifier as a prefix to indicate that an element or attribute name (such as Model) is in a non-default namespace.

```
<target:Model>Spitfire</target:Model>
```

You declare a *default namespace* by specifying xmlns without a subsequent colon, as in the following start-tag.

```
<Insured xmlns="http://www.IBM.com/software">
```

In the absence of other namespace syntax, the element name (Insured, in this case) is in the default namespace, as is the name of each element descended from that element.

The start-tag of the XML root element often includes one or more namespace declarations, as shown here.

```
<wsdl:definitions
    xmlns:soap="http://schemas.xmlsoap.org/wsdl/soap/"
    xmlns:tns="http://www.transunion.com/"
    xmlns:wsdl="http://schemas.xmlsoap.org/wsdl/"
    xmlns:xsd="http://www.w3.org/2001/XMLSchema">
```

Namespace Rules

Before we review an example, consider the following rules:

- Any namespace declaration is *in scope* (that is, available) in the element in which the declaration appears and in the element's descendant elements.

- An element name that is in the scope of a default namespace and is not prefixed is in the default namespace.

- An attribute name can never be in a default namespace:

    - If the attribute name has a prefix, the name is in the namespace referenced by that prefix.

    - If the attribute name is not prefixed, the name is outside any namespace. You can never use a default namespace to reference an attribute.

- A default namespace can be overridden for a given element and for all the descendant elements. In the following example, the element name CarPolicy is in the PolicySpace namespace; and the element names Vehicle, Make, and Model are in the VehicleSpace namespace.

```
<CarPolicy xmlns="PolicySpace" PolicyType="Auto">
    <Vehicle xmlns="VehicleSpace" Category="Sedan">
        <Make>Honda</Make>
        <Model>Accord</Model>
    </Vehicle>
</CarPolicy>
```

- A default namespace can be removed from scope for a given element and for all the descendant elements. In the following example, the names Vehicle, Make, and Model are not in any namespace because the default namespace is set to an empty string ("").

```
<Vehicle xmlns="" Category="Sedan">
   <Make>Honda</Make>
   <Model>Accord</Model>
</Vehicle>
```

- Multiple non-default namespaces can be available for a given element and for all descendant elements, and those namespaces are also available for the attributes in those elements. In the following example, the element names Order and Customer are in OrderSpace, while the element names Company and Buyer are in CustSpace, as is the attribute Number.

```
<ord:Order xmlns:ord="OrderSpace">
   <ord:Customer xmlns:cust="CustSpace">
       <cust:Company cust:Number="123">
       ABC
       </cust:Company>
       <cust:Buyer>
       Smith
       </cust:Buyer>
   </ord:Customer>
</ord:Order>
```

Namespace Example and Terminology

Consider the XML shown in Listing 4.2.

```
<?xml version="1.0" encoding="ISO-8859-1"?>
<!- an order ->
<Order xmlns="http://www.ibm.com/software"
    xmlns:prod="http://www.ibm.com/next">
   <Customer CustID="IBM" Code="1234">
     <prod:Product prod:ID="0123">
        <prod:Type>Blackboard</prod:Type>
        <prod:Quantity>2</prod:Quantity>
     </prod:Product>
     <prod:Product prod:ID="0456">
        <prod:Type>Whiteboard</prod:Type>
        <prod:Quantity>3</prod:Quantity>
     </prod:Product>
     <prod:Product prod:ID="0789"/>
   </Customer>
</Order>
```

Listing 4.2: Sample XML with namespaces

In this example two element names, Order and Customer, are in the default namespace, http://www.ibm.com/software. The element names Product, Type, and Quantity are in the namespace http://www.ibm.com/next. Given the prefix in front of the attribute name ID in the Product element, the name ID is also in that second namespace. The names of the Customer element's CustID and Code attributes are not in a namespace.

The following terminology is in use:

- The name of a namespace (such as http://www.ibm.com/software) is the *namespace URI*.

- The element or attribute name can include a prefix and a colon (as in prod:Quantity). A name in that form is called a *qualified name*, or *QName*, and the identifier that follows the colon is called a *local name*. If a prefix is not in use, neither is the colon, and the QName and local name are identical.

- An XML identifier (such as a local name) that has no colon is sometimes called an *NCName*. (The *NC* comes from the phrase *no colon*.)

XML Schema

The next sections introduce XML Schema definitions, or XSDs. You use an XML Schema to describe the values permitted in an XML document and the relationships among the document's elements. For details about the XML Schema definition language, see the Web site *http://www.w3.org/TR/xmlschema-0*.

Data Type

To understand an XSD, you first need to understand the notion of *data type*. A data type is an identifier that specifies a set of values along with operations able to act on those values. In most computer languages, for example, an integer can include digits and can be mathematically combined with other numbers.

In general, we use data types to validate user input, to avoid runtime errors, and to increase the efficiency of runtime code. Data types also allow a meaningful categorization of data, so that, for instance:

- Each use of an employee ID is based on a data type named Employee-ID.

- Each employee record has the same hierarchy, with data types such as Employee-ID, Name, and Age.

- A known set of validations is in use when a data type such as Name (always containing Last-Name and First-Name) is used in different ways, whether for an employee record or a customer-contact record.

Data types are described in various ways. With some simplification, we can characterize XML Schema types as fitting into one of four basic categories: primitive, derived, simple, and complex.

A *primitive type* is a data type that does not include another and is not derived from another. Examples include Boolean, decimal, and string.

A *derived type* is based on a primitive type and is provided by XML Schema. The type nmtoken, for example, is a subset of a string, with no spaces anywhere.

A *simple type* can be a primitive type or a derived type, but it also can be derived from another simple type by a developer. We want to emphasize a particular use of types in business development, so we'll use the phrase *simple type* to refer only to a developer-derived simple type. If you read XML specifications, however, be aware that the phrase "simple type" can include primitive and derived types.

A simple type retains every operation of the type on which the simple type is based but adds data restrictions that reflect business rules. Given a base type of string, for example, you might create a simple type called Employee-ID and allow only the letters A through J followed by five digits. The meaningfulness of the name Employee-ID helps developers and business analysts to think and communicate clearly. In addition, type checking at different points in the development cycle can ensure that all employee IDs conform to the restrictions specified in the definition of the type.

A *complex type* is a data type that is composed of other data types. An example might be called Employee-Record, which includes a simple type called Employee-ID, a complex type called Name, an integer called Age, and so on. Any data type in the composition may be primitive, derived, simple, or complex. When you create a complex type, you give names even to the primitive and derived types that are included in that complex type. As always, meaningful names are helpful.

A type doesn't contain values but identifies what values are possible. An employee-record type, for example, doesn't refer to a specific employee, but expresses the format needed to describe an employee. A *variable*, in contrast, contains data that fulfills the type requirements. A variable of an employee-record type, for example, can hold the employee ID, name, and age of a specific employee. The variable is said to be an *instance* of the type.

As we stated earlier, a data type allows specific values and operations. A string, for example, can be concatenated with a string, but not with an integer. In relation to a given value, however, you can sometimes ignore or override those restrictions. You can concatenate the string "The year was " with the integer 2000, for example, but only if the integer is first converted to a string. Conversions may happen automatically or by the developer's *cast*, which is a directive that converts a value from one type to another.

Computer languages are sometimes categorized as either *weakly typed*, to the extent that data-type conversions happen automatically, or *strongly typed*, to the extent that the conversions happen only as a result of an explicit cast. A weakly typed language requires less discipline at development time; but a strongly typed language allows for faster processing at run time because less type checking is required then.

Purpose of an XML Schema

You author an XML Schema (sometimes called an XML Schema definition, or XSD) to describe the values that are allowable in each element and attribute in an XML document and to characterize the relationship of one element to another. In short, an XSD describes an XML vocabulary.

In SOA, the XSD has two primary purposes:

- to tell SOA-related tools (often in an integrated development environment) how to construct the code that operates "behind the scenes" to make possible a data exchange between the requester and a specific service

- to assign validation rules that restrict the kind of data accepted by an endpoint at run time

The XSDs for a particular service must be available at each endpoint of a transmission. In the case of a Web service, an XSD is often embedded in a Web Services Description Language (WSDL) file, as described in Chapter 5. The XSD usually is not transferred with the business data.

Structure of an XML Schema

An XML Schema specifies a *content model*, which is an allowable set of *content* (names and types) for elements, along with equivalent details on the attributes of each element. An XML stream that conforms to the rules established in the XML Schema is called an *instance document*, and we can refer to the elements and attributes in that stream as *instance elements* and *instance attributes*, respectively.

As the example in Listing 4.3 shows, an XML Schema is itself written in XML.

```
<?xml version="1.0" encoding="ISO-8859-1"?>

<schema xmlns="http://www.w3.org/2001/XMLSchema"
xmlns:target="http://www.IBM.com/HighlightInsurance"
targetNamespace="http://www.IBM.com/HighlightInsurance"
elementFormDefault="unqualified">
    <annotation>
        <documentation xml:lang="en">
            An example XML Schema Definition (XSD).
        </documentation>
    </annotation>
    <element name="Insured">
        <complexType>
            <choice minOccurs="1" maxOccurs="unbounded">
                <element name="CarPolicy">
                    <complexType>
                        <choice maxOccurs="unbounded">
                            <element name="Vehicle"
                                     type="target:VehicleType"/>
                            <element name="Driver"
                                     type="target:DriverType"/>
                        </choice>
                        <attribute name="PolicyType"
                                   type="string" default="Auto"/>
                    </complexType>
                </element>
                <element name="HomePolicy" type="target:HomePolicyType"/>
```

Listing 4.3: Sample XML Schema definition (part 1 of 2)

```
            </choice>
            <attribute name="CustomerID" type="string" use="required"/>
        </complexType>
    </element>

    <complexType name="VehicleType">
        <group ref="target:VehicleGroup"/>
        <attribute name="VIN" use="required">
            <simpleType>
                <restriction base="string">
                    <minLength value="4"/>
                    <maxLength value="26"/>
                </restriction>
            </simpleType>
        </attribute>
        <attribute name="Category" type="string"/>
    </complexType>

    <group name="VehicleGroup">
        <sequence>
            <element name="Make" type="string"/>
            <element name="Model" type="string"/>
        </sequence>
    </group>

    <!- The complex types DriverType and HomePolicyType are not shown ->
</schema>
```

Listing 4.3: Sample XML Schema definition (part 2 of 2)

Global and Local Types

Any data types that are immediate children of the schema element are *global*, which means you can use the type name when assigning characteristics to elements or attributes anywhere in the Schema. An example of a global type is VehicleType.

```
<schema>
    <complexType name="VehicleType">
        .
        .
    </complexType>
</schema>
```

Other data types you declare are *local*, which means that they affect only their parent, in which case a type name is unnecessary.

```
<element name="Insured">
   <complexType>
      .
      .
   </complexType>
```

A data type that has no name is sometimes called an *anonymous type*.

Simple and Complex Types

A global or local type can be simple or complex. A *simple type* is a data type that indicates the allowable text content for an element or attribute, as in the following lines.

```
<attribute name="VIN" use="required">
   <simpleType>
      <restriction base="string">
         <minLength value="4"/>
         <maxLength value="26"/>
      </restriction>
   </simpleType>
</attribute>
```

Here, the subordinate restriction element includes two kinds of details:

- A *base type*, which is the type from which the simple type will be derived. The base type is a global simple type, a derived type, or a primitive type.

- A set of *facets* (that is, characteristics) and related values. In this case, a restriction is in place for a minimum number of characters (minLength) and a maximum number of characters (maxLength).

  Instead of a restriction element, we could have used a list element (to allow content to be a series of values of the base type) or a union element (to allow content to represent any of several base types).

A *complex type* is a data type that includes elements, attributes, or both, as in the following lines.

```
<element name="CarPolicy">
   <complexType>
      <choice maxOccurs="unbounded">
         <element name="Vehicle" type="target:VehicleType"/>
         <element name="Driver" type="string"/>
      </choice>
      <attribute name="PolicyType"
                  type="string" default="Auto"/>
   </complexType>
</element>
```

Here, the subordinate choice element shows that

- any number of child elements are valid, as indicated by the maxOccurs attribute setting

- a given child element can be called Vehicle (of type VehicleType) or Driver (a string)

Instance attributes are optional by default. CarPolicy has an optional PolicyType attribute, for example, and the default value of PolicyType is *Auto*.

VehicleType is another complex type, which includes a group of elements (type VehicleGroup, as described in the next section) and the attributes VIN and Category.

```
<complexType name="VehicleType">
   <group ref="target:VehicleGroup"/>
   <attribute name="VIN" use="required">

      .
      .

   </attribute>
   <attribute name="Category" type="string"/>
</complexType>
```

Groups

A *group declaration* is essentially a data type that specifies a list of elements. An example of a group declaration is VehicleGroup.

```
<group name="VehicleGroup">
   <sequence>
      <element name="Make" type="string"/>
      <element name="Model" type="string"/>
   </sequence>
</group>
```

Instance elements are required unless the minimum-occurrence (minOccurs) attribute is set to *0*. (The default value of minOccurs is *1*.) The element VehicleGroup, for example, indicates that each child instance element (Make and Model) is required.

Sequencing

A complex type or group might include a *sequencing element*:

- The sequence element means that the instance elements must be in the specified order.

- The all element means that the instance elements can be in any order.

- The choice element means that the instance document can include a subset of elements.

Let's look at two examples.

Insured (the root element of the XML instance document) must include at least one CarPolicy or HomePolicy instance element and can include any number of those elements in any combination or order.

```
<element name="Insured">
    <complexType>
        <choice minOccurs="1" maxOccurs="unbounded">
            <element name="CarPolicy">
                <complexType>
                    .
                    .
                </complexType>
            </element>
            <element name="HomePolicy"
                     type="target:HomePolicyType"/>
        </choice>
        <attribute name="CustomerID" type="string"
                   use="required"/>
    </complexType>
</element>
```

Incidentally, the Insured instance element also must include a CustomerID attribute, as indicated by the value of use.

As shown in VehicleGroup, the Make instance element must precede Model.

```
<group name="VehicleGroup">
    <sequence>
        <element name="Make" type="string"/>
        <element name="Model" type="string"/>
    </sequence>
</group>
```

Simple and Complex Content

You can derive a complex type from an existing (base) type. The derived type will have characteristics of the base type

- with *extensions*, which are added attributes, content, or both

- with *restrictions*, which are exclusions of the existing attributes, content, or both

For example, you can use the simpleContent Schema element to add attributes to an instance element that has text content. Consider the Options element, which we described earlier.

```
<Options>
    <TemporaryRental MaximumDays="10"/>
    <Towing/>
</Options>
```

Here is a related XML Schema element.

```
<element name="Options">
    <all>
        <element name="TemporaryRental" type="TemporaryRentalType"/>
        <element name="Towing" type="boolean" default="true"/>
    </all>
</element>

<complexType name="TemporaryRentalType" default="true">
    <simpleContent>
        <extension base="boolean">
            <attribute name="MaximumDays"
                       type="integer" default="10"/>
            <attribute name="MaxDollarPerDay"
                       type="decimal" default="25.99"/>
        </extension>
    </simpleContent>
</complexType>
```

Within the TemporaryRental Type element, the simple content element specifies that any instance element based on that type has Boolean text (value *true* or *false*, with a default) and can include the optional attributes Maximum Days (which takes an integer value) and MaxDollarPerDay (which takes a decimal value). Each attribute value has a default, too.

You might use the element simpleContent to create a type that restricts aspects of an existing complex type, which itself has simple content. Here's an example.

```
<complexType name="PremiumRentalType" default="true">
    <simpleContent>
        <restriction base="TemporaryRentalType">
            <attribute name="MaximumDays" use="required"/>
            <attribute name="MaxDollarPerDay" use="prohibited"/>
        </extension>
    </simpleContent>
</complexType>
```

Given the new definition, you could allow an instance element (of whatever name) and base that element on the complex type PremiumRentalType. Only one attribute is valid, and it's required. The modified MaxDollarPerDay attribute is not valid in the instance element because, in the Schema attribute definition, the value of use is *prohibited*.

You also can use the complexContent Schema element

- to extend a complex type — for example, to add elements or attributes

- to restrict a complex type — for example, to remove elements or attributes, to change element characteristics such as the minimum number of occurrences, or to change attribute characteristics

Schemas and Namespaces

An XML processor uses namespace details to process an instance document, and the primary source of the namespace details can be either the instance document or the related Schema. Different SOA implementations handle the issue differently, but in any case, settings in the Schema indicate which source to use:

- If the source is the Schema, less namespace information appears in the instance document. In this case, the instance document is easier to understand and maintain, especially when the Schema organization is complicated. Also, the Schema author has the flexibility to merge or split Schemas, with less chance that the reorganization will mean changes to the existing XML instance documents.

- If the source of namespace details is the XML instance document, that document shows namespace information to a wider audience, and the XML processor may run faster.

In the schema element of our sample XML Schema definition, we set the attribute elementFormDefault to *unqualified*, which means that most instance elements are not qualified with a namespace name. Instead, the Schema is the source of namespace details for every element other than the root element. The *unqualified* setting is the default.

The schema element includes other namespace details, too:

- The namespace http://www.w3.org/2001/XMLSchema is the default namespace, but this namespace is often associated with the prefix xs or xsd, as shown later in a WSDL file. That namespace refers to identifiers such as attribute, which is the name of an element in the XML Schema itself.

- The attribute targetNamespace specifies the target namespace, which is used as a category for each name you're adding. The target namespace includes the names of the elements and attributes that will be allowed in your XML instance document and includes the names of any types you create.

- As you can see, the name of the target namespace is also in a second namespace declaration. The purpose of that second declaration is to allow references to any data-type information that you (as the author of the XML Schema) specify in the Schema. The following lines, for example, reference the namespace that is identified by the prefix target and points to VehicleType, which is a data type in the Schema.

```
<element name="Vehicle"
         type="target:VehicleType"/>
```

Aside from the types you create, a set of XML Schema types is available in the default namespace (http://www.w3.org/2001/XMLSchema). For that reason, the use of string in the following declaration is valid in our example.

```
<element name="Make" type="string"/>
```

Last, the documentation element in our example includes the prefix xml, which refers to a namespace that is defined by the XML specification. The language of the documentation element is American English, as indicated by the following entry.

```
xml:lang="en-US"
```

Data-type Reuse

To organize your Schemas in a way that benefits your company over time, store the reusable types in a set of Schema files that other Schemas can access. The types must be global. A Schema gains access to the reusable types by either of two declarations: include or import.

The include declaration is the preferred choice when the Schema being accessed either has no target namespace or has the same target namespace as the accessing Schema. The import declaration is necessary when the accessed Schema has a target namespace that differs from the target namespace of the accessing Schema.

Instance Document

The Schema described earlier validates the instance document shown in Listing 4.4.

```
<?xml version="1.0" encoding="ISO-8859-1"?>

<root:Insured
      xmlns:root="http://www.highlight.com/Insurance"
      xmlns:xsi="http://www.w3.org/2001/XMLSchema-instance"
      xsi:schemaLocation=
          "http://www.ibm.com/HighlightInsurance Insurance.xsd"
      CustomerID="5">
    <CarPolicy PolicyType="Auto">
        <Vehicle VIN="A123">
            <Make>Honda</Make>
            <Model>Accord</Model>
        </Vehicle>
        <Vehicle VIN="A456">
            <Make>Ford</Make>
            <Model>Mustang</Model>
        </Vehicle>
    </CarPolicy>
```

Listing 4.4: Sample XML instance document (part 1 of 2)

```
  <CarPolicy PolicyType="Antique Auto">
    <Vehicle VIN="B321">
      <Make>Triumph</Make>
      <Model>Spitfire</Model>
    </Vehicle>
    <Vehicle VIN="B654">
      <Make>Buick</Make>
      <Model>Skylark</Model>
    </Vehicle>
    <Vehicle VIN="B987">
      <Make>Porsche</Make>
      <Model>Speedster</Model>
    </Vehicle>
  </CarPolicy>
</root:Insured>
```

Listing 4.4: Sample XML instance document (part 2 of 2)

We qualify Insured with the target namespace because that name is defined in a global element of the XML Schema. We cannot qualify the other names without causing a Schema validation error, because the Schema element elementFormDefault is set to *unqualified*.

After we declare a non-default namespace and use it to qualify Insured, we use the prefix xsi to specify an XML-related namespace and to set the attribute schemaLocation.

```
xsi:schemaLocation=
        "http://www.ibm.com/HighlightInsurance Insurance.xsd"
```

The setting of schemaLocation repeats the target namespace and tells the location of the XML Schema. The attribute setting is only a hint to the XML processor, which may be configured to use a different Schema.

CHAPTER 5

Established SOA Standards

In most cases, you use the following open-standard technologies when developing a Web service.

- *Web Services Description Language (WSDL)* is an XML format for describing how to access a service.

- *SOAP* is an XML format for transmitting data to and from a Web service. The runtime message includes business data (as defined in the WSDL definition) and may contain Quality-of-Service (QoS) details too, including (for example) the security details needed to gain access to the service. Although QoS details may be defined in the WSDL definition, those details are increasingly likely to be defined only when a system administrator uses an SOA runtime product to configure the message.

  SOAP was once called Simple Object Access Protocol and is now known only as SOAP.

- *Universal Description, Discovery, and Integration (UDDI)* is a set of rules for registering and retrieving details about a business and its services. Some of the registered details are in the form of WSDL definitions.

WSDL and SOAP have become enormously important, with UDDI less so. The three standards are interrelated to some extent. Figure 5.1 depicts the relationship.

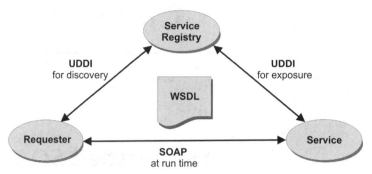

Figure 5.1: Established SOA standards

As the figure suggests, a WSDL definition describes a Web service. A UDDI-compliant service registry can help companies to discover that description. At run time, SOAP-based messages carry business data that conforms to the description.

The World Wide Web Consortium (W3C) is the sponsoring organization for WSDL and SOAP. The Organization for the Advancement of Structured Information Standards (OASIS) has an equivalent role for UDDI.

WSDL

WSDL is an XML format that tells how to access a Web service. Increasingly, this format is used to describe the interface of any kind of service.

You use a WSDL definition to communicate the service interface to developers, who use the information to invoke the service. A WSDL definition also ensures that runtime access is handled correctly on both the requester and service sides of the transmission.

A WSDL definition is cumbersome, resembling a box with many wrapped objects inside, some embedded in others. If you were rewriting the words of an old Stevie Wonder song, you might say, "Isn't she clunky?"

"Yes" is the short answer, and that's why the WSDL definition is usually created for you by an automated tool, though you may want to customize the definition. Among the reasons for the complexity:

- To allow flexibility at WSDL development time. The fine distinctions between one element type and the next allow for greater reuse of different kinds of information (for example, messages).

- To allow vocabulary extensions that are precisely targeted to support new functionality, including functionality that WSDL's designers may not have foreseen.

- To support a wide range of runtime behaviors. In particular, a WSDL definition can describe a complex service interface:

  - A service can include several operations that interact with requesters. A particular order-processing service can include three operations, for example: one for receiving an order from an existing corporate customer, one for receiving an order from an unknown individual, and one for reporting on the status of an order.

  - A single operation also might support multiple message exchange patterns (MEPs), as when the message sent in one invocation requires a response but the message sent in a second invocation does not.

Definitions written in WSDL 1.1 are commonplace and usually support only the following MEPs, which were covered in Chapter 2:

- a one-way pattern, in which the requester invokes the service with an input message but does not receive a response

- a request-response pattern, in which the requester invokes the service with an input message and receives a response, which may be a fault message

In the future, use of WSDL 2.0 is likely to result in a more widespread use of other MEPs.

You can include a WSDL definition in a single file or divide the definition into several files. Listing 5.1 shows the outline of a typical WSDL 1.1 definition.

```
<definitions>
    <types> </types>
    <message>
        <part> </part>
    </message>
    <portType>
        <operation>
            <input> </input>
            <output> </output>
            <fault> </fault>
        </operation>
    </portType>
    <binding>
        <operation> </operation>
    </binding>
    <service>
        <port> </port>
    </service>
</definitions>
```

Listing 5.1: Outline of a WSDL 1.1 definition

In the next sections, we review the WSDL 1.1 definition for a service called getMotorVehicleRecord, which is provided by a fictional Department of Motor Vehicles (DMV). Highlight Insurance invokes this service to verify the details in an insurance-policy request. Listing 5.2 shows the complete WSDL definition.

```
<wsdl:definitions
    name="MotorVehicleRecordsService"
    xmlns:soap="http://schemas.xmlsoap.org/wsdl/soap/"
    xmlns:tns="http://www.dmv.org/"
    xmlns:wsdl="http://schemas.xmlsoap.org/wsdl/"
    xmlns:xsd="http://www.w3.org/2001/XMLSchema"
    targetNamespace="http://www.dmv.org/">

    <wsdl:types>
        <xsd:schema targetNamespace="http://www.dmv.org/">
            <xsd:element name="getMotorVehicleRecord">
                <xsd:complexType>
                    <xsd:sequence>
                        <xsd:element name="VIN" type="xsd:string"/>
                        <xsd:element name="State" type="xsd:string"/>
                        <xsd:element name="Category" type="xsd:string"/>
                    </xsd:sequence>
                </xsd:complexType>
            </xsd:element>
```

Listing 5.2: WSDL definition for the getMotorVehicleRecord service (part 1 of 2)

```
                <xsd:element name="getMotorVehicleRecordResponse">
                    <xsd:complexType>
                        <xsd:sequence>
                            <xsd:element name="RequestID" type="xsd:string"/>
                        </xsd:sequence>
                    </xsd:complexType>
                </xsd:element>
            </xsd:schema>
        </wsdl:types>

        <wsdl:message name="getDMVRecordRequest">
            <wsdl:part element="tns:getMotorVehicleRecord"
                       name="DMVRecordRequest" />
        </wsdl:message>
        <wsdl:message name="getDMVRecordResponse">
            <wsdl:part element="tns:getMotorVehicleRecordResponse"
                       name="DMVRecordResponse" />
        </wsdl:message>

        <wsdl:portType name="DMVRecord">
            <wsdl:operation name="getMotorVehicleRecord">
                <wsdl:input message="tns:getDMVRecordRequest" />
                <wsdl:output message="tns:getDMVRecordResponse" />
            </wsdl:operation>
        </wsdl:portType>

        <wsdl:binding name="MotorVehicleRecordsSOAPBinding"
                      type="tns:DMVRecord">
            <soap:binding style="document"
                          transport="http://schemas.xmlsoap.org/soap/http" />
            <wsdl:operation name="getMotorVehicleRecord">
                <soap:operation soapAction=""/>
                <wsdl:input>
                    <soap:body use="literal" />
                </wsdl:input>
                <wsdl:output>
                    <soap:body use="literal" />
                </wsdl:output>
            </wsdl:operation>
        </wsdl:binding>

        <wsdl:service name="MotorVehicleRecordsService">
            <wsdl:port binding="tns:MotorVehicleRecordsSOAPBinding"
                       name="MotorVehicleRecordsSOAPPort">
                <soap:address location="http://www.dmv.org/" />
            </wsdl:port>
        </wsdl:service>
    </wsdl:definitions>
```

Listing 5.2: WSDL definition for the getMotorVehicleRecord service (part 2 of 2)

We review the two kinds of details included in a WSDL definition: service-interface details and additional access details. For a complete description of WSDL, see the following W3C documents:

- *Web Services Description Language (WSDL) 1.1*, available at *http://www.w3.org/TR/wsdl*.

- *Web Services Description Language (WSDL) Version 2.0 Part 1: Core Language*, available at *http://www.w3.org/TR/wsdl20*.

Service-Interface Details

The following sections identify WSDL elements that are used to describe a service interface.

The definitions Start-tag

The definitions element is the root element of the WSDL definition. Listing 5.3 shows the start-tag of the definitions element in our example.

```
<wsdl:definitions
    name="MotorVehicleRecordsService"
    xmlns:soap="http://schemas.xmlsoap.org/wsdl/soap/"
    xmlns:tns="http://www.dmv.org/"
    xmlns:wsdl="http://schemas.xmlsoap.org/wsdl/"
    xmlns:xsd="http://www.w3.org/2001/XMLSchema"
    targetNamespace="http://www.dmv.org/">
```

Listing 5.3: Sample definitions start-tag

That start-tag includes several attributes, and understanding all but the first requires an understanding of namespaces, which were described in Chapter 4.

The first attribute, name, is solely for documentation. The last attribute, targetNamespace, specifies the target namespace, which contains each name you're adding to the WSDL file. The target namespace contains the value of the name attribute of each message element, for example. The target namespace specified in the definitions start-tag, however, does not include the names you add in the file's XML Schema definition (XSD), which has a targetNamespace attribute that applies solely to that Schema. In many cases, the two target namespaces are the same.

Namespace declarations in the definitions start-tag indicate a default namespace (which is specific to WSDL) and define a set of prefixes that can be used to reference other namespaces. Our example features three prefixes: tns refers to the target namespace identified in the definitions element; xsd refers to the target namespace identified in the XML Schema; and soap refers to a SOAP-specific namespace.

The types Element

The WSDL definition's types element describes the data available for building the input and output messages. In our example, that element includes the XML Schema definition shown in Listing 5.4.

```
<wsdl:types>
    <xsd:schema targetNamespace="http://www.dmv.org/">
        <xsd:element name="getMotorVehicleRecord">
            <xsd:complexType>
                <xsd:sequence>
                    <xsd:element name="VIN" type="xsd:string"/>
                    <xsd:element name="State" type="xsd:string"/>
                    <xsd:element name="Category" type="xsd:string"/>
                </xsd:sequence>
            </xsd:complexType>
        </xsd:element>
        <xsd:element name="getMotorVehicleRecordResponse">
            <xsd:complexType>
                <xsd:sequence>
                    <xsd:element name="RequestID" type="xsd:string"/>
                </xsd:sequence>
            </xsd:complexType>
        </xsd:element>
    </xsd:schema>
</wsdl:types>
```

Listing 5.4: XML Schema definition

In keeping with the preferred message format (called *document-literal wrapped*), this XSD begins with a *wrapper element* for the request message. That element has the same name as the operation being invoked and includes or references a complex type that describes the message.

The previous types element is appropriate for our example because the collection of data types is probably unique to a specific service interface. An alternative is appropriate, however, when you're defining a data-type collection that is likely to be reused. We'll continue with this example to show you the alternative types element (Listing 5.5).

```
<wsdl:types>
   <xsd:schema>
      <xsd:import namespace="http://www.dmv.org/"
                  schemaLocation="GetMVRecord.xsd">
      </xsd:import>
   </xsd:schema>

   <xsd:element name="getMotorVehicleRecord">
      <xsd:complexType>
         <xsd:sequence>
            <xsd:element name="recordSearchInfo"
                         type="xsd1:MVRecordSearchInfo"/>
         </xsd:sequence>
      </xsd:complexType>
   </xsd:element>
   <xsd:element name="getMotorVehicleRecordResponse">
      <xsd:complexType>
         <xsd:sequence>
            <xsd:element name="response"
                         type="xsd1:MVRecordResponse"/>
         </xsd:sequence>
      </xsd:complexType>
   </xsd:element>
</wsdl:types>
```

Listing 5.5: Alternative types element

We've used the preferred message format again, but in this case we've referenced the complex types, stored the types separately, and used an import statement to make the types available in the WSDL file. This approach yields several benefits. It lets the business developer change the types without affecting the WSDL file. In addition, the types can be used in multiple WSDL files; can be the basis of extensions and restrictions, as shown in Chapter 4; and can be the basis of a shortcut used in Business Process Execution Language (BPEL), as shown in Chapter 8. The types also can be stored in a repository that is made available throughout the business. However implemented, the repository can guide designers and programmers in a variety of projects.

Listing 5.6 shows the separately stored types in an XSD file. We comment further on the message format later.

```
<?xml version="1.0" encoding="ISO-8859-1"?>

<xsd:schema xmlns:xsd="http://www.w3.org/2001/XMLSchema"
            targetNamespace="http://www.dmv.org/"
            xmlns:tns="http://www.dmv.org/">

    <xsd:complexType name="MVRecordSearchInfo">
        <xsd:sequence>
            <xsd:element name="VIN" type="xsd:string" />
            <xsd:element name="State" type="xsd:string" />
            <xsd:element name="Category" type="xsd:string" />
        </xsd:sequence>
    </xsd:complexType>

    <xsd:complexType name="MVRecordResponse">
        <xsd:sequence>
            <xsd:element name="RequestID" type="xsd:string" />
        </xsd:sequence>
    </xsd:complexType>
</xsd:schema>
```

Listing 5.6: Types stored in an XSD file

The message Element

Each message element in the WSDL definition defines an input, output, or fault message and includes one or more part elements, each referring to a data type. Listing 5.7 shows the message elements for our example.

```
<wsdl:message name="getDMVRecordRequest">
    <wsdl:part element="tns:getMotorVehicleRecord"
               name="DMVRecordRequest" />
</wsdl:message>
<wsdl:message name="getDMVRecordResponse">
    <wsdl:part element="tns:getMotorVehicleRecordResponse"
               name="DMVRecordResponse" />
</wsdl:message>
```

Listing 5.7: Sample message elements

In some cases, you'll see multiple part elements in a message element, usually meaning that each part element represents a parameter of the service and that the order of part elements corresponds to the order of parameters. The best practice in most situations, however, is to organize the WSDL definition as our example is organized: each message includes only one part element, and the types element identifies the parameters, if any.

In any case, the content of a message element is used only if referenced by a descendant of a portType element, which we review next.

The portType Element

The portType element defines the service interface and can include multiple operation elements, each describing how to invoke a specific operation. Listing 5.8 shows the portType element for our example.

```
<wsdl:portType name="DMVRecord">
    <wsdl:operation name="getMotorVehicleRecord">
        <wsdl:input message="tns:getDMVRecordRequest" />
        <wsdl:output message="tns:getDMVRecordResponse" />
    </wsdl:operation>
</wsdl:portType>
```

Listing 5.8: Sample portType element

Included in an operation element are none, some, or all of the following subordinate elements:

- an input element, which defines an input message (but not every service requires an input beyond the operation name)

- an output element, which defines an output message, if any

- zero to many fault elements, each defining a fault message (that is, an error message)

In most cases, each subordinate element refers to a message element. In a complex case, the operation element may include a parameterOrder attribute to override the parameter order that a related message element specified.

WSDL 2.0 replaces the portType element with the interface element, which is similar.

Additional Access Details

We now review WSDL elements that cause the data to be formatted in a particular way and to be sent to a specific location over a specific transport protocol.

As before, WSDL allows for complexity. You may want to support a wide variety of requesters, including some that process SOAP-based messages and some that do not. You also may want to associate a service with multiple locations, as is useful to distinguish between test- and production-level versions of a service or to ensure that a service is available when a network fails or when many requesters are attempting access.

In the usual case, all requester messages are formatted in the same way and are sent to a single location over a single transport protocol.

The binding Element

The binding element associates a portType element with most of the additional details needed to structure a runtime transmission. Listing 5.9 shows an example.

```
<wsdl:binding name="MotorVehicleRecordsSOAPBinding"
              type="tns:DMVRecord">
   <soap:binding style="document"
                 transport="http://schemas.xmlsoap.org/soap/http" />
   <wsdl:operation name="getMotorVehicleRecord">
      <soap:operation soapAction=""/>
      <wsdl:input>
         <soap:body use="literal" />
      </wsdl:input>
      <wsdl:output>
         <soap:body use="literal" />
      </wsdl:output>
   </wsdl:operation>
</wsdl:binding>
```

Listing 5.9: Sample binding element

The type attribute in the binding element refers to a portType element by name.

Some child elements of the binding element represent extensions to WSDL, as needed for a particular message format (such as SOAP) and transport protocol (such as HTTP).

When you work with SOAP over HTTP, you may be asked to choose a binding style (*rpc* or *document*) and, less often, a use (*literal* or *encoded*).

The binding style represents a message sub-format:

- A value of *rpc* means that the operation name goes into the transmitted message.

- A value of *document* means that the operation name does not go into the transmitted message.

The binding element should specify *document* in almost all cases. Incidentally, the values *rpc* and *document* only reflect how to structure a message and do not correspond to the two kinds of service interface described in Chapter 2.

The *use* value concerns how the runtime transmission is structured for data-type validation:

- *literal* means that the transmitted data will conform to the details you specify in the WSDL types element and will be structured simply, as in this example.

  ```
  <VIN>A123</VIN>
  ```

- *encoded* means that the transmitted data will reference data types in attributes, as in this example:

  ```
  <VIN xsi:type="xsd:string">A123</VIN>
  ```

The binding element should specify *literal* in almost all cases.

For more information about your formatting choices, go to *http://www.ibm.com/ developerworks*, and search for the quoted string "Which style of WSDL should I use?"

Let's briefly mention two other details:

- Each operation element in the binding element is associated with a same-named operation element in the portType element.

- The soapAction attribute is placed in the transmitted message for inspection by a receiving server but is being discontinued in WSDL 2.0. In most cases, assign an empty string.

Not shown in our example is reference to the SOAP Header elements that include Quality of Service details. You can specify an *explicit header*, in which case QoS details are defined in the binding element and in the elements that describe the service interface. The effect in one sense is quite simple: the requester includes QoS-related arguments in the service invocation. When an explicit header is in use, however, you're mixing QoS and business detail, and the mixing is undesirable:

- Over time, your company wants to benefit from a division of labor, with different people working on different kinds of detail, at best in different files that are combined to form a single WSDL definition. This division of labor allows use of people who specialize in security or other issues.

- The developer of the requester code shouldn't need to code QoS-specific arguments or even necessarily to know about the type of QoS data that must be transmitted. As much as possible, you want the developer to focus on business issues.

As an alternative, you can specify an *implicit header*, in which case the QoS details are described only in the binding element and have no effect on service parameters. Some analysts suggest that this option is the best available, as it separates QoS data definition from parameter definition, and an SOA runtime product can ensure that QoS details are included in the transferred message.

The problem in both cases is that you lose flexibility. Describing QoS data in the WSDL definition means that you're required to use QoS details whenever you deploy the service. You might want to deploy a service and use a security scheme in some cases (for example, when connecting with a business partner) but avoid a security scheme in others (for example, when the requester and service are in the same company).

The direction in the industry is to describe QoS details outside the WSDL definition. This book emphasizes the greater flexibility that comes from making QoS decisions at configuration time or even later, as when the requester and service negotiate the rules of their interaction at run time.

We'll return to the QoS issue later in the book, when we describe Service Component Architecture.

The service Element

The last major element of a WSDL definition is service, which completely describes the structure of every possible transmission. Listing 5.10 shows an example.

```
<wsdl:service name="MotorVehicleRecordsService">
    <wsdl:port binding="tns:MotorVehicleRecordsSOAPBinding"
               name="MotorVehicleRecordsSOAPPort">
        <soap:address location="http://www.dmv.org/" />
    </wsdl:port>
</wsdl:service>
```

Listing 5.10: Sample service element

Included are a set of port elements, each of which references a binding element by name and includes an address. The meaning of multiple port elements is that the related service can be accessed at any of several locations.

A WSDL port represents a deployed endpoint. An endpoint reference (which allows access of an endpoint at run time) is different from a port description primarily because the reference includes details that are meaningful only at run time.

SOAP

SOAP is an XML format for transmitting data to and from a Web service. An automated tool creates the SOAP file, which includes details from the WSDL definition. For details on SOAP that go beyond our introduction, see the following primer: *http://www.w3.org/TR/2003/REC-soap12-part0-20030624*.

SOAP Format

The major elements in the transmitted SOAP message are as follows:

- the Envelope element, which is the root and usually includes namespace declarations.

- the Header element, which includes Quality of Service details. The Header element is optional; if it is present, each of its immediate children is called a *header block*.

- the Body element, which includes business data.

Listing 5.11 depicts the overall structure of a SOAP message.

```
<Envelope>
  <Header>
    <!- header blocks go here ->
  </Header>
  <Body>
    <!- business data goes here ->
  </Body>
</Envelope>
```

Listing 5.11: Structure of a SOAP message

Example

We created the SOAP output shown in Listing 5.12 using IBM Rational Application Developer.

```
<SOAP-ENV:Envelope
    xmlns:SOAP-ENV="http://schemas.xmlsoap.org/soap/envelope/"
    xmlns:q0="http://www.dmv.org/"
    xmlns:xsd="http://www.w3.org/2001/XMLSchema"
    xmlns:xsi="http://www.w3.org/2001/XMLSchema-instance">
    <SOAP-ENV:Body>
        <q0:getMotorVehicleRecord>
            <VIN>A123</VIN>
            <State>NC</State>
            <Category>sport</Category>
        </q0:getMotorVehicleRecord>
    </SOAP-ENV:Body>
</SOAP-ENV:Envelope>
```

Listing 5.12: Sample SOAP output

The Envelope element start-tag includes namespace details. The prefixes SOAP-ENV, xsd, and xsi are commonplace, even though this specific SOAP transmission doesn't use them. Use of the q0 prefix (in place of the WSDL-specific tns prefix) is a detail specific to Rational Application Developer. At the other end of the transmission, the namespace Universal Resource Identifier (URI) is important, but the identity of the prefix that references the URI is not.

Header Blocks

As Web-based SOA runtimes become more advanced, header blocks will become more important; and the content of those blocks will increasingly conform to the open-standard *WS-** specifications being developed by various organizations.

The header block can include details that are needed to fulfill the kind of QoS options described in Chapter 2. The block can also indicate whether conditional processing is required, as when the service returns a log of its activity during some invocations but not others.

You can set header blocks explicitly in the WSDL file that contributes to the SOAP message. More likely, however, is that your SOA runtime product adds header blocks in accordance with data structures and values that are established at configuration time.

The extra details provided by header blocks may not be meaningful at a particular intermediary or at the final destination. To allow you to control a variety of cases, SOAP lets you set the following attributes in any header block:

- The mustUnderstand attribute indicates whether a given *SOAP engine* (a kind of XML processor) must handle the header block. By default, the value of *false* is transmitted, which means that handling is not required.

- The actor attribute identifies the SOAP engine to which the mustUnderstand attribute applies. By default, mustUnderstand applies to the message's final destination.

A SOAP engine that handles a header block must remove that block, although the processor can always add the equivalent header block or any other.

In SOAP 1.2, the role attribute replaces actor and identifies, not an intermediary, but a specific role whose name and purpose are defined by an intermediary. As in Version 1.1, however, the default behavior is to process the header block at the message's final destination.

Like business data, the data in a header block usually conforms to an XML Schema definition.

SOAP Body

The SOAP body includes business data, such as that shown in Listing 5.13.

```
<SOAP-ENV:Body>
    <q0:getMotorVehicleRecord>
        <VIN>A123</VIN>
        <State>NC</State>
        <Category>sport</Category>
    </q0:getMotorVehicleRecord>
</SOAP-ENV:Body>
```

Listing 5.13: Sample SOAP body

The data is structured in a way that reflects a WSDL format called *document-literal wrapped*, which means that

- on receiving the message, the service accesses the operation name (getMotorVehicleRecord) and can easily dispatch the message to that operation
- the elements lack the encoded data-type attributes (as shown earlier) that would otherwise degrade performance
- every data value can be validated by an XML Schema definition

SOAP at Run Time

We now outline how the SOAP engine fits into a larger scheme.

The main purpose of the SOAP engine is to convert data between a language-specific format and the format used in the transmitted message. A data conversion is required on both the requester and service sides of the transmission.

When the requester is written in Java, the runtime events are often as shown in Figure 5.2. On the client side, the requester invokes a JAX-RPC stub, which is Java code that your development environment created for you, in most cases. The Java code is based on service-specific details in a WSDL definition and lets you invoke the service as if you were invoking a local function.

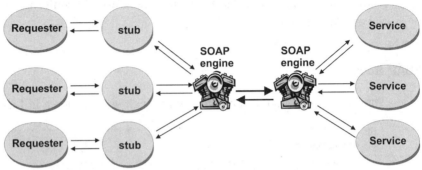

Figure 5.2: SOAP at run time

The stub frees the requester from interacting directly with the SOAP engine. In response to the stub's access, the engine converts data from the Java data types into a SOAP format and transmits the data.

On receiving a return message, if any (it may be business data or an error message), the stub uses the information from the WSDL definition again, in this case to convert data from a SOAP format into the data types expected by the requester.

On the service side, the SOA runtime code responds to its invocation by using a service-side WSDL definition to create data that the service can use. That WSDL definition is equivalent to the definition used during creation of the client-side stub.

The SOA runtime code submits the data to the service. When the service returns data, the SOA runtime first uses the service-side WSDL definition to convert data from the native-language data types into a SOAP format. The service then returns the message to the client.

When intermediaries are in use, the message is passed from one SOAP engine to another, and data conversions occur as needed when a message is transmitted first over one transport protocol, then over another.

UDDI

UDDI is a set of rules for registering and retrieving details about a business and its services. As you design a program, you might search a UDDI registry for Web services to invoke in your code. You also might create a program that queries a UDDI registry at run time to access a set of similar services because (for example) each provides price information for a specific product. The latter use of UDDI is less common, however.

A UDDI registry might include details on business services (not just on software), but the major purpose of such a registry is to publicize what Web services are available in a particular domain such as a business or industry. The publicity exposes redundant Web services and promotes reuse.

Other purposes are possible, especially in products that build on the UDDI standard. Those UDDI-compliant products provide sophisticated user interfaces so that users are better able to register, review, and compare information. The products may track the planning and fulfillment of project tasks when a company is updating Web services so that the software complies with Service Level Agreements (SLAs) or industry standards. UDDI-compliant products also may hold additional details. Use of the word *repository* in some products suggests that SLAs, WSDL definitions, and supporting documentation of all kinds are immediately available and are not merely on a remote site that is referenced by the UDDI registry.

Among the categories of information in a UDDI registry entry:

- *business entity*, which usually includes

    ♦ basic information such as business name and address

    ♦ a set of classifications, such as by industry or by a category of products offered

    ♦ a reference to the services provided by the business

- *publisher assertion*, which indicates a business relationship, as when one business is a subsidiary of another

- *business service*, which usually includes the service name and description

- *binding template*, which includes a service's access point such as a phone number (as might be appropriate for a non-software service) or a URL (for a Web service)

When interacting with a UDDI registry, you may be exposed to the following terms:

- *tModel* (technical model) is a data structure that references a specification such as a WSDL definition.

- *Category bag* is a list of entries. Each entry identifies an instance of a category, as in the following examples:

  - One category bag indicates that a business is in a particular geographical area (such as Connecticut) and handles a particular product (such as insurance).

  - A second category bag indicates that a service is described with a particular kind of specification (such as a WSDL definition) and fulfills a particular kind of purpose (such as providing a stock quote).

- *Identifier bag* is a list of similar entries — for example, a list of corporate tax IDs for use in different jurisdictions.

SOAP is the basis for the transfer of data to and from a registry. In the message shown in Listing 5.14, the UDDI directive get_businessDetail retrieves business-specific information that was stored at some previous time.

```
<Envelope xmlns=
   "http://schemas.xmlsoap.org/soap/envelope/">
   <Body>
      <get_businessDetail generic="2.0" xmlns="urn:uddi-org:api_v2">
         <businessKey=
            "uddi:AB0E435D-890B-1358-6DE2-6349816453F5">
         </businessKey>
      </get_businessDetail>
   </Body>
</Envelope>
```

Listing 5.14: Sample message containing a UDDI directive

For further details about UDDI, see the following Web site, which is operated by OASIS: *http://www.uddi.org.*

CHAPTER 6

Introduction to XPath

We introduced XML and showed how it made possible the three best-known SOA standards: WSDL, SOAP, and UDDI. We'd like to progress now to *Business Process Execution Language (BPEL)*, which is used to create services that orchestrate real-world business processes.

We can describe how each service (called a *BPEL process*) accepts messages from Web services A and B and sends related messages to Web services X and Y. But first we need to review how the BPEL process queries a message to retrieve specific data and how it calculates and compares values, which may be derived from the queried data.

If we're to do more than transfer data from here to there, we need a lower-level language; by default, BPEL 2.0 relies on *XPath 1.0*.

In addition to its use in BPEL, XPath (which stands for *XML Path Language*) is used in Service Component Architecture (SCA) and Service Data Objects (SDO), to isolate specific values. XPath is also central to XQuery 2.0, which we expect will become a widely used technology for accessing business data. Moreover, XPath plays a key role in XML Stylesheet Language Transformations (XSLT), a language for reorganizing data to accommodate the input requirements of different services, to handle calculations and comparisons more easily, and to allow use of a single XML source from which you derive a variety of outputs.

This chapter describes the first version of XPath and may be sufficient for your work in the language. If you're working with XPath 2.0, you'll need details that are available elsewhere — for example, in Michael Kay's work, *XPath 2.0 Programmer's Reference* (Wrox Press, 2004). Unless otherwise stated, our comments apply in either case.

XPath is a language for *addressing* (that is, accessing) the values in *XML source*, which is either an XML document or a variable based on XML. The language is also used for creating numeric, string, and Boolean expressions. Those expressions can include XML-stored values, as well as literals, operands, function calls, and other XPath expressions.

The defining aspect of XPath is the *location path*, which is the syntax for addressing XML-based values. To get you started with that syntax, this chapter offers examples and informal descriptions. Language specifications are at the following W3C sites: *http://www.w3.org/TR/xpath* (for XPath 1.0) and *http://www.w3.org/TR/xpath20* (for XPath 2.0).

Our explanations don't assume that you're trying our examples or creating your own, but if you wish to gain practical experience, you can set up a Windows 2000/NT/XP environment as described in Appendix B. An alternative for Java programmers is to use the Java API for XML Processing (JAXP), as noted in the following article: *http://www-128.ibm.com/developerworks/library/x-javaxpathapi.html.*

Nodes

The XPath processor reads the XML source and includes the information in a series of data structures called *nodes*, which include only the information necessary for data access. An XPath node doesn't provide detail, for example, on whether an attribute value was embedded in single or double quotation marks.

Seven different kinds of nodes are related to one another in a tree structure that is specific to XPath. The purpose of four of the seven nodes is straightforward. Each *element, attribute, comment,* and *processing-instruction node* has information that was derived from a corresponding aspect of the XML source. Each *text node* has information on the text value of an XML element. Each *namespace node* has information on the namespaces that are in scope for a given element. Last, the single *root node* (what XPath 2.0 calls the *document node*) has information on the entire XML document.

In the tree structure built from the following example, the children of the root node are, in order, a comment node, an element node, and another comment node.

```
<?xml version="1.0" encoding="ISO-8859-1"?>
<!- here is an insured ->
<Insured></Insured>
<!- end of file ->
```

The root node is not the same as the *root element*, which is the ancestor of all other elements in the XML source. The root node is more inclusive; it is the ancestor of the element node that was derived from the root element.

```
<?xml version="1.0" encoding="ISO-8859-1"?>
<!-- CarPolicy applicant -->
<Insured CustomerID="5">
    <CarPolicy PolicyType="Auto">
        <Vehicle Category="Sedan">
            <Make>Honda</Make>
            <Model>Accord</Model>
        </Vehicle>
        <Vehicle Category="Sport" Domestic="True">
            <Make>Ford</Make>
            <Model>Mustang</Model>
        </Vehicle>
    </CarPolicy>
    <CarPolicy PolicyType="Antique">
        <Vehicle Category="Sport">
            <Make>Triumph</Make>
            <Model>Spitfire</Model>
        </Vehicle>
        <Vehicle Category="Coupe" Domestic="True">
            <Make>Buick</Make>
            <Model>Skylark</Model>
        </Vehicle>
        <Vehicle Category="Sport">
            <Make>Porsche</Make>
            <Model>Speedster</Model>
        </Vehicle>
    </CarPolicy>
</Insured>
```

Listing 6.1: Sample XML document

The XPath nodes have no details on the XML declaration. They also lack details on a DOCTYPE declaration, which is present when a validation mechanism called a Document Type Definition (DTD) is in use.

You can access specific data by referencing the nodes in a sequence that leads from the root node to the nodes of interest. Every node has a string value, so you gain access to a unit of business data as soon as you reference (in particular) an element or attribute node. Consider, for example, the XML document shown in Listing 6.1.

Here's a kind of XPath expression (called a *location path*) for accessing the make of the vehicles whose Category value is *Coupe*.

```
/Insured/CarPolicy/Vehicle[@Category='Coupe']/Make
```

As we describe this expression in the following paragraphs, we refer to nodes by a type name, as when we say Vehicle node.

The initial virgule (/) in the expression indicates that the search for data starts at the root node. The set of characters between one virgule and the next represents a *location step*. Each location step selects nodes based on criteria that you specify.

The first step (Insured) brings the search to the node that is subordinate to the root node and has details on the root element. The Insured node refers to a single element, but the general rule is important: location steps provide access to a *node set*, which is a group of nodes that (with exceptions) are arranged in *XML-source order* (an order that reflects the sequence of content in the XML source) or is an empty set. An empty set is the outcome when no node conforms to the selection criteria.

We will have more to say about ordering in due time.

In general terms, a location path is an XPath expression that resolves to a node set. An *absolute location path* is one that starts at the root node, and a *relative location path* is one that starts in the middle of a node tree.

The second step in our sample expression (CarPolicy) brings us to a node set that has multiple members — specifically, a set of all CarPolicy nodes that are children of the Insured node.

The third step (Vehicle[@Category='Coupe']) continues the path, referencing all Vehicle nodes that are children of any CarPolicy node that is itself a child of the Insured node. The brackets ([]) and the syntax internal to them is a *predicate*, which contains a Boolean expression or (as shown later) an abbreviation that is expanded to a Boolean expression. The XPath processor selects only the nodes for which the expression evaluates to *true*.

In this case, the location step means "access all the Vehicle nodes, with the further restriction that the string value of the Category attribute node is *Coupe*." When you refer to an attribute node in a predicate, you precede the name with the "at sign" (@), as shown.

Here's another predicate, outside our example.

```
[@Exterior='white' and @Interior='red']
```

You might read this as, ". . . with the further restriction that the exterior is white and the interior is red."

Continuing with our main example, the fourth step (Make) completes the path, referencing the Make node for the Vehicle nodes whose Category attribute value is *Coupe*. In this case, the overall expression resolves to an element node whose string value is *Buick*.

XPath cannot create nodes or add detail to an XML source. You can use XPath in the context of XSLT, however, to create output that is based on, first, an XML source and, second, a set of directions (including XPath expressions) that are supplied in an XML stylesheet. If you use the instructions in Appendix B to try out XPath expressions, you'll be creating an output with XSLT.

Avoiding Errors

We interrupt this description of a language to give you some practical pointers on avoiding errors.

First, if you work with the environment described in Appendix B, you'll find that the XPath expression causes an error if the syntax is incorrect but does not cause an error if names or values are not in the XML under review. (You receive no error message, for example, if you type Category instead of @Category.) That lack of errors doesn't extend to every other product that incorporates XPath, however. When you work in BPEL, you'll find that an empty set itself may cause an error if you copy an empty set to a variable.

Second, when you work with XPath in an XML file rather than through a user interface, consider the following points:

- Delimit a string with single quotes (or the characters ') if the string is in an expression that is delimited by double quotes. Similarly, delimit a string with double quotes (or the characters ") if the string is in an expression that is delimited by single quotes. Use of the same kind of quotation marks for the string and the expression ends the expression prematurely.

- To express comparison operators that include angle brackets, use the following characters:
  - > for greater than (>)
  - < for less than (<)
  - >= for greater than or equal to (>=)
  - <= for less than or equal to (<=)

- Use & if you wish to type an ampersand (&).

Last, when you're working on a real-world problem, try to recall a namespace-related issue that we now describe.

If an XML element is in the default namespace, you cannot access the element node by name unless the XPath expression uses a prefix when referring to that name. In the following XML source, for example, CarPolicy is in namespace defaultNamespace.

```
<other:Insured xmlns="defaultNamespace"
               xmlns:other="otherNamespace">
    <CarPolicy type="Antique"/>
</other:Insured>
```

The next XPath expression, however, resolves to an empty set because CarPolicy is not being addressed correctly.

```
/other:Insured/CarPolicy
```

To access the CarPolicy node, you can use syntax (as shown later) for accessing a node without referencing a node name at all. The solution that applies more often, however, is to ensure that the XPath expression has access to and uses the appropriate namespace.

To demonstrate the solution, we need to show the XPath expression in its native habitat, inside an XML file. Assume, for example, that the XPath expression resides in the from element of a BPEL process, as shown next.

```
<from xmlns:abcde="defaultNamespace"
      xmlns:other="otherNamespace">
   $myVariable/other:Insured/abcde:CarPolicy
</from>
```

The BPEL variable ($myVariable) that begins the XPath expression contains XML-based data such as a transmitted message. In this case, the specific variable contains the other:Insured node that we just described. The location path that follows the variable identifies how to access the data inside that variable.

Do you see what we've done? The XML element that contains the XPath expression has the information necessary to ensure that the XPath expression works. Specifically, the XPath expression has access to a prefix (abcde) that in turn refers to the namespace URI called defaultNamespace. The namespace problem is fully solved because CarPolicy is being addressed with a prefix that refers to defaultNamespace.

Context

Let's return to the language itself.

The XPath processor evaluates a location path one step at a time, and each node that is selected during a given step provides a *context*, which is information that limits which nodes are available in the next step.

As suggested in Figure 6.1, if we descend the node tree /Insured/CarPolicy/Vehicle one generation at a time

- a single Insured node provides a context that limits us to selecting (at most) the two CarPolicy nodes

- the first of the CarPolicy nodes provides a context that limits us to selecting (at most) the first two Vehicle nodes

- the second CarPolicy node provides a context that limits us to selecting (at most) the last three Vehicle nodes

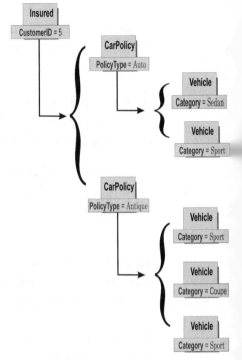

The node that provides a context at a given time is called the *context node*.

Perhaps the best way to understand a location path is to consider the location-path characters that act as operators. As we saw earlier, if an expression begins with a virgule, the search starts at the root node. The essential point, however, is that if the virgule is placed between one location step and the next (in CarPolicy/Vehicle, for example), the XPath processor selects *in turn* each node (in this

Figure 6.1: Context

case, each CarPolicy node) that was retained by the location step at the left of the virgule. The node selected at a given time is the context node. The processor then uses that node when evaluating the location step at the right of the virgule. The virgule completes its operation only when, for each context node, the XPath processor evaluates the right-side location step.

Similarly, the presence of a predicate (in Vehicle[@Category='Coupe'], for example) causes the XPath processor to select *in turn* each node (in this case, each Vehicle node) that was retained by the syntax that immediately precedes the predicate in the same location step. The selected node is the context node. The processor retains that node only if the predicate evaluates to *true*. The predicate completes its operation only when, for each context node, the XPath processor evaluates the predicate.

In both cases, the node used "in turn" is the context node.

Our definition of context node is the one you need as you explore location paths, but be aware that we're using a subset of the W3C definition, which states that the context node is the node being processed at a given time. The W3C definition and the explanations required to make it meaningful are geared to developers of XPath processors.

The word "context" is included in additional terms. In some cases, *context position* reflects the position of the context node in the sequence of possible context nodes. That position ranges from 1 to the *context size*, which is the number of nodes in the set of nodes that are each used (in turn) as a context node. In a broader sense, *context position* reflects the position of a node in a node set, and *context size* is the number of nodes in that set. We'll show the different uses of these terms as appropriate.

You can use a *positional predicate*, which is a predicate that restricts the addressed nodes based on the context position. For example, the following expression restricts the selection to the second Vehicle child within each CarPolicy node.

```
/Insured/CarPolicy/Vehicle[position()=2]
```

Those nodes represent *Ford Mustang* and *Buick Skylark*. As described later, however, the only string value that is displayed (if you're trying out these examples) is *Ford Mustang*.

If the comparison operator is an equal sign (=), an abbreviated form of a positional predicate is valid. The last expression can be stated as follows.

```
/Insured/CarPolicy/Vehicle[2]
```

Other operators are valid, too, as listed later. You can select the nodes at any position greater than 1, for example.

```
/Insured/CarPolicy/Vehicle[position()&gt; 1]
```

Here, the returned nodes represent *Ford Mustang*, *Buick Skylark*, and *Porsche Speedster*. However, only *Ford Mustang* is displayed as a string value.

You can verify the number of returned nodes by using the XPath function *count*, which takes a node set as its only argument. The next example returns the value *3*.

```
count(/Insured/CarPolicy/Vehicle[position()&gt; 1])
```

Examples

We have more to tell before we present "Location Steps in Summary," a later section that concisely explains what location steps do. For now, let's look at some more examples.

- As mentioned, /Insured/CarPolicy/Vehicle makes available all Vehicle nodes that are children of any CarPolicy child within Insured. The following expression resolves to the node whose string value is *Buick*.

```
/Insured/CarPolicy/Vehicle[@Category='Coupe']/Make
```

- In contrast, /Insured/CarPolicy[1]/Vehicle is more restrictive, making available all Vehicle nodes that are children of the first CarPolicy child within Insured. The following expression resolves to an empty set.

```
/Insured/CarPolicy[1]/Vehicle[@Category='Coupe']/Make
```

- /Insured/CarPolicy[last()] selects (within Insured) the last CarPolicy node, which is the node whose PolicyType attribute has the string value *Antique*.
- /Insured/CarPolicy[last()]/Vehicle[last()] selects the third Vehicle node within the second CarPolicy node. That Vehicle node has details on the *Porsche Speedster*.

Let's talk about the returned nodes whose string values are not available to you. The following expression resolves to a set of two Make nodes (one for *Ford*, one for *Buick*).

```
/Insured/CarPolicy/Vehicle[2]/Make
```

Only the first Make node seems to be available. The reason is that most XPath processors (such as the ones used with BPEL) provide the string value only of the first returned node.

The following expression returns an empty set.

```
/Insured/CarPolicy/Vehicle[2]/Make[2]
```

The set is empty because each of the two Vehicle nodes selected by /Insured/CarPolicy/Vehicle[2] has only one Make child, and the predicate [2] refers not to the whole expression but to the Make node.

How do you access only the Make node that refers to *Buick*? The solution is to use parentheses, which selects a node set that can be filtered by a predicate. In the next example, the XPath processor makes available only the second node in the node set.

```
(/Insured/CarPolicy/Vehicle[2]/Make)[2]
```

Incidentally, a parenthetical expression is valid only at the beginning of a location path in XPath 1.0. The next expression is valid only if you're working with XPath 2.0.

```
<!- not a valid expression with XPath 1.0 ->
/Insured/CarPolicy/(Vehicle)
```

Now, let's look again at the effect of the last() function. The following expression returns, for each CarPolicy node, the Make child of the second Vehicle element:

```
/Insured/CarPolicy/Vehicle[2]/Make[last()]
```

The value of last() is *1*, and although the XPath processor returns two nodes (one for *Ford*, one for *Buick*), the only returned string value is *Ford*.

The following expression returns the last Make node of the nodes returned from the parenthesized expression:

```
(/Insured/CarPolicy/Vehicle[2]/Make)[last()]
```

The value of last() is *2*, and the related string value is *Buick*.

A predicate operates in the context of the previous location steps and the syntax that precedes the predicate in the same location step. Therefore . . . what is the result of the next expression?

```
/Insured/CarPolicy/Vehicle[@Category='Sport'][2]/Make
```

This expression evaluates to a single node whose string value is *Porsche*. The reason is that the predicate [2] is operating on each node set that is created by the syntax Vehicle[@Category='Sport']:

- Subordinate to the first CarPolicy node is a node set that contains all Vehicle nodes whose Category attribute equals *Sport*. One node is present, and its Make child has the string value *Ford*. When applied to this set, the predicate [2] yields an empty set.

- Subordinate to the second CarPolicy node is a node set that also contains all Vehicle nodes whose Category attribute equals *Sport*. Two nodes are present, and their Make children have the respective string values *Triumph* and *Porsche*. When applied to this set, the predicate [2] yields the second node.

Here's a variation:

```
/Insured/CarPolicy/Vehicle[@Category='Sport'][last()]/Make
```

Each of the branches mentioned earlier now contributes one node that is returned by last(). The overall expression yields a node set whose string values are *Ford* and *Porsche*, though only the string *Ford* is immediately available.

Order counts, even within a location step. The next example returns the Make node for the second Vehicle child within each CarPolicy node, with the further restriction that the value of attribute Category is *Sport*:

```
/Insured/CarPolicy/Vehicle[2][@Category='Sport']/Make
```

The string value of the single returned node is *Ford*.

Parts of a Location Step

A location step includes, at most, three kinds of details: an axis specification, a node test, and predicates.

An *axis specification* includes a range of nodes for subsequent consideration. The most common axis specification is child, whose use means that the location step accesses *children* of the context. Our examples used the child specification, but child is the default and so was not required in our syntax. If you assign an axis specification explicitly, you must follow it with two colons (for example, child::).

By varying the axis specification

- you can indicate how to select nodes in a given location step; for example, you can include all descendant nodes rather than stepping down the tree one generation at a time

- you can indicate in which direction to seek nodes for selection; for example, you can include nodes that are siblings rather than children or descendants

A *node test* is a criterion to compare against each of the nodes included in an axis specification. That test is either a node name to be matched (as in our prior examples) or a preset value.

Predicates are optional and further restrict the set of nodes that are selected.

Axis Specifications

This section lists the thirteen axis specifications. As you read through the list, note the following distinction. The *forward axes* are the axis specifications that assign context-position numbers to nodes in XML-source order. The *reverse axes* are the axis specifications that assign context-position numbers to nodes in reverse XML-source order.

The XML processor always returns nodes in XML-source order, regardless of whether you use a forward or reverse axis. Only the context-position number that is assigned to each node is affected by the axis direction, as we'll show later.

The axis specifications are as follows:

- ancestor is a reverse axis that includes the parent of the context node, the parent of the parents, and so on, up the tree.

- ancestor-or-self is a reverse axis that includes the context node from the previous location step, along with (as you'd guess) the parent of the context node, the parent of the parents, and so on, up the tree.

- attribute is described later.

- child is a forward axis that includes the children of the context node and is the default axis specification.

- descendant is a forward axis that includes the children of the context node, the children of those children, and so on, down the tree.

- descendant-or-self is a forward axis that includes the context node from the previous location step, along with (right!) the children of the context node, the children of the children, and so on, down the tree.

- following is a forward axis that includes all nodes subsequent to the context node, including subsequent siblings but excluding children and other descendants.

- following-sibling is a forward axis that includes all the next siblings (the first through the last) of the context node.

- namespace is described later.

- parent is a reverse axis that includes the parent of the context node; however, the context position is 1 at most.

- preceding is a reverse axis and includes all prior nodes, including prior siblings and text nodes, but excluding parents and other ancestors.

- preceding-sibling is a reverse axis and includes all previous siblings (the first through the last) of the context node.

- self includes the context node. The axis is considered forward, but the context position is 1 at most.

In general, you can restrict the selection of nodes by using attribute values in predicates. Only two axis specifications, however, actually include attribute nodes or (what is similar) namespace nodes.

The attribute axis specification includes attribute nodes. This specification selects nodes only if the context node is an element node. In the XPath model:

- The parent of an attribute node is an element node and is accessible through the parent or ancestor axis specification. The converse relationship is not true, however: an attribute node is not a child of an element node. You can access an attribute node in two ways: by the attribute axis specification when the context node is an element, and by the self axis specification when the context node is an attribute.

- A namespace URI in a declaration such as xmlns = 'www.ibm.com' or xmlns:tns = 'www.ibm.com' is available through the namespace axis specification but not through the attribute axis specification.

- The order of attribute nodes within an element node can vary from one XPath processor to another. (In general in XML, attributes are unordered.)

The namespace axis specification includes namespace nodes. In XPath 2.0, this rarely used specification is *deprecated* (is made a target for future removal from the language). Therefore, you may want to skim or skip the next paragraph.

The namespace specification selects nodes only if the context node is an element node. The string value of a namespace node is a namespace URI. In the XPath model:

- Each element node includes a namespace node that represents the XML system namespace. (The XML system namespace allows use of attributes such as xml:lang, which identifies a human language.) The string value of the namespace node is *http://www.w3.org/XML/1998/namespace*.

- Each element node also includes a node for each namespace that is in scope for the XML element. Consider the following XML document:

```
<?xml version="1.0" encoding="ISO-8859-1"?>
<other:Insured xlmns="defaultNamespace"
xmlns:other="otherNamespace">
   <CarPolicy/>
</other:Insured>
```

The related CarPolicy node includes namespace nodes whose string values are *defaultNamespace* and *otherNamespace*.

- The parent of a namespace node is an element node. The converse relationship is not in effect, however: a namespace node is not a child of an element node. You can access a namespace node in two ways: by the namespace axis specification when the context node is an element, and by the self axis specification when the context node is a namespace node.

- The order of namespace nodes within an element node can vary from one XPath processor to another.

You can categorize axis specifications in a different way:

- Six axis specifications provide access vertically, up and down the node tree: ancestor, ancestor-or-self, child, descendant, descendant-or-self, and parent. In relation to BPEL, you'll primarily use child and, on occasion, descendant.

- Six axis specifications provide access horizontally, across the node tree: attribute, following, following-sibling, namespace, preceding, and preceding-sibling. In relation to BPEL, you'll probably use only attribute and on occasion, following and following-sibling.

  The attribute and namespace specifications do not concern the relationship of one element node to another but let you access nodes derived from details that are internal to an XML element.

- The self specification stands alone and is used on occasion in BPEL.

Node Tests

As mentioned, a *node test* is a criterion to compare against each of the nodes included in an axis specification. Several preset node tests are available:

- *
- comment()
- text()
- node()
- processing-instruction()

*

The asterisk (*) node test retains all the element nodes and no others in a given axis specification, except in two instances. In the case of the attribute specification, the asterisk retains all the attribute nodes and no others. In the case of the namespace specification, the asterisk retains all the namespace nodes and no others.

The asterisk provides a way to include a node without referencing a name. In relation to our main example, the following expression accesses the second CarPolicy node.

```
/Insured/*[2]
```

comment( )

The comment() node test retains comment nodes, which are children and siblings of element nodes or are children of the root node. Consider the following XML document.

```
<?xml version="1.0" encoding="ISO-8859-1"?>
<!- here is an Insured ->
<Insured><CarPolicy><!- Cancelled -></CarPolicy></Insured>
```

The next expression resolves to the contents of the second comment, including the space that precedes and follows the word *Cancelled*.

```
/descendant::comment()[2]
```

text( )

The text() node test retains text nodes, which are children and siblings of element nodes or are children of the root node. In relation to our main example, the following expression returns a single text node, and the string value is *Buick*.

```
/Insured/CarPolicy/Vehicle[@Category = 'Coupe']/Make/text()
```

If you wish to access multiple text nodes for subsequent string processing, you can select an element node that has descendant element nodes. For example, assume that the Material element includes no line break in the next XML document.

```
<?xml version="1.0" encoding="ISO-8859-1"?>

<Material>Leather<Product>Bucket Seats</Product>
<Quantity>20</Quantity></Material>
```

The XPath expression /Material provides the following string value, which represents the content of the three text nodes that are descendants of the Material node.

LeatherBucket Seats20

Also, the string value of the root node (which is expressed by a virgule) resolves to the same text nodes as does the root element node (which is subordinate). Either of the following expressions resolves to the string *Bucket Seats*.

```
/descendant::text()[2]
/Material/descendant::text()[2]
```

Last, you may become perplexed about the location of text nodes that include or are composed of white space (carriage return, spaces, tabs). Consider the following Material element, for example.

```
<Material>Leather
  <Product>Bucket Seats</Product>
  <Quantity>20</Quantity>
</Material>
```

Three text nodes are children of that element:

- the string *Leather* followed by the white space that is between the end of *Leather* and the left angle bracket of the Product start-tag

- the white space between the right angle bracket that ends the Product element and the left angle bracket of the Quantity start-tag

- the white space between the right angle bracket that ends the Quantity element and the left angle bracket of the Material end-tag

You can access any of those text nodes by a positional predicate. Here's a location path that returns white space.

```
/Material/text()[2]
```

XPath does not retain any space that precedes the first element node.

node( )

The node() node test retrieves all nodes in a given axis specification:

- In the attribute axis specification, the test retrieves only attribute nodes.

- In the namespace axis specification, the test retrieves only namespace nodes.

- Otherwise, the test retrieves all nodes in the axis specification.

processing-instruction( )

The processing-instruction() node test retrieves a set of processing-instruction (PI) nodes, which are children and siblings of element nodes or are children of the root node. Here's an XML document with a single processing instruction:

```
<?xml version="1.0" encoding="ISO-8859-1"?>
<Material>Leather
   <?HandleThis how="somehow"   ?>
   <Product>Leather Seats</Product>
   <Quantity>20</Quantity>
</Material><?HandleThat how="another way"   ?>
```

The next expression returns the contents of the instruction, including the spaces that follow the phrase *how="somehow"*.

```
/Material/processing-instruction('HandleThis')
```

The node test can identify a processing-instruction node by specifying a PI target, such as *HandleThis*, but the test is also valid without specifying a PI target. The next expression returns two nodes.

```
count(/descendant::processing-instruction())
```

The XML declaration statement (which starts with <?xml) is not a processing instruction and is not available to an XPath expression.

Predicates

As noted earlier, a predicate restricts the context nodes based on some criterion, as specified in a Boolean expression. A later section suggests some of the flexibility that is available to you. XPath 1.0 will convert any expression to a Boolean expression, but that behavior may or may not yield the result you intend. We'll give you a hint of the issues now.

A predicate can restrict your selection to a context node that has a specified string value. Either of the following, equivalent location paths, for example, return the second Make node from our main example.

```
/descendant::Make[self::node()='Ford']
/descendant::Make[.='Ford']
```

However, if you use a string where a Boolean is expected, the value of the expression is always *true*. Any of the following location paths selects all five Make nodes.

```
/Insured/descendant::Make['Ford']
/Insured/descendant::Make['false']
/Insured/descendant::Make['true']
```

In each case, the string value of the first returned node is *Honda*.

You can use an XPath function in a predicate. Let's consider two examples.

The starts-with() function returns *true* if the second string argument is at the beginning of the first. Each of the following expressions returns the one Model node whose string value is *Skylark*.

```
/descendant::Model[starts-with(self::node(),'Sky')]
/descendant::Model[starts-with(.,'Sky')]
```

The contains() function returns *true* if the second string argument is within the first. Each of the following expressions also returns the one Model node whose string value is *Skylark*.

```
/descendant::Model[contains(self::node(),'lark')]
/descendant::Model[contains(.,'lark')]
/descendant::Model[contains(.,'Sky')]
```

Last, you can use a predicate to test for the presence of an attribute or of an immediately subordinate element. Here's an expression that returns *5*, which is the number of Vehicle nodes that are parents of a Make node.

```
count(/descendant::Vehicle[Make])
```

The next expression returns *2*, which is the number of Vehicle nodes that include the Domestic attribute.

```
count(/descendant::Vehicle[@Domestic])
```

Abbreviations

The XPath 1.0 location-path abbreviations are as follows:

- You can omit child::.

- A short form is available for a predicate that contains only a position value with an equal sign. The predicate [2] is a short form of [position()=2]. No short form is available for a predicate such as [position() < 2], which has an operator other than an equal sign. Also, if you use a Boolean operator, you must use the long form for the position value. The predicate [position()=1 or position()=5] is not expressed as [1 or 5], for example.

- The at sign is used in front of an attribute name in a predicate but also functions as a short form of attribute::. In our main example, the following location path selects the string value *5*.

```
/Insured/@CustomerID
```

- The double virgule (//) lets you step through many levels of the tree, with the children of the context node potentially included as one of the selected nodes. The formal definition is /descendant-or-self::node()/.

You can use the double virgule at the beginning of a location path or in the middle. Each of the next expressions includes all Vehicle nodes that are the first children of their parents.

```
//Vehicle[1]
/Insured//Vehicle[1]
```

In our case, each expression makes available the nodes for *Honda Accord* and *Triumph Spitfire*, displaying only the string value *Honda Accord*.

If your XML source includes hundreds of lines and if you use the double virgule at the start of a location path rather than in the middle, the processing time may be too long for your purpose.

The following example (not an abbreviation) may seem similar to //Vehicle[1], but selects only the first Vehicle node in the document.

```
/descendant::Vehicle[1]
```

The displayed string value is *Honda Accord*.

- A single period (.) is a short form for the context node; specifically, the period is a short form of self::node(), as noted earlier.

```
/descendant::Make[.='Ford']
```

- A double period (..) is a short form of parent::node(), which is the parent of the context node. The following example returns the five Vehicle nodes, starting with the one for *Honda Accord*.

```
/descendant::Make/..
```

Examples with Descendants and Siblings

Some axis specifications cause behavior that you might not expect. Let's try examples with the descendant specification (which is straightforward) and with the following-sibling specification (which is less so).

The string value of the next expression refers to the third of the Insured node's Vehicle descendants whose Category value is *Sport*.

```
/Insured/descendant::Vehicle[@Category='Sport'][3]/Make
```

The string value is *Porsche*.

The string value of the following expression also is *Porsche*, which refers to the fifth Vehicle descendant of the Insured node.

```
/Insured/descendant::Vehicle[last()]/Make
```

The following expression selects two nodes — specifically, the second Vehicle descendant of each CarPolicy node. The displayed string value is *Ford*, from the first of the two selected nodes.

```
/Insured/CarPolicy/descendant::Vehicle[last()]/Make
```

We'll now introduce the union (|) operator, which selects nodes based on a prior and subsequent location path. The following expression retrieves one Vehicle node whose Category attribute value is *Sedan* and two whose Category attribute is *Sport*.

```
/descendant::CarPolicy[1]/Vehicle[@Category='Sedan']/Make | /descen-
dant::CarPolicy[2]/Vehicle[@Category='Sport']/Make
```

The string value of the first retrieved node is *Honda*.

When you work with child or descendant elements, the position value [2] is the second child or descendent; but when you work with siblings, the position value [2] refers to the second sibling (forward or backward, depending on the axis specification). In the following expression, five Vehicle nodes are used at different times as the context node for the second-to-last location step (following-sibling::Vehicle), which selects three unique nodes.

```
/Insured/CarPolicy/Vehicle/following-sibling::Vehicle/Make
```

The string values of the selected Make nodes are as follows:

- *Ford* is the only string value that is immediately available. That value is present because the expression selected all subsequent siblings of the first Vehicle child of the first CarPolicy node.

- *Buick* is available if you use parentheses and the predicate [2], as in previous examples. That value is present because, in relation to the second CarPolicy node, the expression selected all subsequent siblings of the first Vehicle child.

- *Porsche* is available if you use parentheses and the predicate [3]. That value is present because, in relation to the second CarPolicy node, the expression selected all subsequent siblings of the first and second Vehicle nodes and then removed the duplicate node that has string value *Porsche*. XPath 1.0 expressions never provide a duplicate node, although the option to retrieve duplicate nodes is available in XPath 2.0.

The following expression returns only one node because in only one case is a sibling a *second* sibling, two nodes away from a context node.

```
/Insured/CarPolicy/Vehicle/following-sibling::Vehicle[2]
```

The expression resolves to the string value *Porsche Speedster*, and the string value of the relevant context node is *Triumph Spitfire*.

Consider a variation:

```
/Insured/descendant::Vehicle/following-sibling::Vehicle[2]
```

The effect is precisely the same as that of the previous expression. The sibling relationships of the Vehicle nodes are not dependent on the CarPolicy context node. The node for *Ford Mustang* is never a sibling of the node for *Triumph Spitfire*, for example, no matter the location path.

Examples with a Reverse Axis

Let's explore the effect of using a reverse axis. As we said earlier, the meaning of reverse axis is that the context-position numbers are assigned in reverse XML-source order.

In the following case, the XPath processor returns the first-level ancestor node of each Make node.

```
/descendant::Make/ancestor::*[1]
```

The XPath processor returns five Vehicle nodes, each of which is the first ancestor of a Make node. The ancestor nodes are returned in XML-source order, not in reverse order. The string value of the first returned node is *Honda Accord*.

In the following case, the XPath processor returns the third-level ancestor node of each Make node.

```
/descendant::Make/ancestor::*[3]
```

The third-level ancestor node of every Make node is the Insured node. The string value is the concatenation of all text nodes in the XML source and contains the make and model of all five cars.

Last, notice the difference between our first ancestor example and the following one, which includes parentheses.

```
(/descendant::Make/ancestor::*)[3]
```

The parenthetical expression returns eight nodes (five Vehicle nodes, two CarPolicy nodes, and the Insured node). The predicate selects the third of those nodes in XML source order; in other words, it selects the first Vehicle node, whose string value is *Honda Accord*.

Location Steps in Summary

Now we can give you a big story in a few words. For a given location step, the XPath processor handles one context node at a time and fulfills four steps in relation to each context node:

1. Selects all nodes in the axis specification.

2. Retains each node that passes the node test.

3. Assigns a number to each retained node in a way that reflects the XML-source order (for forward axes) or that reflects the opposite (for reverse axes).

4. Processes each predicate in turn, in a loop that acts as follows:

    a. Reviews the Boolean expression.

       As described earlier, the predicate can include one or more values to be tested against position() and may include a value returned from last(). The XPath processor compares the test values against the numbers assigned in step 3. The value returned from last() is the highest number that was assigned in step 3.

    b. Retains all nodes for which the Boolean value in the predicate is *true* and removes the rest.

    c. Reassigns a number to each node, as needed to respond to the removal of nodes during step 4b.

XPath 1.0 always removes duplicate nodes, and XPath (whether 1.0 or 2.0) returns the nodes in XML-source order.

Other Aspects of XPath 1.0

We've described location paths at length and now sprint through aspects of XPath 1.0 that are more like other languages. For additional details, refer to descriptions in your product documentation, which should include product-specific extensions, if any.

Expressions

XPath 1.0 expressions resolve to

- Boolean values that are directly available by invoking the functions true() and false()

- strings

- numbers (double-precision, 64-bit floating point)

- node sets

In relation to Booleans, strings, and numbers, the XPath 1.0 processor automatically converts from one type to another in accordance with the XPath functions string(), number(), and Boolean():

- When a comparison of one operand to another is based on the equal sign or the not-equal sign (!=), data-type conversions occur as follows:

  - A comparison that includes a Boolean is a Boolean comparison.

  - A non-Boolean comparison that includes a number is a numeric comparison.

  - A comparison that lacks Booleans and numbers is a string comparison.

- When a comparison of one operand to another uses <=, <, >=, or >, the comparisons are numeric.

- A zero is equivalent to a Boolean *false*, and any non-zero number is equivalent to a Boolean *true*.

- A string with any value is equivalent to a Boolean *true*, and a string with no characters is equivalent to a Boolean *false*.

- The characters *NaN* mean *not a number* and may appear in a situation where you've tried to convert a string such as *Hello!* to a number.

In relation to node sets, the following rules are in effect:

- A comparison of two node sets evaluates to *true* if the string value of any node in the first node set is the same as a string value of any node in the second. The following example resolves to *true* because each of the two node sets includes a node whose string value is *Sport*:

```
/descendant::CarPolicy[1]/Vehicle/@Category =
    /descendant::CarPolicy[2]/Vehicle/@Category
```

One implication is that an equality comparison of one node to another is a comparison of string values and is never a comparison to determine whether the nodes are the same.

- A comparison of a node set to a number evaluates to *true* if the string value of a node in the node set can be converted to that number, as in the next example.

```
/Insured/@CustomerID = 5
```

- A comparison of a node set to a string evaluates to *true* if the string value of a node in that node set is equivalent to the string, as in the next example.

```
/Insured/@CustomerID = '5'
```

- A node set evaluates to *true* in a Boolean comparison if the node set includes at least one node. The following evaluates to *true* because the XML source includes at least one Make element whose string value is *Porsche* and at least one Model element whose string value is *Mustang*.

```
/descendant::Make[.='Porsche'] and /descendant::Model[.='Mustang']
```

As mentioned earlier, a predicate can accept any Boolean expression. The following expression returns any Vehicle node whose Make child has the string value *Ford* and whose Model child has the string value *Mustang*.

```
/descendant::Vehicle[child::Make = 'Ford'][child::Model = 'Mustang']
```

That expression returns the second Vehicle node, as does the next expression, which is the same but omits references to the child axis specification.

```
/descendant::Vehicle[Make = 'Ford'][Model = 'Mustang']
```

Last, we want to shed light on a confusing aspect of Boolean logic in XPath. Our focus is twofold: the effect of the not-equal operator when it is used to compare a node set and a string, and the effect of the not() function, which returns the opposite of the Boolean value that is passed to it.

We offer four examples:

- The first expression evaluates to *true* if one or more Make nodes has the string value *Buick*.

```
/descendant::Make = 'Buick'
```

- The second expression evaluates to *true* if no Make node has the string value *Buick*.

```
not (/descendant::Make = 'Buick')
```

That is, the example evaluates to *false* if any Make node has the string value *Buick*.

- The third expression evaluates to *true* if one or more Make nodes has a string value that is not *Buick*:

```
/descendant::Make != 'Buick'
```

That is, the example evaluates to *false* only if every Make node has the string value *Buick*.

- The fourth expression evaluates to *true* only if every Make node has the string value *Buick*.

```
not(/descendant::Make != 'Buick')
```

The subtle difference in meaning between the second and third expressions causes a big difference between the first and fourth.

Consider the first and third expressions again and ask yourself, "What do the following Boolean expressions have in common?"

```
/descendant::Make[position() &lt; 3] =
    /descendant::Make[position() &lt; 3]

/descendant::Make[position() &lt; 3] !=
    /descendant::Make[position() &lt; 3]
```

Both Boolean expressions evaluate to *true*. The first expression evaluates to *true* because at least one node in the first node set has the same string value as at least one node in the second node set. The second expression evaluates to *true* because at least one node in the first node set has a string value that is different from the string value of at least one node in the second node set.

Aren't you glad you asked?

Numeric and Boolean Operators

Table 6.1 lists the numeric and Boolean XPath operators in order of decreasing precedence. The operators in a given cell are processed in left-to-right order in a given expression.

Table 6.1: XPath numeric and Boolean operators	
Operator	**Meaning**
*	Multiply
div	Divide
mod	Use modular arithmetic, where the output is negative only if the dividend is negative:
	• 7 mod 3 yields 1
	• 7 mod 3 yields 1
	• -7 mod -3 yields -1
	• -7 mod -3 yields -1
+	Plus
-	Minus
<=	Less than or equal to
<<	Less than
>=	Greater than or equal to
>>	Greater than
=	Equal
!=	Not equal
and	Boolean and
or	Boolean or

Functions

The next sections give a brief overview of most XPath 1.0 functions. For further details, see your product documentation.

Returns a Boolean

Each function in Table 6.2 returns a Boolean.

Table 6.2: XPath 1.0 functions that return a Boolean value	
Function	**Meaning**
contains(string, string)	Indicates whether the first argument includes a string equal to the second argument. Given our main example, each the following expressions resolves to true because the string *lark* is within the string *Skylark*.
	contains('Skylark','lark') contains(descendant::Model[4],'lark') contains(descendant::Model[position() >= 4],'lark')
	The first argument in the third expression returns the nodes whose string values are *Skylark* and *Speedster*; however, only the first node is available, and the only tested string value is *Skylark*.
	The next expression resolves to *false* because string operations are case-sensitive.
	contains('Skylark,'LARK')
false()	Returns *false*
not(Boolean)	Returns the opposite value to the value of the argument.
starts-with (string, string)	Indicates whether the first argument starts with a string equal to the second argument. Given our main example, each the following expressions resolves to *true* because the string *Sky* is at the beginning of the string *Skylark*.
	starts-with('Skylark','Sky') starts-with(descendant::Model[4],'Sky') starts-with(descendant::Model[position() >= 4],'Sky')
	The first argument in the third expression returns the nodes whose string values are *Skylark* and *Speedster*; however, only the first node is available, and the only tested string value is *Skylark*
	The next expression resolves to *false* because string operations are case-sensitive.
	starts-with('Skylark','SKY'
true()	Returns *true*.

Returns a String

Each function in Table 6.3 returns a string.

Table 6.3: XPath 1.0 functions that return a string (Part 1 of 2)	
Function	**Meaning**
concat(string, string, . . .)	Concatenates any number of string arguments. The following expression resolves to *Buick Skylark*. concat('Buick ', 'Sky', 'lark')
name(node set)	Returns the name of the first node in the node set. Given our main example, the following expression resolves to *CarPolicy*, which is the name of the first retrieved node name(/Insured/*)
normalize-space(string)	Removes leading and trailing spaces and removes all but one space when multiple white-space characters (carriage returns, spaces, tabs) are between other characters. The following expression resolves to *Buick Skylark* normalize-space(' Buick Skylark ')
substring(string, number, number)	Returns a substring of the first argument, starting at a specified position (the first number). The substring continues for a specified number of characters (the second number) or (if the second number is omitted) returns the rest of the string. Each of the following expressions resolves to *Speed* substring('Porsche Speedster', 9, 5) substring('Porsche Speed', 9)
substring-after(string, string)	Returns a substring of the first argument, starting at one position after the first occurrence of the second string. The following expression resolves to a space, then Speedster. substring-after('Porsche Speedster', 'e')
substring-before(string, string)	Returns a substring of the first argument, starting at the beginning of the first argument and ending at one position before the first occurrence of the second string. The following expression resolves to *Porsche,* then a space. substring-before('Porsche Speedster', 'S')

Table 6.3: XPath 1.0 functions that return a string (Part 2 of 2)

Function	Meaning
translate(string, string, string)	Returns a variant of the first argument: • Changes any character that matches a character listed in the second argument • Substitutes a character listed in the third argument. If no substitution value is listed there, the character is not returned from the function The second and third arguments are a matching array of characters. If the third argument is longer than the second, the extra positions have no effect. If the third argument is shorter than the second, the missing position removes a character from the returned string. The second example in the next table shows a character removal.

Invocation	Returns
translate('98786', '8', 'X')	9X7X6
translate('98786', '87', 'X')	9XX6
translate('98786', '87', 'XPA')	9XPX6

Returns a Number

Each function in Table 6.4 returns a number.

Table 6.4: XPath 1.0 functions that return a number (part 1 of 2)	
Function	**Meaning**
ceiling(number)	Returns the value of a numeric expression, rounded upward to the greater integer. Here are examples: | Invocation	Returns | |---|---| | ceiling(2) | 2 | | ceiling(2.01) | 3 | | ceiling(-2) | 2 | | ceiling(-2.01) | -2 | | ceiling(-2.99) | -2 |
count(node set)	Returns the number of nodes in a node set. Given our main example, the following expression resolves to *5*. count(/descendant::Vehicle[Make])
floor(number)	Returns the value of a numeric expression, rounded downward to the lesser integer. Here are examples: | Invocation	Returns | |---|---| | floor(2) | 2 | | floor(2.99) | 2 | | floor(-2) | -2 | | floor(-2.01) | -3 | | floor(-2.99) | -3 |
last()	Returns the context size, as described earlier. In our main example, the value of last() in the following expression is 2. (/Insured/CarPolicy/Vehicle[2]/Make)[last()]
round(number)	Returns the value of a numeric expression, rounded to the nearest integer. The next examples show the effect of mid points. | Invocation	Returns | |---|---| | round(2.499) | 2 | | round(2.5) | 3 | | round(-2.5) | -2 | | round(-2.501) | -3 |
string-length(string)	Returns the number of characters in the argument. Given our example, the following invocation returns *5* (the number of letters in *Honda*). string-length(/descendant::Make[1])

Table 6.4: XPath 1.0 functions that return a number (part 2 of 2)

Function	Meaning
sum(node set)	Returns the sum of the numeric values in each node in a node set. If the node includes non-numeric text, the returned value is *NaN* (not a number).

Consider the following XML source

```
<?xml version="1.0"?>
<Options>
  <Towing>50</Towing>
  <Rental>20</Rental>
</Options>
```

The following expression resolves to 70.

```
sum(/Options/*)
```

CHAPTER 7

Introduction to BPEL

Business Process Execution Language (BPEL) is an XML-based language for creating a *process*, which is a set of logical steps (called *activities*) that guide a workflow like the following one:

1. Accept a request for an insurance quote.

2. If the submitted details are appropriate, calculate the quote and include it in the response.

3. Otherwise, say "No" and include a justification.

A BPEL process fulfills a workflow primarily by accessing one service after another. Each of those services is called a *partner service*.

Each BPEL activity is equivalent to a function call in a programming language or to a box in a flowchart. The receive activity waits for an inbound message, for example, and the invoke activity transmits an outbound message. Activities are categorized as either *basic* or *structured*. Basic activities (such as receive and invoke) do discrete tasks. Structured activities (such as if and while) specify an order or condition that affects the circumstance for running a set of other, embedded activities, which may be basic, structured, or both.

The running time for a BPEL process can be far longer than in other kinds of software. An insurance-claims process, for example, might wait to receive additional data from a specific customer for as long as the claim is active, even for years.

Listing 7.1 shows an excerpt from the BPEL process ProcessQuote.

```
<process name= "ProcessQuote">

    <!- omitted namespaces, as well as
        imports of WSDL and XSD definitions ->
    <partnerLinks>
        <partnerLink name="ProcessQuote"
            partnerLinkType="ProcessQuotePLT" myRole="ProcessQuoteRole" />
        <partnerLink name="mainframeQuoteMgr"
            partnerLinkType="PartnerLinkPLT" partnerRole="partnerRole" />
    </partnerLinks003E

    <variables>
        <variable name="quoteRequest"
                messageType="placeQuoteRequestMsg" />
        <variable name="highlightQuote"
                messageType="placeQuoteResponseMsg" />
        <variable name="buildQuoteReq"
                messageType="buildQuoteRequestMsg" />
        <variable name="newHighlightQuote"
                messageType="buildQuoteResponseMsg" />
    </variables>

    <sequence>
        <receive name="processQuoteRequest" createInstance="yes"
                operation="placeQuote" partnerLink="ProcessQuote"
                portType="ProcessQuote" variable="quoteRequest">
        </receive>

        <assign name="AssignQuoteReq">
            <copy>
                <from variable="quoteRequest" part="placeQuoteParameters">
                    <query>/quoteInformation</query>
                </from>
                <to variable="buildQuoteReq" part="buildQuoteParameters">
                    <query>/customerQuoteInfo</query>
                </to>
            </copy>
        </assign>

        <invoke name="CalculateQuote" inputVariable="buildQuoteReq"
                operation="buildQuote" outputVariable="newHighlightQuote"
                partnerLink="mainframeQuoteMgr" portType="QuoteManagement" />
```

Listing 7.1: Excerpt from BPEL process ProcessQuote (part 1 of 2)

```
            <assign name="AssignQuoteRes">
            <copy>
                <from variable="newHighlightQuote" part="buildQuoteResult">
                    <query>/quote</query>
                </from>
                <to variable="highlightQuote" part="placeQuoteResult" >
                    <query>/quote</query>
                </to>
            </copy>
        </assign>
        <reply name="processQuoteResponse"
                operation="placeQuote" partnerLink="ProcessQuote"
                portType="ProcessQuote" variable="highlightQuote" />
    </sequence>
</process>
```

Listing 7.1: Excerpt from BPEL process ProcessQuote (part 2 of 2)

This excerpt

1. creates *partner links*, which give details on the relationship between the BPEL process and each partner service

2. assigns *variables*, which are memory areas that are each described by a Web Services Description Language (WSDL) message but could have been described by an XML Schema element or type

3. receives a quote request

4. uses XPath syntax to copy data from the received message to a variable that is used for invoking another service

5. invokes the other service, which calculates and returns a quote

6. copies the quote details to another variable and in this way formats the response message

7. replies to the invoker, which may have been a Web application or a service

We'll not describe every detail, just yet.

In general, activities may

- run in a preset sequence

- run in a loop

- run on condition that a Boolean expression evaluates to *true*

- run immediately or wait for some period of time, even years

- run in response to an event that occurs after the process starts (specifically, in response to an inbound message, a calendar date and clock time, or the passing of time)

- run in an order that differs for different instances of the same process

That last option implies *concurrency*, which is a kind of processing in which several activities are issued more or less at the same time. A process may enable the receipt of messages from different services, for example, without requiring that one receipt precede another. Or a process may invoke several services without requiring that one invocation precede another. The general rule is that a service may fulfill several *parallel streams* (often called *branches*), each of which is a series of activities, with different streams running at once.

BPEL also has mechanisms for

- *fault handling*, as needed to respond to business errors (such as a request for an excessive credit line) and to technical errors (such as a network failure)

- *compensation*, as needed to reverse an action (such as a product purchase) that succeeded but was later found to be undesirable

- *correlation*, as needed to direct a message to the correct instance of a BPEL process

Two kinds of BPEL processes are possible. A *BPEL executable process* is itself a Web service and acts as the hub in a service orchestration. The software that runs an executable process is called a *BPEL engine*. One executable process can invoke another, with the effect of connecting one orchestration to another, as Figure 7.1 illustrates.

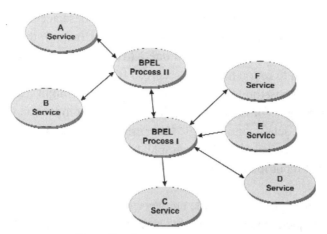

Figure 7.1: Connected orchestrations

A *BPEL abstract process* is similar to a BPEL executable process but includes a subset of the information. The abstract process is a description of business logic and can be used for the following purposes:

- to specify the behavior of one business unit or partner in a collaboration with others.

- to provide a design guide for programmers in your company and in partnering companies.

- to be an input to commercial software that creates skeletal code for a service implementation. The output may be in Java or some other language.

A BPEL abstract process can include all the content of a BPEL executable process, but omits implementation details in most cases.

When you create a BPEL process, you use two additional kinds of language. A *query language* lets you search for values that are embedded in an XML structure such as a message. An *expression language* lets you calculate numeric and date-time values, manipulate strings, and make comparisons. By default, BPEL uses XPath 1.0 in all cases. If your BPEL engine also lets you use an alternative language (such as Java) to create expressions, you can use XPath or the alternative at different points in the same process.

BPEL does not directly support file or database access and was not designed for extensive computation or string handling. However, the function doXslTransform lets you transform data from one XML structure to another. You might use the function to reorganize data received from one service, making the data appropriate for transmission to a second service. You also might use doXslTransform to reorganize data for internal use, either for easy comparison (for example, to place product details into a single table after receiving data from multiple suppliers) or for easy calculation (for example, to sum prices after receiving details about different input materials).

The next sections provide an overview of BPEL executable processes, and a subsequent chapter highlights event handlers and selected activities. Our comments reflect the WS-BPEL 2.0 specification, which was written under the guidance of the Organization for the Advancement of Structured Information Standards (OASIS). The specification is at *http://www.oasis-open.org/committees/documents.php?wg_abbrev=wsbpel*.

The following proposals for extending BPEL are under review by several companies:

- *BPEL4People* proposes a way to model human interactions as services: *http://www.ibm.com/developerworks/webservices/library/specification/ws-bpel4people*.

- *BPEL Extensions for Sub-Processes* proposes use of modular code in BPEL processes: *http://www.ibm.com/developerworks/webservices/library/specification/ws-bpelsubproc*.

- *BPELJ* proposes a use of Java in BPEL processes, as well as access of Java Enterprise Edition code from BPEL processes: *http://www.ibm.com/developerworks/library/specification/ws-bpelj*.

Use of WSDL

A BPEL process can use a WSDL definition as the source of the data types used in variable declarations. (Any missing data types must be provided by a separate XML Schema.) As explained in the next sections, the process also references three WSDL extensions that are specific to BPEL: *partner link type*, *property*, and *property alias*.

- Each partner link type is the basis of one or more partner links, which each describe the business relationship of the process and a partner service.

- Each property gives a name to an important subset of business data.

- Each property alias *maps* a property to a type of message; that is, the alias identifies where the property data is located in a particular type of message.

Although a WSDL definition may include binding and location detail for a given service or requester, the BPEL process never accesses that detail, which is called an *endpoint reference*. Instead, the endpoint reference is specified by one of three sources: by the administrator of the BPEL server at configuration time; by an SOA product at run time (as described in our review of Service Component Architecture); or by the BPEL process at run time (as described in our review of the BPEL assign activity).

PartnerLinkType

A partner link type specifies the roles that are enacted during a runtime conversation between the BPEL process and a partner service. The simplest partner link type declares a single role and relates that role to a WSDL port type:

```
<partnerLinkType name="ProcessQuotePLT">
    <role name="ProcessQuoteRole">
        <portType name="ProcessQuote" />
    </role>
</partnerLinkType>
```

A single role is appropriate when only one port type is involved — that is, when every communication between the BPEL process and the partner service starts from the same direction. (In a synchronous communication, the same port-type operation describes the request and response messages.)

A partner link type specifies two roles when two port types are involved — that is, when a callback is in use, as explained in Chapter 2. Here's an example of a partner link type that defines two roles:

```
<partnerLinkType name="MotorVehicleRecordsLT">
    <role name="motorVehicleRecordsService"
          portType="MotorVehicleRecords" />
    <role name="motorVehicleRecordsCallback"
          portType="MotorVehicleRecordsCallback" />
</partnerLinkType>
```

When you create a partner link type, you're not concerned with whether the BPEL process or the partner service fulfills a specific role. If the partner service is also a BPEL process, the two processes can use the same partner link type to describe the relationship between them. When you write a process, however, you use a partner link type to create a *partner link* (Figure 7.2), which is a kind of variable that (in a sense) "chooses a side" by indicating

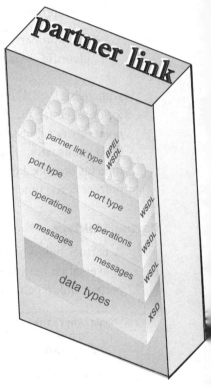

- the role of the process you're creating (in other words, which port type describes the operations provided by the process); or

- the role of the partner service (in other words, which port type describes the operations provided by that service); or

- both, but only if the partner link type declares two roles.

The BPEL engine uses the partner link to help manage the conversation between the two partners.

Figure 7.2: Partner link

Properties and Property Aliases

In Chapter 2, we mentioned use of identifiers (purchase-order numbers, invoice numbers, and so on) that help direct a message to the correct service instance at run time. Those identifiers *correlate* the processing done by one instance (which receives a purchase order) with the processing done by other instances (which submit an invoice, acknowledge receipt of payment, and so on).

When you work with BPEL, you can define WSDL-based constructs called properties and property aliases to perform the correlation function. The availability of these constructs provides several benefits.

First, as you code a BPEL process, you can use the same name (such as CustomerID) to access the same data in differently structured variables — for example, in a variable that holds a purchase order and in a variable that holds an invoice. This repeated use of the same name lets you focus on the business meaning of the data.

Second, properties make maintenance is easier. If an inbound message includes a customer ID, and a change occurs in the position of that ID, you don't necessarily change the logic in the BPEL process. If you've used properties well, you can simply change the property alias that associates the name CustomerID with a specific position in the variable.

Third, you can define a BPEL *correlation set*, which is essentially a list of constants (for example, a customer ID followed by an invoice number). Those constants help direct an inbound message to the correct instance of the BPEL process. They also allow automatic validation of positions in an outbound message. If the first element in an outbound message is expected to include a particular customer ID and does not, an error occurs at run time.

Let's consider an example.

Listing 7.2 shows a WSDL definition that describes the message placeQuoteRequestMsg.

```
<wsdl:message name="placeQuoteRequestMsg">
    <wsdl:part name="placeQuoteParameters"
               element="placeQuote" />
</wsdl:message>

<xsd:element name="placeQuote">
    <xsd:complexType>
        <xsd:sequence>
            <xsd:element
               .name="quoteInformation"
               type="CustomerQuoteInformation"/>
        </xsd:sequence>
    </xsd:complexType>
</xsd:element>
```

Listing 7.2: Message placeQuoteRequestMsg WSDL definition (part 1 of 2)

```
<xsd:element name="placeQuote">
   <xsd:complexType>
      <xsd:sequence>
         <xsd:element
            name="quoteInformation"
            type="CustomerQuoteInformation"/>
      </xsd:sequence>
   </xsd:complexType>
</xsd:element>

<xsd:complexType name="CustomerQuoteInformation">
   <xsd:sequence>
      <xsd:element name="applicant" type="NameAddress"
                   minOccurs="0" />
      <xsd:element name="dependents" type="NameAddress"
                   minOccurs="0" maxOccurs="unbounded"/>
      <xsd:element name="auto" type="Auto"
                   minOccurs="0" maxOccurs="unbounded"/>
      <xsd:element name="applicantEmailAddr"
                   type="xsd:string" minOccurs="0" />
      <xsd:element name="desiredPolicyInfo"
                   type="PolicyQuoteTerms"
                   minOccurs="0" />
   </xsd:sequence>
</xsd:complexType>
```

Listing 7.2: Message placeQuoteRequestMsg WSDL definition (part 2 of 2)

As shown, the message (placeQuoteRequestMsg) references an XSD element (placeQuote), which in turn references a type (CustomerQuoteInformation). The type has a field for an email address (applicantEmailAddr).

In another WSDL definition, you declare a property (emailAddr):

```
<property name="emailAddr" type="xsd:string" />
```

The property is of the same type (xsd:string) as the email address.

In this WSDL definition, you also declare a property alias:

```
<propertyAlias
   propertyName="emailAddr"
   messageType="placeQuoteRequestMsg"
   part="placeQuoteParameters" >
   <query>
      /quoteInformation/applicantEmailAddr
   </query>
</propertyAlias>
```

The alias declaration ensures that you can use the property name to refer to the appropriate field in a BPEL variable such as this one:

```
<variable name="quoteRequest"
          messageType="placeQuoteRequestMsg" />
```

The important point about this variable declaration is the messageType element, which indicates that the structure of the variable reflects the same message definition as the one referenced in the propertyAlias element. By the way, the variable is declared in a BPEL process, not in WSDL.

The propertyAlias element's messageType and part attributes refer by name to the message and part elements in the WSDL message definition. The query element identifies a search string, which is in a query language (XPath 1.0, by default). At run time, the BPEL engine uses the search string (hereafter called a *query*) to access the email address that resides in an appropriately structured variable.

You could have included other property aliases for the same property, in each case referring to a different WSDL message definition.

Assume that in the BPEL process, you declare these two variables:

```
<variable name="quoteRequest"
          messageType="placeQuoteRequestMsg" />
<variable name="theAddress" type="xsd:string" />
```

The process later receives a message into quoteRequest:

```
<receive name="processQuoteRequest"
         createInstance="yes"
         operation="placeQuote"
         partnerLink="ProcessQuote"
         portType="ProcessQuote"
         variable="quoteRequest">
</receive>
```

You can access the email address from quoteRequest by invoking the function getVariableProperty, which is in a BPEL-specific namespace and takes two arguments (the variable name and the property name):

```
theAddress = bpel:getVariableProperty
             ("quoteRequest", "emailAddr")
```

You can benefit from the convenience of properties even when your BPEL process accesses a variable that contains data other than a message. For example, after retrieving values from different online stores, you might

- retain a list of product names and, for each product, the prices in all stores
- calculate the average price of each product
- use a variable to hold a table, each row of which holds a product name and the average price for the named product

You can refer easily to the product name in every variable that you use in processing. The steps for establishing a property and a set of property aliases are similar to the steps described earlier. In this case, however, each property alias refers to an XML Schema element or type rather than to a WSDL message definition.

BPEL File Structure

The topmost structure of a BPEL executable process can include the elements shown in Listing 7.3 and also can include a BPEL extension element (<extensions>), which is used in relation to other technologies such as Service Component Architecture.

```
<process>
    <import> </import>
    <partnerLinks> </partnerLinks>
    <messageExchanges> </messageExchanges>
    <variables> </variables>
    <correlationSets> </correlationSets>
    <faultHandlers> </faultHandlers>
    <eventHandlers> </eventHandlers>
    <!- The previous two elements include activities,
        as does the subsequent content of the process
        element. Activities can be enclosed in scopes,
        as described later. ->
</process>
```

Listing 7.3: BPEL process elements

Here are highlights of a process definition:

- Each import provides access to a WSDL definition or an XML Schema.

- Each partner link is a kind of specialized variable that describes the relationship between the BPEL process and a partner service.

- Each *message exchange* is an identifier that is used to avoid an ambiguous case in a complex business scenario — specifically, to pair a BPEL activity that receives a message with the activity that issues a reply.

- Each variable contains business data, whether to hold a message or for other use in the process logic.

- Each correlation set is a listing of properties used to correlate service instances.

- Each *fault handler* is a set of activities that run in response to a *fault*, which is a failure in the process.

- Each *event handler* is a set of activities that run concurrently with other activities, in response either to the passage of time or to receipt of a message.

Activities in Brief

Table 7.1 lists the basic activities available to a BPEL-process developer. Table 7.2 lists the structured activities.

Table 7.1: BPEL basic activities	
Basic activity	**Purpose**
assign	Copy one or more values to variables and partner links
compensate	Invoke a set of compensation handlers
compensateScope	Invoke a specific compensation handler
empty	Act as a placeholder
exit	End the process immediately
extensionActivity	Do a task allowed by a technology that extends BPEL
invoke	Invoke a partner service
receive	Receive an inbound message
reply	Reply to an inbound message
rethrow	Re-direct an error from one fault handler to another
throw	Direct an error to a fault handler
validate	Validate one or more variables against their data types
wait	Block processing for a time

Table 7.2: BPEL structured activities	
Structured activity	**Purpose**
extensionActivity	Do a task allowed by a technology that extends BPEL
If (else, elseif)	Process activities conditionally
forEach	Process activities a specified number of times, either sequentially or concurrently
flow	Process activities concurrently
pick (onMessage, onAlarm)	Wait for one of potentially several events to occur
repeatUntil	Process activities in a loop whose subordinate activity always runs at least once
scope	Process activities that can be compensated separately from other activities
sequence	Process activities sequentially
while	Process activities in a loop whose subordinate activity runs zero or more times

Scopes

As suggested in Figure 7.3, the scope is a world of meaning, where the names of some variables and handlers are known and where specific data values and handler effects are available, while the names of other variables and handlers are unknown. A *scope* includes a single activity, which (if structured) can include others. An important characteristic is that a scope can be compensated without interfering with the behavior of activities and handlers in other scopes.

A BPEL process can include many scopes, and they provide a way for you to organize your work. Each scope

- can include one or more scopes, called nested scopes.

- can have peer scopes, which are scopes that are neither nested nor nesting in relation to one another.

- can include (within a nested scope) other nested scopes, to any nesting depth, as

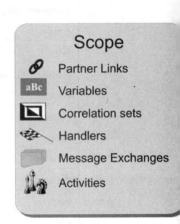

Figure 7.3: Scope

suggested in Figure 7.4. All the nested scopes within a scope are said to be the scope's descendants. All superior scopes are said to be ancestor scopes, and an immediately superior scope is said to be a parent.

Peer scopes

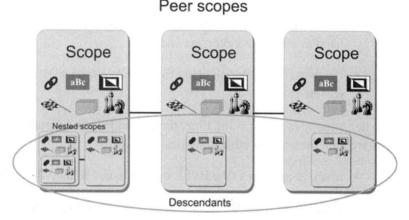

Figure 7.4: Peer and nesting scopes

The rules of access for each category of name (for variables, partner links, and so on) are similar to the rules in other languages. Consider the case of variables:

- Variables declared in the topmost level of a process are global to the process.

- Variables declared in a scope are visible both in the scope and in the scope's descendants.

- Variables declared in a scope are not visible to any ancestor or peer scopes.

- A variable declared in a nested scope hides any same-named variable in a superior scope, and the variable in the superior scope is hidden not only from the nested scope but also from descendants of the nested scope.

A scope can include its own partner links, variables, correlation sets, event handlers, fault handlers, and message exchanges. In addition, two other handlers are available in a scope. A compensation handler is a set of activities that compensate for a change made successfully by the scope and that run after being invoked by a parent scope. A termination handler is a set of activities issued when a running scope is being forced to terminate.

The BPEL engine forces termination in any of the following cases:

- if the BPEL process has faulted

- if an ancestor scope has faulted

- if the scope is in a compensation handler, fault handler, or termination handler and the handler has faulted

- if a particular situation is in effect inside a forEach activity, as described in Chapter 8

When a scope is active at run time, the embedded event handlers are available, along with the scope's other activities. A scope

- is active as soon as the BPEL engine issues an activity in the scope

- is active until the BPEL engine gives control to a different scope (other than a descendant) or to the top level of the process

- begins and ends several times if embedded in a loop or event handler

A scope is said to have completed successfully if no faults occur in the scope. A fault may occur in a nested scope, however, and if the fault is handled without affecting the scope that encloses the nested scope, the enclosing scope may complete successfully.

If a fault occurs in a scope, the scope is said to have failed, and compensation is unavailable. Last, if the scope is in a loop, compensation is available only for the scope instances that succeeded.

Message Exchanges

A message exchange is an identifier that helps to define the association between an inbound message and the reply activity that responds to the inbound message. We provide an example in Chapter 8.

Variables

A variable is a data area that is based on a WSDL message definition (called a *message type*) or on an XML Schema element or type. In many cases, a variable is complex, not merely an integer or a string.

Listing 7.4 shows a few variable declarations.

```
<variables>
    <variable name="quoteRequest"
            messageType="placeQuoteRequestMsg" />

    <variable name="theAddress" type="xsd:string">
      <from variable="quoteRequest"
          property="emailAddr" />
      </from>
    </variable>

    <variable name="theAddress02" type="xsd:string">
      <from variable="quoteRequest"
          part="placeQuoteParameters" >
        <query>
            /quoteInformation/applicantEmailAddr
        </query>
      </from>
    </variable>

    <variable name="currentStatus"
            type="xsd:string"
      <from>
          <literal>approved</literal>
      </from>
    </variable>

    <variable name="myRequestID"
            element="placeQuote"/>
</variables>
```

Listing 7.4: Sample variable declarations

You initialize a variable by including a from element in the declaration. A variable is initialized when the scope begins or, for global variables, when the process begins.

The sources of data are the same as the sources in an assign activity, which we describe later.

Variables and XPath

As mentioned in Chapter 6, you prefix a BPEL variable name with a dollar sign ($) if you need to access data from that variable. If the variable is based directly on an XSD type, use a location path that skips the type name and (as appropriate) uses names declared in the type. For example, assume that the BPEL variable named applicant is directly based on the following XSD type:

```
<xsd:complexType name="NameAddress">
    <xsd:sequence>
        <xsd:element name="first" type="xsd:string"
                     minOccurs="1" />
        <xsd:element name="last" type="xsd:string"
                     minOccurs="1"/>
    </xsd:sequence>
</xsd:complexType>
```

Here is the XPath expression for accessing the content of the variable field named last.

```
$applicant/last
```

Similarly, if the variable is based on an XSD element, use a location path that skips the element name and (as appropriate) uses names declared in the related XSD type. For example, assume that the BPEL variable named dmvResponse is directly based on the following XSD element.

```
<xsd:element name="retrieveLicenseStatusResponse">
    <xsd:complexType>
        <xsd:sequence>
            <xsd:element name="valid" type="xsd:boolean"/>
        </xsd:sequence>
    </xsd:complexType>
</xsd:element>
```

Here is the XPath expression for accessing the content of the variable field named valid.

```
$dmvResponse/valid
```

A variation occurs if the variable is based on a WSDL message definition. To derive the variable name used in the XPath expression, prefix the BPEL variable name with a dollar sign. Then, add a period and the name of a message part.

Assume that the BPEL variable named dmvResponse is based on the following WSDL message definition, which refers to the same XSD element as mentioned in the previous example.

```
<wsdl:message name="retrieveLicenseStatusResponseMsg">
    <wsdl:part name="retrieveLicenseStatusResult"
               element="retrieveLicenseStatusResponse"/>
</wsdl:message>
```

Here is the XPath expression for accessing the content of the variable field named valid.

```
$dmvResponse.retrieveLicenseStatusResult/valid
```

As shown, you use a location path that skips the XSD element name specified in the WSDL message definition.

Partner Links

As noted earlier, the BPEL engine uses a partner link to help manage the conversation between two partners. Each partner link is a kind of variable that is based on a partner link type and contains an endpoint reference. You can use the BPEL assign activity to copy an endpoint reference to or from a given partner link.

Each activity that accesses a service in any way requires a partner link. Here is a declaration based on a partner link type that defines only one role.

```
<partnerLinks>
    <partnerLink name="ProcessQuote"
                 partnerLinkType="ProcessQuotePLT"
                 myRole="ProcessQuoteRole"/>
</partnerLinks>
```

The attribute myRole indicates that the role is enacted by the BPEL process. Specifically, the BPEL process provides the operations described in the port type that is related to the role ProcessQuoteRole.

Let's look at a second, similar declaration. Here, the attribute partnerRole indicates that the role (related to another port type) is enacted by the partner service.

```
<partnerLinks>
    <partnerLink name="mainframeQuoteMgr"
                 partnerLinkType="PartnerLinkPLT"
                 partnerRole="handleMainframe" />
</partnerLinks>
```

Here is a declaration based on a partner link type that defines two roles.

```
<partnerLinks>
    <partnerLink name="MotorVehicleRecords"
                 partnerLinkType="MotorVehicleRecordsLT"
                 myRole="motorVehicleRecordsCallback"
                 partnerRole="MotorVehicleRecords">
</partnerLinks>
```

Multiple partner links can be based on the same partner link type. The case arises, for example, when you use the same service interface to interact with multiple vendors.

Correlation Sets

An application must maintain data integrity when messages are exchanged between services. A manufacturer that receives orders, for example, must not mix data for one order with the data for another.

A BPEL process addresses this issue with correlation sets, each of which is a list of properties whose values are expected to remain constant throughout a process or throughout a specific scope, even as data is transmitted to and from partner services.

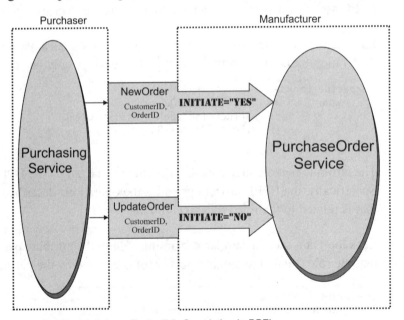

Figure 7.5: Correlation in BPEL

As Figure 7.5 illustrates, the BPEL process PurchaseOrder is maintaining a long-term conversation with a purchasing service. The process maintains a correlation set that includes two properties: customer ID and order number. The correlation set is *initiated* (assigned constant values) when a new order arrives. The process keeps those constant values separate from values that are received from any message or are transmitted as part of any message.

You reference a correlation set only in activities that receive or transmit data:

- in each inbound activity that may require the BPEL engine to direct a message to a specific service instance

- in an outbound activity, if you want to verify that the property values at the time of transfer are correct

- in any inbound or outbound activity that initiates the correlation set

In the third case, the values must remain unchanged in later inbound or outbound activities throughout the scope to which the correlation set applies or (outside a scope) throughout the process.

In the PurchaseOrder process example, an inbound activity initiates the correlation set. In an example that involves an outbound activity, the PurchaseOrder process exchanges order-specific data with another service (not shown in the figure). That secondary service checks the availability of parts and invokes the PurchaseOrder service with a callback that may provide only a partial response.

Correlation in this case involves not only the customer ID and order number but also a tracking code. When the BPEL process submits the initial request to the secondary service, the BPEL process initiates the new correlation set. The constant values that are assigned for that second correlation set are maintained separately from the constant values that were assigned for the first.

As suggested by this example, a BPEL process might use a variety of different correlation sets.

Initiation Attributes

Whenever you reference a correlation set in an activity, you indicate whether the activity is initiating the correlation set. In particular, you assign one of the following values to the initiate attribute that is specific to the correlation set: *no*, *yes*, or *join*.

The attribute's default value, *no*, means that the activity must not initiate the correlation set. In our example, a request to update an existing order does not assign new constant values. Instead, the BPEL engine uses the values in the inbound message to direct processing to a service instance associated with a correlation set that was already initiated. BPEL throws a fault if the activity determines that the inbound message has unexpected values or that the correlation set was not initiated previously.

If you set the initiate value to *no* for an outbound message, the BPEL process verifies that the values being sent are consistent with what was received or transmitted earlier.

An initiate value of *yes* means that the activity must initiate the correlation set. In our example, the receipt of a new order (probably in the first receive activity) causes initiation. BPEL throws a fault if the activity determines that the correlation set was initiated previously.

The third value possible initiate value is *join*. That value is used (for example) if you issue multiple receive activities concurrently and the same correlation set is required for each activity. The effect of *join* is that the first-running activity initiates the correlation set, and the BPEL engine directs the other messages to the correct service instance. If the activity determines that the correlation set has unexpected values, BPEL throws a fault.

In an invoke activity that invokes a service synchronously, you use the pattern attribute in addition to the initiate attribute. The need arises because the correlation sets referenced for the outbound message of the invoke activity may be different from the correlation sets referenced for the message returned to the BPEL process.

For each correlation set referenced in the synchronous invoke activity, you specify one of three values for the pattern attribute. A *request* value means that the correlation-set initiate attribute refers to the message sent to the partner service. A *response* value means that the correlation-set initiate attribute refers to the message returned to the BPEL process. A *request-response* value means that the correlation-set initiate attribute refers to both messages.

Effect of Correlation Errors

During synchronous invocation, if the message returned to the BPEL process has unexpected values, the values are received into one or more variables for use in fault processing. A transfer is not completed in other cases of correlation fault, regardless of the activity.

Fault Handling

A fault can come from any of the following sources:

- A partner service returns an error message. In this case, the fault name and data are described in the WSDL definition.

- The SOA runtime product returns an error, as when a partner service is unavailable or a network fails. In this case, the fault name and data are described (at best) in product documentation.

- The BPEL engine reports a runtime problem. Again, check your product documentation. You also can review the BPEL specification, which lists the faults (called *standard faults*) that are thrown by any standards-compliant BPEL engine.

- Your BPEL process issues a throw activity in response to a business problem. In this case, your company is defining the fault name and data and should be keeping a record of those definitions so they can be reused in other processes.

The primary purpose of fault handling is to minimize the effect of an error so that the usual work of the business can continue.

After a fault occurs in a given scope, the scope has failed and is not available for compensation by a parent scope. The BPEL engine selects a scope-specific fault handler, terminates other handlers and activities in the current scope, terminates each descendant scope that is still running, and runs the fault handler.

The fault handler can respond in various ways and often issues a compensate activity to invoke compensation handlers in nested scopes that completed successfully. If, on completion, the fault handler issues the rethrow activity, processing continues in a fault handler in the parent scope. The parent scope has failed and is not available for compensation by its parent scope. If the fault handler does not issue the rethrow activity, normal processing resumes either in the parent scope or (if the faulting scope was nested directly in the process) at the top level of the process.

If a fault reaches the top level of the process or originates there, the BPEL engine terminates the process and informs the SOA runtime product of the failure.

Selection at Run Time

A fault handler is composed of a catch or optional catchAll element, with embed-ded activities. The outline shown in Listing 7.5 has three fault handlers.

```
<faultHandlers>
    <catch faultName="oneFault"
        faultVariable="oneVariable"
        faultElement="getDMVRecordElement">
        <empty/>
    </catch>
    <catch faultName="twoFault">
        <empty/>
    </catch>
    <catch
        faultVariable="threeVariable"
        faultMessageType="getDMVRecordRequest">
        <empty/>
    </catch>
    <catchAll>
        <empty/>
    </catchAll>
</faultHandlers>
```

Listing 7.5: Fault handler outline

Each fault handler has selection criteria, which include (optionally) the fault name and the type of data.

If you specify a variable name, the BPEL process implicitly declares a variable that receives data and is local to the fault handler. The declaration is based on either an XML Schema element or a WSDL message type.

The BPEL engine selects the fault handler whose selection criteria most closely mirror the fault. Let's wade into a description of "most closely."

If the fault has a name but no data, the BPEL engine selects the fault handler whose selection criteria match exactly. If no such fault handler is available, the engine selects the catchAll handler. If the fault has data, the BPEL engine selects the fault handler whose selection criteria match exactly; or (if necessary) match nearly, with an exact match on fault name as long as no data type is specified in the selection criteria; or (if necessary) match nearly, when no fault name is specified in the selection criteria but an exact match is found on the data type. If no fault handlers conform to those rules, the engine selects the catchAll handler.

Here are some results when the fault handlers for a given scope are as shown in the preceding figure:

- If the scope throws a fault named *oneFault* and the fault has no data, the BPEL engine selects the catchAll handler.

- If the scope throws a fault named *twoFault*, the BPEL engine selects the fault handler named *twoFault* regardless of whether the fault has data.

- If the scope throws a fault named *unknown* and the fault has data that corresponds with a message of type getDMVRecordRequest, the BPEL engine selects the third fault handler.

If any fault handler issues a rethrow activity, the data presented to the fault handler of the parent scope is identical to the original data, even if the original fault handler changed the data or did not include a variable to accept the data.

If you don't include a catchAll handler in a given scope or at the process level, the BPEL engine provides the following default:

```
<catchAll>
    <sequence>
        <compensate/>
        <rethrow/>
    </sequence>
</catchAll>
```

The Inner Life of a Fault Handler

A fault handler can be quite complex, with internal scopes, and a fault can occur in a fault handler. Here are a few details, which you can skip if your head hurts:

- The top level of a fault handler (for example, the handler called *one*) cannot include a fault, compensation, or termination handler; and no default handlers are available at that level.

- A scope nested directly in the fault handler cannot include a compensation handler. This second restriction is caused by the first, as you have no way to invoke a compensation handler except from a fault, compensation, or termination handler in a parent scope.

- A fault in a fault handler is always thrown to a parent scope, regardless of whether you issue a rethrow activity.

- A fault in a fault handler is ultimately thrown to the process — specifically, to the parent scope of the scope that contains the fault handler (in our case, the fault handler called *one*).

Exiting in Response to a Fault

Two attributes of the process element affect fault handling.

First, if you set the exitOnStandardFault attribute to *yes* rather than to its default *no* value, a BPEL standard fault exits the process without causing invocation of a fault or termination handler. The only standard fault that is unaffected by this attribute is the concurrency-related fault *bpel:joinFailure*.

Second, thettribute suppressJoinFailure affects how the process responds to the standard fault *bpel:joinFailure*. The details are later in this chapter, in the section on advanced concurrency.

Compensation Handling

As indicated earlier, compensation for a successfully completed scope occurs under the guidance of a compensation handler, which reverses the scope's effect in response to a business development such as a cancelled purchase.

Imagine that scope in a BPEL process invokes a data-access service to record a customer's purchase. The service commits the changes because a multi-user database should not (and perhaps cannot) stay in an uncommitted state for days. The parent scope, however, runs an event handler for days more, waiting for a cancellation message for as long as the customer is allowed to cancel. If the message comes, the event handler issues a fault, and the fault handler invokes a compensation handler that in turn invokes a service to revise the database.

Invocation of a compensation handler always comes from a parent scope — specifically, from a fault, compensation, or termination handler that issues either of two activities: compensateScope or compensate.

The compensateScope activity invokes the compensation handler of a specific nested scope. Here, a failure in scope A causes invocation of the compensation handler in scope B:

```
<scope name="A">
   <compensationHandler>
     <compensateScope target="B">
   </compensationHandler>
   <scope name="B">
      <compensationHandler>
          <!- a basic or structured activity is here ->
      </compensationHandler>
   </scope>
</scope>
```

The compensate activity invokes the compensation handler in each nested scope, in most cases in an order that is opposite to the order of scope completion. That behavior is guaranteed, however, only when the initiation of one scope depends on the completion of another, as is true when nested scopes run in sequence. Otherwise, the order is specific to a BPEL engine.

The compensate activity does not handle descendant scopes other than the immediately nested scopes. The assumption is that an invoked compensation handler will itself invoke the compensation handlers at the next descendant level.

The name of a scope embedded in a loop refers to all the scope instances that run in that loop, and the compensate or compensateScope activity from the parent scope invokes a *group* of compensation handlers, as appropriate.

A compensation handler has access to all values that were in effect when the scope completed, including the values of variables, correlation sets, and partner links. A problem can arise, however, if scopes are running at the same time as the one being compensated. You can ensure that changes to shared variables in one scope do not affect the values of variables in another. For details on isolating one scope from another, see the description of the scope activity in Appendix C.

If you do not specify a compensation handler for a given scope, the BPEL engine uses the following default.

```
<compensationHandler>
    <compensate/>
</compensationHandler>
```

A compensation handler (for example, a handler named *inProcess*) can be internally complex, and you can use embedded compensation handlers to ensure (as much as possible) that the activities in handler *inProcess* succeed or fail as a unit, rather than leaving some changes compensated and some uncompensated.

Two rules apply to the internals of a compensation handler. First, the top level cannot include a fault, compensation, or termination handler; and no default handlers are available at that level. Second, a scope nested directly in the compensation handler cannot include a compensation handler.

A business process might need to undo a compensation that completed successfully, but the question arises, "How many reversals are supported?" A compensation that compensates for a previous compensation might need. . . . You see the issue.

A BPEL process offers no routine way to undo the effects of a compensation handler that completed successfully. A business process ultimately relies on personal intervention.

Termination Handling

As noted earlier, a termination handler is a set of activities that are issued when a running scope is being forced to terminate. If you do not specify a termination handler for a given scope, the BPEL engine uses the following default:

```
<terminationHandler>
    <compensate/>
</terminationHandler>
```

The rules that apply to the internals of a compensation handler apply here as well, with the added restriction that a fault handler in a termination handler cannot rethrow a fault.

Introduction to Concurrency

We'll explore concurrency by example.

Imagine an online music store that caters to children and requires two kinds of information: preference information from the child, and credit-card details from a parent. You can fulfill those requirements at more or less the same time, in two parallel streams, and we can assume that completion of both streams is required before some other action occurs — for example, before you inform partner companies about the new customer.

In a more complex case, one stream can be internally dependent on another. The process might send a thank-you note to the child, for example, only after the parent's credit is approved, as shown in Figure 7.6.

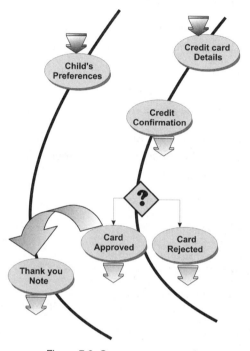

Figure 7.6: Concurrency example

When activities run concurrently and one activity is forced to wait for another, the activities are said to be *synchronized* when the second activity starts.

You may say, "If a thank-you note requires that the process receive preferences and gain credit approval, you don't need a concurrent stream for the note-sending activity at all. The note-sending activity can start later, after you inform the partner companies."

That's true. BPEL provides alternate ways to accomplish the same purpose. If one activity in your business depends on the successful completion of another activity, you can enforce the dependency by writing a BPEL process in either of the following ways:

- by including the two activities in a sequence activity, where an embedded · · activity runs subsequent to another embedded activity in an unchanging order

- by fulfilling two tasks:

    - Place both activities in a flow activity, where an embedded activity runs concurrently with another embedded activity.

    - Establish a *link* between the two activities. Name a link, assign the link as a *source* in the activity that must occur earlier, and assign the link as a *target* in the activity that must occur later.

Listing 7.6 shows an outline of a flow activity that enforces a dependency but does not fulfill the business requirement. We'll describe the activity and make the necessary changes.

```
<flow>
    <links><link name= "creditApproval"/> </links>

    <sequence name="interactWithChild">
        <receive name="acceptPreferences"/>
        <invoke name="sendNote">
            <targets>
                <target linkName="creditApproval"/>
            </targets>
        </invoke>
    </sequence>

    <sequence name="interactWithParent">
        <receive name="creditCardDetails"/>
        <invoke name="creditConfirmation"/>
        <if name="approved">
            <condition> ... </condition>
                <invoke name="informPartnerCompanies">
                    <sources>
                        <source linkName="creditApproval"/>
                    </sources>
                </invoke>
        <else/>
        </if>
    </sequence>
</flow>
```

Listing 7.6: Sample flow activity outline

In the outline, two activities run concurrently. The sequence activity named *interactWithChild* accepts the child's preferences and sends a thank-you note. The sequence activity named *interactWithParent* receives credit-card details, confirms the parent's credit-worthiness, and, if credit is approved, informs the partner companies.

A link called *creditApproval* enforces a dependency, as indicated by the use of the target and source elements. The process will not send a note to the child unless the parent-related invoke activity succeeds. In general terms, a *target activity* depends on one or more *source activities.*

The problem is that the target activity is dependent on informing the partner companies and is not dependent on approving the parent's credit.

"The solution," you may say, "is to move the link source from the invoke activity to the if activity."

```
<if name="approved">
    <condition> ... </condition>
    <sources> <source linkName="creditApproval"/> </sources>
    <invoke name="informPartnerCompanies"/>
<else/>
</if>
```

The change seems sensible but creates a new problem. The source activity is now the if activity, which can complete successfully even if the else logic (if any) is invoked. Assuming no fault occurs, the process sends a note to the child regardless of whether the parent's credit is approved.

Let's do as follows:

- Introduce the BPEL empty activity to the if activity, to help us enforce a precise synchronization.

- Use a BPEL sequence activity as a container in the if activity.

```
<if name="approved">
    <condition> ... </condition>
    <sequence name="oneActivity">
        <empty>
            <sources>
                <source linkName="creditApproval"/>
            </sources>
        </empty>
        <invoke name="informPartnerCompanies"/>
    </sequence>
<else/>
</if>
```

In this case, the empty activity is a container for the link source, and the sequence activity is a syntactic requirement. An if activity can include no more than one activity between the if start tag and the next else or elseif activity, if any.

That example fulfills the business need.

"Wait!" you say as you synchronize your thoughts with what you've read. "Can link sources and targets be in any BPEL activity?"

They can, although a few restrictions apply. It is not valid, for example, to place a link source (or link target) inside a loop while the related link target (or link source) is outside the loop, as in the following outline.

```
<!- Not Valid! ->
<flow>
    <links><link name="sentFinalContract"/> </links>
    <invoke name="sendIt">
        <sources>
            <source linkName="sentFinalContract"/>
        </sources>
    </invoke>
    <while name="loop">
        <sequence name="oneActivity">
            <empty>
                <targets>
                    <target linkName="sentFinalContract"/>
                </targets>
            </empty>
            <invoke name="sendPartyInvitation"/>
        </sequence>
    </while>
</flow>
```

Here is a possible solution:

```
<flow>
    <links><link name="sentFinalContract"/> </links>
    <invoke name="sendIt">
        <sources>
            <source linkName="sentFinalContract"/>
        </sources>
    </invoke>
    <while name="loop">
        <targets>
            <target linkName="sentFinalContract"/>
        </targets>
        <invoke name="sendPartyInvitation"/>
    </while>
</flow>
```

Advanced Concurrency

BPEL supports complex synchronization scenarios:

- A target activity may depend on several source activities.

- Several target activities may depend on the same source activity.

To see how the ideas fit together, consider the outline shown in Listing 7.7, which is from a service that verifies customer details at Highlight Insurance. Two aspects of the outline are of interest and are explained next: transition conditions, as declared in the transitionCondition elements, and join conditions, as declared in the joinCondition elements.

```
<flow name="approveAndPurchase">
    <links>
        <link name="CreditLink1"/>
        <link name="DMVLink1"/>
        <link name="DMVLink2"/>
    </links>

    <invoke name="RunCreditCheck">
        <sources>
            <source linkName="CreditLink1">
                <transitionCondition>
                    $checkResponse.creditCheckResult/valid
                </transitionCondition>
            </source>
        </sources>
    </invoke>

    <sequence>
        <invoke name="CheckApplicantWithDMV">
            <sources>
                <source linkName="DMVLink1">
                    <transitionCondition>
                        $dmvResponse.retrieveLicenseStatusResult/valid
                    </transitionCondition>
                </source>
            </sources>
        </invoke>

        <invoke name="CheckDependentsWithDMV">
            <sources>
                <source linkName="DMVLink2">
                    <transitionCondition>
                        $dmvResponse.retrieveLicenseStatusResult/valid
                    </transitionCondition>
```

Listing 7.7: Advanced concurrency example (part 1 of 2)

```
                    </source>
                  </sources>
                </invoke>
              </sequence>

              <sequence name="Accepted">
                <targets>
                  <target linkName="CreditLink1" />
                  <target linkName="DMVLink1" />
                  <target linkName="DMVLink2" />
                  <joinCondition>
                    $CreditLink1 and $DMVLink1 and $DMVLink2
                  </joinCondition>
                <targets>
                <assign name="copyAcceptanceData" />
                <invoke name="sendAcceptanceNote"/>
              </sequence>

              <sequence name="Rejected">
                <targets>
                  <target linkName="CreditLink1" />
                  <target linkName="DMVLink1" />
                  <target linkName="DMVLink2" />
                  <joinCondition>
                      not($CreditLink1 and $DMVLink1 and $DMVLink2)
                  </joinCondition>
                </targets>
                <assign name="copyRejectionData" />
                <invoke name="sendRejectionNote"/>
              </sequence>
            </flow>
```

Listing 7.7: Advanced concurrency example (part 2 of 2)

Transition Conditions

A *transition condition* is a Boolean expression that is specific to a link source. When a source activity completes successfully, the BPEL engine evaluates the transition condition for each link source in that activity and assigns the value to each of the related links.

In response to a policy request, for example, Highlight Insurance verifies details with a credit agency and with the DMV, using parallel streams to save time. If *RunCreditCheck* (the invoke statement that contacts a credit agency) succeeds (which means, ends without a fault), the link *CreditLink1* is set to *true* or *false*, depending on the credit agency's response. A similar assignment occurs for each of the two DMV-related invocations.

If multiple link sources are present for a single activity, the order of evaluation is the order of the source elements. If a transition condition is not present for a given source activity that succeeds, the value of the link is *true*.

When a source activity fails (ending with a fault), the transition condition evaluates to *false*. That rule does not apply, however, in the following cases:

- The source activity is a scope.

- A fault occurs in that scope.

- The scope's fault handler completes without throwing a fault.

In that situation, the BPEL engine evaluates the transition condition as if the scope had succeeded. As always, the default transition condition is *true*.

Join Condition

A *join condition* is an expression that is specific not to a link target but to a target activity. The target activity can run only when two conditions apply:

- The BPEL engine resolves every related link source to *true* or *false*.

- The join condition for the target activity evaluates to *true*.

In our example, if the credit and DMV checks resolve to *true*, the sequence named *Accepted* runs. If any check resolves to *false*, the sequence named *Rejected* runs.

The join condition can include only the value of each link, plus Boolean operators that combine the values. The default join condition combines the link values so that if any of the links are *true*, the target activity runs.

If a join condition evaluates to *false*, processing continues normally or the BPEL engine throws the fault *bpel:joinFailure*. The specific outcome depends on the value of attribute suppressJoinFailure in the target activity. If the value of that attribute is *yes*, processing continues normally. The implication is that processing can skip activities for which the join condition was false until an activity is reached that is valid to run. The skipping of target activities during normal processing is called *dead path elimination*.

If a join condition fails and the value of attribute suppressJoinFailure is *no*, the BPEL engine throws a fault.

If you do not specify a value for the attribute suppressJoinFailure, a value is derived from the nearest enclosing activity or process for which you did specify a value, even if that enclosing activity is outside the flow activity. The default value for the process-level suppressJoinFailure attribute is *no* so that you don't need to change a default setting to ensure that fault handling occurs.

In the following outline, the value of attribute suppressJoinFailure in the invoke activity is *yes*.

```
<flow suppressJoinFailure="yes">
    <links><link name="creditApproval"/> </links>
    <sequence>
        <receive/>
        <invoke>
            <targets>
                <target linkName="creditApproval"/>
            </targets>
        </invoke>
    </sequence>
    <sequence>
        .
        .
    </sequence>
</flow>
```

In the next outline, the value of attribute suppressJoinFailure in the invoke activity is also *yes*.

```
<flow suppressJoinFailure="no">
    <links><link name="creditApproval"/> </links>
    <sequence suppressJoinFailure="yes">
        <receive/>
        <invoke>
            <targets>
                <target linkName="creditApproval"/>
            </targets>
        </invoke>
    </sequence>
    <sequence>
        .
        .
    </sequence>
</flow>
```

If no enclosing activity specifies a value, you can assign a default value at the process level. Here, the value of attribute suppressJoinFailure in the invoke activity is also *yes*:

```
<process suppressJoinFailure="yes">
    <flow>
        <links><link name="creditApproval"/> </links>
        <sequence>
            <receive/>
            <invoke>
                <targets>
                    <target linkName="creditApproval"/>
                </targets>
            </invoke>
        </sequence>
        <sequence>
            .
            .
        </sequence>
    </flow>
</process>
```

CHAPTER 8

BPEL Activity Highlights

This chapter highlights selected BPEL activities, as well as event handlers.

As noted earlier, BPEL activities are divided into two categories. A *basic activity* does a task such as assigning a value to a variable. A *structured activity* embeds other activities (basic or structured) and specifies an order or condition that affects the circumstance in which those activities run.

Any activity can include either or both of the following optional, standard attributes: name and suppressJoinFailure. The name attribute's value is used for documentation and possibly for display in a BPEL editor, but the attribute has an additional use in compensation. The compensateScope activity uses the name value to refer to a particular scope or invoke activity, as described later.

The suppressJoinFailure attribute affects what happens in a flow activity after a join condition fails. If the attribute value is *yes*, the BPEL engine issues the activity that logically follows the target activity. If the attribute value is *no*, the BPEL engine throws a fault.

Start Activities

In a BPEL process, the first activity (other than flow, scope, or sequence) must be a *start activity*, which is an activity that can create an instance of the BPEL process. A start activity must be able to receive a message and must have a createInstance attribute that is set to *yes*. Two kinds of start activities are available:

- a receive activity

- a pick activity that contains only onMessage events

A flow activity causes concurrent processing, so a start activity embedded in that activity isn't necessarily the first to run. Two rules apply. First, every activity that may run first in the process must be a start activity. The following outline isn't valid because in the second receive activity, the createInstance attribute is set to *no* by default, and that activity can be issued before the BPEL engine creates the process instance.

```
<!- Not Valid! ->
<process>
    <flow>
        <receive createInstance="yes"/>
        <receive/>
    </flow>
</process>
```

Second, if multiple start activities are in a flow activity and any of them reference correlation sets, these activities must reference at least one correlation set in common; also, the initiate attribute for each of the common correlations must be set to *join*, as in the following outline.

```
<process>
    <correlationSets>
        <correlationSet name="invoiceSet"
          properties="invoiceNumber countryCode">
        </correlationSet>
    </correlationSets>
    <flow>
        <receive createInstance="yes">
          <correlations>
              <correlation set="invoiceSet" initiate="join"/>
          </correlations>
        </receive>
        <receive createInstance="yes">
          <correlations>
              <correlation set="invoiceSet" initiate="join"/>
          </correlations>
        </receive>
    </flow>
</process>
```

assign Activity

The assign activity copies sources to targets.

A source can be a literal, an expression, a property, a partner link, a variable, or a part of a variable; and you may use a query element to retrieve data from a variable that is based on a message type. The same kinds of sources are available when you initialize a variable.

A target can be a property, a partner link, an expression, a variable, or a part of a variable; and you may use a query element or expression to identify a field in which to place a value.

Your BPEL engine also may provide an *extension assign operation*, which is an assignment that is not defined in the language itself.

The assign activity can copy multiple values, as shown in Listing 8.1.

```
<assign name="assignValues">
    <copy>
        <from variable="temporaryVariable"/>
        <to variable="quoteRequest"/>
    </copy>
    <copy>
        <from variable="quoteRequest"
              part="placeQuoteParameters"/>
            <query>
                /quoteInformation/applicantEmailAddr
            </query>
        </from>
        <to variable="emailAddress"/>
    </copy>
    <copy>
        <from variable="mvRecord" property="licenseNumber"/>
        <to variable="vehicleLicense"/>
    </copy>
    <copy>
        <from>$input.msgPart/descendant::Make[.="Ford"]</from>
        <to variable="output"/>
    </copy>
</assign>
<assign name="assignLink">
    <copy>
        <from partnerLink="dmv"
              endpointReference="partnerRole"/>
        <to variable="partnerDMVrole"/>
    </copy>
</assign>
```

Listing 8.1: assign activity

The copies occur in sequential order, and the values assigned earlier are available for later operations in the same assign activity.

The assign activity includes the validate attribute, which defaults to *no*. If that attribute is set to *yes*, every variable changed in the assign activity is subject to being compared against the WSDL or XML Schema definition on which the variable is based. A validation failure causes the runtime *bpel:invalidVariables* fault, but some BPEL engines turn off the validation for better performance.

Literals

The following examples demonstrate use of the assign activity to copy literals.

For a simple type:

```
<assign>
    <copy>
        <from>
            <literal>Main Street</literal>
        </from>
        <to variable="address"/>
    </copy>
</assign>
```

For a string (such as *<You&Me>*) that must be hidden from the BPEL engine:

```
<assign>
    <copy>
        <from>
            <literal>
                <![CDATA[<You&Me>]]>
            </literal>
        </from>
        <to variable="printString"/>
    </copy>
</assign>
```

For an empty string:

```
<assign>
    <copy>
        <from>
            <literal />
        </from>
        <to variable="emptyString"/>
    </copy>
</assign>
```

For a complex type:

```
<assign>
   <copy>
      <from>
         <literal>
            <VehicleList>
               <OneVehicle/>
            </VehicleList>
         </literal>
      </from>
      <to variable="AllVehicles"/>
   </copy>
</assign>
```

For a type that must be qualified by a namespace prefix:

```
<assign>
   <copy>
      <from>
         <literal>
            <highlight:VehicleList xmlns:highlight="abc">
               <highlight:OneVehicle/>
            </highlight:VehicleList>
         </literal>
      </from>
      <to variable="AllVehicles"/>
   </copy>
</assign>
```

Types and Namespaces

In general, a source and target in an assign activity must have compatible types. You cannot assign a string to a variable that is based on type xsd:int, for example, nor can you assign a variable based on a message type to a variable that is not based on a message type.

Let's look at a few other requirements:

- If the source is a variable of a given message type, the target must be a variable of the same message type.

- If the source is a variable of a given XSD element or type, the target must be a variable of the same XSD element or type.

- If the source is a combination of variable name and part, the definition of the target must be identical at the level of the XSD element or type definition. (Zzzzz. . . .)

Listing 8.2 shows an example of two message definitions, which may be in different WSDL files, and Listing 8.3 shows the element on which each message part is based.

```
<wsdl:message name="receiveMsg">
    <wsdl:part element="highlightXSD:transferElement"
               name="receivePart"/>
</wsdl:message>

<wsdl:message name="sendMsg">
    <wsdl:part element="highlightXSD:transferElement"
               name="sendPart"/>
</wsdl:message>
```

Listing 8.2: Sample message definitions

```
<xsd:schema xmlns:xsd="http://www.w3.org/2001/XMLSchema"
            targetNamespace=
                "http://com.highlight/policy/xsd/"
            xmlns:highlightXSD=
                "http://com.highlight/policy/xsd/">

    <xsd:element name="transferElement">
        <xsd:complexType>
            <xsd:sequence>
                <xsd:element name="msgInfo"
                             type="highlightXSD:NoticeType"/>
            </xsd:sequence>
        </xsd:complexType>
    </xsd:element>

    <xsd:complexType name="NoticeType">
        <xsd:sequence>
            <xsd:element name="noticeID"
                         type="xsd:string" />
            <xsd:element name="fields"
                         type="xsd:string" />
        </xsd:sequence>
    </xsd:complexType>
</xsd:schema>
```

Listing 8.3: Sample element definition

Listing 8.4 shows an `assign` statement that works if you've created a variable for each message type. The statement works, however, only because the message parts are based on the same element, which means that the data types (including namespaces and local names) are identical.

```
<assign name="copyNotice">
    <copy>
        <from variable="receiveVariable" part="receivePart" />
        <to variable="sendVariable" part="sendPart" />
    </copy>
</assign>
```

Listing 8.4: Sample assign activity for message parts based on same XSD element

The name of any XSD type is a combination of namespace (which is often represented by a prefix) and local name, regardless of whether the type is xsd:int or a complex type that you created. If the source in your assign activity is a variable name and property, for example, the type of the target must be the same as the type of the property.

You may not be thinking about namespaces, however, when the source of an assign activity has one of the following formats:

- a query, literal, or other expression

- a combination of variable name and property

In this case, the source resolves to a value of a particular type, which is usually a simple type. The number *7* or the Customer ID *ABC* is what it is. If the target in the first case accepts an integer, and if the target in the second case accepts a string, all is well.

A target must have the appropriate type in all cases, but you're likely to be aware of namespace issues only in some.

Use of an Expression As the Target

In some cases, you can use an expression to identify the field that receives data. The situation applies when the to element includes either of the following:

- a variable based on a message type, followed by a query that identifies a field in that variable

- an expression that identifies a field in a variable

Here's an example of each variation.

```
<assign name="DefaultQuoteAssignment">
    <copy>
        <from><literal>false</literal></from>
        <to variable="highlightQuote" part="placeQuoteResult">
            <query>/quote/quoteProvided</query>
        </to>
    </copy>
    <copy>
        <from><literal>false</literal></from>
        <to>$myVariable/quote/quoteProvided</to>
    </copy>
</assign>
```

In each case, the statement writes "false" to the quoteProvided field.

Use of Partner Links

Let's focus for a moment on assigning endpoint references. When the source is a partner link, you specify myRole or partnerRole to identify the endpoint reference being copied. When the target is a partner link, however, you don't specify myRole or partnerRole because you can assign the endpoint reference only for the partner service.

One source of endpoint references might be configuration settings in an SOA runtime product. Another source might be a directory of services.

One partner service might provide the endpoint reference that is necessary to access another. In that case, the BPEL process

- issues an input-message activity (such as a receive activity) to accept the endpoint reference from the first service into a variable

- includes the variable in an assign activity, to copy the endpoint reference to a partner link

- includes the partner link in an invoke activity, to access the other service

In another scenario, you can access a service that has the same interface as an often-accessed service but resides at a different location. In that case, the BPEL process

- declares a partner link and sets one of the partner-link attributes (initializePartnerRole) to require that the SOA runtime product initialize the partner link with an endpoint reference.

- includes the partner link in an invoke activity.

- also includes the partner link in a fault handler that runs only if the first invoke activity fails. The fault handler copies a second endpoint reference into the partner link and retries the service invocation.

Listing 8.5 shows a literal endpoint reference. The sref:service-ref element is provided with BPEL and conforms to whatever data is required to describe a particular kind of endpoint reference. We show subordinate elements for an example.

```
<assign>
    <copy>
        <from>
            <literal>
                <sref:service-ref>
                    <addr:EndpointReference>
                        <addr:Address>
                            http://com.highlight/policy/ProcessPolicy/
                        </addr:Address>
                        <addr:ServiceName>
                            RegistrationService
                        </addr:ServiceName>
                    </addr:EndpointReference>
                </sref:service-ref>
            </literal>
        </from>
        <to partnerLink="PolicyPL" />
    </copy>
</assign>
```

Listing 8.5: Literal endpoint reference

Attributes of Each Copy Element

Each copy element of the assign activity includes two attributes:

- If keepSrcElementName is set to *yes*, not only is content copied, but the root XML element name in the source replaces the root element name in the target.

- If ignoreMissingFromData is set to *yes*, missing data from the source of the copy has no effect; otherwise, missing data causes the runtime *bpel:selectionFailure* fault.

Both attributes default to *no*.

fromParts and toParts

Consider the following scenario:

1. You issue a receive activity that accepts data into a variable.

2. You issue an invoke activity that submits the same data to another service.

In general, you cannot use the same variable to receive and submit data. Even if the message structure is the same (two strings and an integer, for example), messages in most cases are defined in different WSDL namespaces, as shown in a later example. If a variable based on one message definition is expected but a variable based on another message definition is used, a validation error occurs at design or run time.

One way around the problem is to use an assign activity between the receive and invoke activities. A second way, however, lets you avoid defining a variable that is specific to a message:

1. Define a variable that holds only the business data that you want to transfer into and out of your BPEL process. That variable is based on an XSD element or type.

2. Reference the variable in each activity that transfers data.

The fromParts and toParts syntax makes the second alternative possible.

Imagine, for example, a BPEL process that accepts a greeting for subsequent distribution by mail. An operation in that service might use the message definition shown in Listing 8.6.

```
<wsdl:definitions
    name="ReceiveNotice"
    xmlns:wsdl="http://schemas.xmlsoap.org/wsdl/"
    targetNamespace="http://com.highlight/policy/"
    xmlns:highlightXSD="http://com.highlight/policy/xsd/">
    .
    .
    <wsdl:types>
        <xsd:schema>
            <xsd:import namespace="http://com.highlight/policy/xsd/"
                        schemaLocation="PolicyDefinitions.xsd">
            </xsd:import>
        </xsd:schema>
    </wsdl:types>
    .
    .
    <wsdl:message name="receiveMsg">
        <wsdl:part element="highlightXSD:transferElement"
                   name="receivePart"/>
    </wsdl:message>
</wsdl:definitions>
```

Listing 8.6: ReceiveNotice message definition

Also imagine the BPEL process invoking a mailing service that uses the message definition shown in Listing 8.7.

```
wsdl:definitions
    name="SendNotice"
    xmlns:wsdl="http://schemas.xmlsoap.org/wsdl/"
    targetNamespace="http://com.highlight/printer/"
    xmlns:highlightXSD="http://com.highlight/policy/xsd/">
    .
    .
    <wsdl:types>
        <xsd:schema>
            <xsd:import namespace="http://com.highlight/policy/xsd/"
                        schemaLocation="PolicyDefinitions.xsd">
            </xsd:import>
        </xsd:schema>
    </wsdl:types>
    .
    .
    <wsdl:message name="sendMsg" >
        <wsdl:part element="highlightXSD:transferElement"
                   name="sendPart"/>
    </wsdl:message>
</wsdl:definitions>
```

Listing 8.7: SendNotice message definition

Our assumption is that the message part in each definition uses the same XSD element (in this case, transferElement), as defined in the same namespace (in this case, http://com.highlight/policy/xsd/). Use of the same namespace prefix (highlightXSD) is a convention.

The purpose of the process outlined in Listing 8.8 is to transfer data from the inbound message (the greeting) to the outbound message (the mail content). You may be unfamiliar with some of the syntax, which demonstrates use of a receive, assign, and invoke activity. Be aware that in the invoke activity, inputVariable provides data for transmission to the service being invoked.

```
<process
    .
    .
    xmlns:tns1="http://com.highlight/policy/"
    xmlns:tns2="http://com.highlight/printer/">

    <!- import of a third WSDL
        that holds partner link type is not shown ->
    <import namespace="http://com.highlight/policy/"
        location="../highlight/policy/ReceiveNotice.wsdl"
        importType="http://schemas.xmlsoap.org/wsdl/" />
    <import namespace=" http://com.highlight/printer/"
        location="../highlight/printer/SendNotice.wsdl"
        importType="http://schemas.xmlsoap.org/wsdl/" />

    <variables>
        <variable name="receiveVariable"
                messageType="tns1:receiveMsg" />
        <variable name="sendVariable"
                messageType="tns2:sendMsg" />
    </variables>

    <sequence>
        <receive name="receiveNotice"
                partnerLink="receiveNoticePL"
                portType="tns1:noticePT"
                operation="receiveNoticeOp"
                variable="receiveVariable">
        </receive>

        <assign name="copyNotice">
            <copy>
                <from variable="receiveVariable" part="receivePart" />
                <to variable="sendVariable" part="sendPart" />
```

Listing 8.8: BPEL process that accepts and distributes a greeting (part 1 of 2)

```
            </copy>
        </assign>

        <invoke name="sendLetter"
                partnerLink="sendLetterPL"
                portType="tns2:sendLetterPT"
                operation="sendLetterOp"
                inputVariable="sendVariable" />
    </sequence>
</process>
```

Listing 8.8: BPEL process that accepts and distributes a greeting (part 2 of 2)

An alternative is to use a variable that is based on an XSD element and to use
fromParts and toParts syntax. Listing 8.9 demonstrates this approach.

```
<process
    .
    .
    .
    xmlns:tns1="http://com.highlight/policy/"
    xmlns:tns2="http://com.highlight/printer/"
    xmlns:tns3="http://com.highlight/policy/xsd/">


    <!- XSD import is required. WSDL imports are not shown. ->
    <import namespace=" http://com.highlight/policy/xsd"
        location="../highlight/policy/xsd/PolicyDefinitions.xsd"
        importType="http://www.w3.org/2001/XMLSchema" />

    <variables>
        <variable name="transferVariable"
                element="tns3:transferElement" />
    </variables>

    <sequence>
        <receive name="receiveNotice"
                partnerLink="receiveNoticePL"
                portType="tns1:noticePT"
                operation="receiveNoticeOp"
            <fromParts>
                <fromPart part="receivePart"
                        toVariable="transferVariable" />
                </fromPart>
            </fromParts>
        </receive>
```

Listing 8.9: BPEL process that uses toParts and fromParts instead (part 1 of 2)

```
            <invoke name="sendLetter"
                    partnerLink="sendLetterPL"
                    portType="tns2:sendLetterPT"
                    operation="sendLetterOp"
                <toParts>
                    <toPart part="sendPart"
                            fromVariable="transferVariable" />
                    </toPart>
                </toParts>
            </invoke>
        </sequence>
    </process>
```

Listing 8.9: BPEL process that uses toParts and fromParts instead (part 2 of 2)

The toParts and fromParts syntax supports multi-part messages. As noted earlier, however, the best practice is to define single-part messages.

In summary, when identifying the target of an inbound message (for example, in a receive activity), you have a choice: either specify a variable to receive all the data or use the fromParts syntax. In the latter case, you specify a set of variables, each based on an XSD element or type, along with a message part for each. You can exclude some message parts to avoid accepting data that the process does not use. Each message part is described in the WSDL message element for the operation.

Similarly, when identifying the target of an outbound message in an invoke or reply activity, you have a choice: either specify a variable that contains all the data or use the toParts syntax. In the latter case, you specify a set of variables, each based on an XSD element or type, along with a message part for each. You must ensure that each variable has content. The message part is described in the WSDL message element for the operation.

invoke Activity

The invoke activity invokes a service synchronously or asynchronously.

```
<invoke partnerLink="agent" portType="policyPT"
        operation="requestQuote"
        inputVariable="quoteRequest"
        outputVariable="requestInfo">
</invoke>
```

In relation to this activity, the word "input" and the elements inputVariable and toParts refer to the data that the BPEL process sends to the partner service.

Among the attributes of the invoke activity:

- partnerLink identifies the partner link used to connect to the service.

- portType identifies the port type but is optional because the port type is implied by the partner link and by the role identifier partnerRole in that partner link. Many developers repeat the port type in the invoke activity because they are familiar with the port-type name, and the repetition adds clarity at design time. However, the repetition creates a small dependency: if the partner link type (in the WSDL) changes to refer to a port type that has a different name, the BPEL process is no longer valid.

- operation identifies the service operation to invoke.

- inputVariable identifies a variable that contains the business data being *sent* to the service. Specify this attribute only if you don't specify the toParts element.

- outputVariable identifies a variable that receives the business data being *returned* from the service. Specify this attribute for synchronous processing, but only if you don't specify the fromParts element.

Among the elements in the invoke activity:

- correlations references one or more correlation sets.

- toParts identifies a set of message parts and related variables for data sent to the partner service. Specify this element only if you don't specify the inputVariable attribute.

- fromParts identifies a set of message parts and related variables for data returned to the BPEL process. Specify this element for synchronous processing, but only if you don't specify the outputVariable attribute.

A special form of the invoke activity embeds fault handlers, a compensation handler, or both. This form provides a shortcut to those who are working directly with the XML. Listing 8.10 shows an example.

```
<invoke name="AgentQuoteRequest"
        partnerLink="agent"
        portType="policyPT"
        operation="requestQuote"
        inputVariable="quoteRequest"
        outputVariable="requestInfo">
    <compensationHandler>
        <invoke partnerLink="agent"
                portType="policyPT"
                operation="cancelQuoteRequest"
                inputVariable="requestInfo"
                outputVariable="confirmationInfo" />
    </compensationHandler>
</invoke>
```

Listing 8.10: Sample invoke activity with embedded compensation handler

Listing 8.11 shows an example of the equivalent statements when the scope is declared explicitly.

```
<scope name="AgentQuoteRequest">
    <compensationHandler>
        <invoke partnerLink="agent"
                portType="policyPT"
                operation="cancelQuoteRequest"
                inputVariable="requestInfo"
                outputVariable="confirmationInfo" />
    </compensationHandler>
    <invoke name="AgentQuoteRequest"
            partnerLink="agent"
            portType="policyPT"
            operation="requestQuote"
            inputVariable="quoteRequest"
            outputVariable="requestInfo">
    </invoke>
</scope
```

Listing 8.11: Sample invoke activity with an explicitly declared scope

If the special form of the invoke activity has a name, the BPEL engine accepts that name as the name of an implicit scope, and a compensateScope activity in the immediately higher-level scope can reference the name.

receive Activity

The receive activity waits for a message that matches the detail in the related WSDL operation.

```
<receive name="getQuote"
         partnerLink="agent"
         operation="requestQuote"
         variable="quoteDetails"
         createInstance="yes" />
```

Among the attributes of the receive activity:

- partnerLink identifies the partner link used to connect to the service.

- portType identifies the port type but is optional because the port type is implied by the partner link and by the role identifier myRole in that partner link.

- operation identifies the service operation.

- variable identifies a variable that receives the business data from the service. Specify this attribute only if you don't specify the fromParts element.

- createInstance indicates whether the activity creates a BPEL instance. Valid values are *yes* and *no*. The default is *no*.

- messageExchange references a message exchange.

Among the elements in the receive activity:

- correlations references one or more correlation sets.

- fromParts identifies a set of message parts and related variables to receive business data. Specify the fromParts element only if you don't specify the variable attribute.

reply Activity

The reply activity responds to a message received by one of the following kinds of *inbound message activities (IMAs)*: a receive activity, an onMessage event (within the pick activity), or an onEvent handler.

```
<reply name="confirmQuote"
       partnerLink="agent"
       operation="requestQuote"
       variable="quoteResponse"/>
```

The partner link, port type, and operation used in the reply activity are the same as the partner link, port type, and operation used in the IMA.

Consider the following port type.

```
<wsdl:portType name="agentPT">
    <wsdl:operation name="requestQuote">
        <wsdl:input message="requestMessage" />
        <wsdl:output message="responseMessage" />
    </wsdl:operation>
</wsdl:portType>
```

When the BPEL process is using a combination of IMA and reply activity:

- the message sent by the partner service is described by the input message

- the message returned by the BPEL process is described by the output message

The port type implies synchronous processing, which means that the requester suspends processing while waiting for a response. The requester may treat the invocation as synchronous or asynchronous, however, depending on the runtime software that handles the interaction between the two services.

Among the attributes of the reply activity:

- partnerLink identifies the partner link used to connect to the service.

- portType identifies the port type but is optional because the port type is implied by the partner link and by the role identifier myRole in that partner link.

- operation identifies the service operation.

- variable identifies a variable that contains the business data being sent to the service. Specify this variable only if you don't specify the toParts element.

- faultName identifies a WSDL fault name, as used when sending a fault message to the partner service.

- messageExchange references a message exchange.

Among the elements in the reply activity:

- correlations references one or more correlation sets.

- toParts identifies a set of message parts and related variables for data sent to the partner service. Specify this element only if you don't specify the variable attribute.

forEach Activity

The forEach activity issues its embedded scope repeatedly, either in sequence or concurrently.

Figure 8.1 depicts the sequential forEach activity. As shown, the sequential forEach is similar (but not identical) to a "for loop" in other programming languages, where the logic is expressed by the phrase "for X equals start to finish."

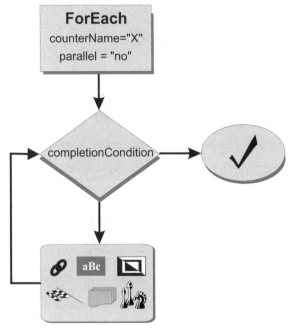

Figure 8.1: Sequential forEach

The maximum number of iterations is specified when the sequential forEach begins, and a counter indicates which iteration is running at a given time.

Figure 8.2 illustrates the concurrent (or *parallel*) forEach activity. As shown, the concurrent forEach also runs the embedded scope repeatedly, but each scope (really, each scope instance) starts at the same time.

The starting number of scope instances is specified when the concurrent forEach begins, and a counter is available to distinguish one scope instance from the next.

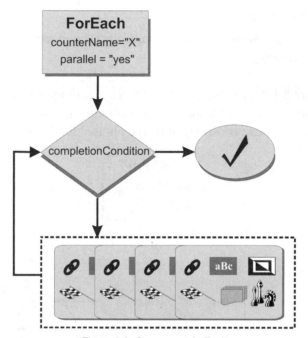

Figure 8.2: Concurrent forEach

Depending on specified options, the forEach activity ends normally

- when all scope instances complete;

- when a preset number of scope instances complete; or

- when a preset number of scope instances complete successfully.

Here's an example of a forEach activity.

```
<forEach counterName="myVar" parallel="yes"
        name="forLoop">
   <startCounterValue>1</startCounterValue>
   <finalCounterValue>5</finalCounterValue>
   <completionCondition>
      <branches successfulBranchesOnly="yes">
         3
      </branches>
   </completionCondition>
   <scope name="forEachScope">
     .
     .
   </scope>
</forEach>
```

Among the attributes of the *forEach* activity:

- counterName is an unsigned integer variable that is implicitly declared in the *forEach scope*, which is the scope in the activity. The variable value is available at run time. Any changes have no effect on the number of scope instances because the number is preset when the forEach activity starts. Moreover, changes are lost after any particular scope instance ends.

- parallel accepts the value *yes* (for the parallel version of the activity) or *no* (for the sequential).

Among the elements in the forEach activity:

- startCounterValue has the starting counter value, which does not change after the forEach activity begins. If the value is greater than that of finalCounterValue, the forEach activity is equivalent to an empty activity.

- finalCounterValue has the maximum counter value, which does not change after the forEach activity begins.

- branches (within the completionCondition element) indicates the number of scope instances whose completion ends the forEach activity. If the number is meant to refer to the number of successfully completed scope instances, set the successfulBranchesOnly attribute to *yes*.

  The specified number must be less than or equal to the maximum number of scope instances that can run in the forEach activity. (The maximum is one more than the difference between startCounterValue and finalCounterValue.)

  When running a parallel forEach activity that has a value in the branches element, the BPEL engine may end the activity only after more completions occur than are specified in that element.

Any of those elements can accept an expression that resolves to a number.

Other Loops

BPEL provides two other loops: while and repeatUntil.

while Activity

The while activity defines a loop that iterates while a Boolean expression at the top of the loop evaluates to *true*. If the expression initially evaluates to *false*, the loop does not run.

```
<while>
    <condition>$numberOfDrivers &lt; 5</condition>
    <sequence>
        .
        .
    </sequence>
</while>
```

repeatUntil Activity

The repeatUntil activity defines a loop that always runs at least once. The loop iterates until the Boolean expression at the bottom of the loop evaluates to *true*.

```
<repeatUntil>
    <sequence>
        .
        .
    </sequence>
    <condition>$numberOfDrivers = 5</condition>
</repeatUntil>
```

pick Activity

The pick activity waits for one of potentially several events to occur, often including a timeout and always including receipt of an inbound message. The activity completes when any one of its immediately embedded activities completes:

- The onMessage event processes an inbound message and is similar to a receive activity.

- The onAlarm event waits for a passage of time or for a specific date and time.

Both those events can embed other activities.

A variation of the pick activity creates an instance of a BPEL process, but in that case, no timeout is possible and any inbound message can create an instance.

In most cases, the pick activity is not concurrent with other activities.

Listing 8.12 shows an example. A further explanation of each embedded activity follows.

```
<pick name="CustomerResponseToQuote">
    <onMessage operation="requestMore"
               partnerLink="ProcessQuotePL"
               portType="ProcessQuotePT"
               variable="furtherConsiderationReq">
        <correlations>
            <correlation initiate="no" set="applicantEMailAddr" />
        </correlations>
        <sequence name="customerWantsUnderwriterToContactPostReview">
            <assign name="copyQuoteForReview">
                <copy>
                    .
                    .
                </copy>
            </assign>
            <invoke name="underwriterFollowupAndCall"
                    partnerLink="UnderwriterPL"
                    portType=" UnderwriterPT"
                    operation="retrieveAndFollowUp"
                    inputVariable="underwriterReview"/>
        </sequence>
    </onMessage>
    <onAlarm>
        <for>'PT5M'</for>
        <invoke .../>
    </onAlarm>
</pick>
```

Listing 8.12: pick activity

onMessage Event

Among the attributes of the onMessage event:

- createInstance indicates whether the activity creates a BPEL instance. Valid values are *yes* and *no*. The default is *no*.

- partnerLink identifies the partner link used to connect to the service.

- portType identifies the port type but is optional because the port type is implied by the partner link and by the role identifier myRole in that partner link.

- operation identifies the service operation.

- variable identifies a variable that receives the business data from the service. Specify the variable attribute only if you don't specify the fromParts element.

- messageExchange references a message exchange.

Among the elements in the onMessage event:

- correlations references one or more correlation sets.

- fromParts identifies a set of message parts and related variables to receive business data. Specify the fromParts element only if you don't specify the variable attribute.

onAlarm Event

The onAlarm event requires the presence of at least one of the following elements:

- for identifies the duration that passes before the alarm is fired. The start time for that duration is when the pick activity begins. Specify this element only if you don't specify the until element.

- until identifies the calendar date and clock time when the alarm is triggered. Specify this element only if you don't specify the for element.

wait Activity

Like the onAlarm event of the pick activity, the wait activity causes a delay for a specified period or until a specified date and time.

```
<sequence>
    <wait>
        <until>'2010-12-25T18:00+01:00'</until>
    </wait>
    <invoke ... />
</sequence>
```

```
<sequence>
    <documentation>
        wait for 1 Year 2 Months and 1 Hour
    </documentation>
    <wait>
        <for>'P1Y2MT1H'</for>
    </wait>
    <invoke ... />
</sequence>
```

Elements nested in the wait activity include the following:

- for identifies the duration that passes before the activity ends. The start time is when the activity starts. Specify this element only if you don't specify the until element.

- until identifies the calendar date and clock time when the activity ends. Specify this element only if you don't specify the for element.

Event Handlers

An event handler is a set of activities that run concurrently with either the primary activity of the same scope or, outside a scope, with the primary activity of the process. The handler also may run concurrently with other event handlers and with other instances of the same handler. Unlike the other handlers (compensation, fault, and termination), the event handler runs during normal processing.

Two kinds of event handlers are available: onEvent and onAlarm.

An onEvent handler processes an inbound message and is similar to a receive activity. You can use this kind of handler for an interaction that occurs only in some process instances, as when a customer cancels a purchase before a product is shipped.

An onAlarm handler waits for a passage of time or for a specific date and time. After firing an initial alarm, the handler can fire an alarm repeatedly at a specified interval. You can use an onAlarm handler to send a renewal notice.

An event handler is enabled when the BPEL process receives its initial message or when the scope that encloses the event handler begins. An event handler is disabled when the process or scope ends. If an event handler is running, though, the BPEL engine allows the activities to complete.

The onEvent handler accepts messages for as long as the handler is enabled, whereas the onAlarm handler does not fire again unless you requested a repetition.

onEvent Handler

The BPEL process implicitly declares a variable that receives data and is local to the scope of the handler. You can receive data only into that implicitly declared variable.

The implicit declaration occurs whether you've specified the variable attribute, along with a message type or XSD element, or the fromParts element. (We've ignored the possibility of several variable declarations, one for each part in the inbound message.) All local variables in the scope of the handler are local to each running instance of the handler.

Among the attributes of the onEvent handler:

- partnerLink identifies the partner link used to connect to the service.

- portType identifies the port type but is optional because the port type is implied by the partner link and by the role identifier myRole in that partner link.

- operation identifies the service operation.

- variable identifies a variable that receives the business data from the service. Specify the variable attribute only if you don't specify the fromParts element.

- messageExchange references a message exchange in a scope that encloses the onEvent handler.

Among the elements in the onEvent handler:

- correlations references one or more correlation sets.

- fromParts identifies a set of message parts and related variables to receive business data. Specify the fromParts element only if you don't specify the variable attribute.

onAlarm Handler

The onAlarm handler requires the presence of at least one of the following elements:

- for identifies the duration that passes before the alarm is fired. The start time for that duration is when the BPEL process receives its initial message or when the scope that encloses the event handler begins. You can specify this element only if you don't specify the until element.

- until identifies the calendar date and clock time when the alarm is triggered. You can specify this element only if you don't specify the for element.

- repeatEvery causes the alarm to be triggered repeatedly and specifies the interval between triggers. The interval begins when the initial trigger fires or, if neither of the other elements is specified, when the BPEL process receives its initial message or when the scope that encloses the event handler begins.

Listing 8.13 shows several onAlarm handler examples.

```
<process>
    <eventHandlers>

        <!- the event fires after 5 minutes ->
        <onAlarm>
            <for>'PT5M'</for>
            <invoke .../>
        </onAlarm>

        <!- the event fires at 9am on Dec 24 2010 ->
        <onAlarm>
            <until>'2010-12-24T09:00+01:00'</until>
            <invoke .../>
        </onAlarm>

        <!- the event fires every 3 hours ->
        <onAlarm>
            <repeatEvery>'PT3H'</repeatEvery>
            <invoke .../>
        </onAlarm>

        <!- the event fires after 5 minutes
            and every day thereafter ->
        <onAlarm>
            <for>'PT5M'</for>
            <repeatEvery>'P1D'</repeatEvery>
            <invoke .../>
        </onAlarm>
    </eventHandlers>
</process>
```

Listing 8.13: onAlarm handlers

You can assign some or all of the element values from data that was received in an inbound message. Also, if you wish to fire the alarm repeatedly but only a specified number of times, you can create a sequential forEach activity and embed an onAlarm handler that doesn't have a repeatEvery element.

Message Exchanges, Revisited

As noted earlier, the BPEL engine can pair a reply activity with an inbound message activity, but only if the paired activities reference the same partner link, operation, and message exchange. The pairing allows the BPEL engine to direct the reply appropriately.

In most cases, the process creates a default message exchange for each activity, and you need to specify only the partner link and operation. An explicit message exchange is necessary at times, as in the following example.

In response to most car-insurance policy requests, the BPEL process CheckCredit requires financial data from the applicant and co-applicant. The process includes a receive activity for each applicant in sequence.

```
<sequence>
    <receive partnerLink="CreditCheck"
             operation="checkFamilyCredit"
             variable="applicantInfo"
             createInstance="yes"
             messageExchange="applicant" />
    <receive partnerLink="CreditCheck"
             operation="checkFamilyCredit"
             variable="spouseInfo"
             createInstance="no"
             messageExchange="spouse" />
</sequence>
```

As shown, the two activities are based on the same partner link and operation and are distinguished only by the message-exchange value. The message-exchange values were defined earlier, as follows.

```
<messageExchanges>
    <messageExchange name="applicant" />
    <messageExchange name="spouse" />
</messageExchanges>
```

Assume that in the subsequent flow activity, shown in Listing 8.14, a calculation occurs at the same time for each applicant (within the sequence activity that we show for simplicity). We cannot know which calculation will end first, but in any case, a reply is necessary to the appropriate applicant, and the message-exchange value is required so that the BPEL engine can match a receive activity and the subsequent reply.

```
<flow>
    <links>
        <link name="ApplicantLink" />
        <link name="SpouseLink" />
    </links>

    <!- assume that activities in each sequence activity
        perform a calculation. The reply statements that follow
        the calculation run concurrently, but must respond to a
        specific request. ->

    <sequence name="Calculate credit report for spouse">
        .
        .
        .
        <sources>
            <source linkName="SpouseLink" />
        </sources>
    </sequence>

    <reply partnerLink="CreditCheck"
           operation="checkFamilyCredit"
           variable="resultSpouse"
           messageExchange="spouse">

        <targets>
            <target linkName="SpouseLink" />
        </targets>
    </reply>

    <sequence name="Calculate credit report for applicant">
        .
        .
        .
        <sources>
            <source linkName="ApplicantLink" />
        </sources>
    </sequence>

    <reply partnerLink="CreditCheck"
           operation="checkFamilyCredit"
           variable="resultApplicant"
           messageExchange="applicant">
        <targets>
            <target linkName="ApplicantLink" />
        </targets>
    </reply>
</flow>
```

Listing 8.14: Use of message exchanges

In general, you must do as follows if multiple IMA-and-reply pairs reference the same partner link and operation and if those activity pairs may run at the same time:

- Declare a message exchange for each IMA-and-reply pair.

- Reference the appropriate message exchange when you define each activity, to make the pairings explicit.

doXSLTransform

Extensible Stylesheet Transformations (XSLT) 1.0 is a language for copying data from an XML source into a second, differently structured text format (called a *result document*), which in most cases is also in XML. Here's the situation in BPEL:

- The primary purpose of XSLT is to reorganize the data received from one service so that the process can transmit the data to another.

- The XML source must contain a single XPath element node, which may contain descendants.

To reorganize data from an XML source, do as follows:

1. Write an extensible stylesheet (XSL), which is an XML file that includes

   ♦ XPath 1.0 expressions that select the data of interest

   ♦ optionally, parameters that accept values from outside the XSL and that help specify what data to review from the XML source, as well as what data to place in the result document

   ♦ XSLT statements that specify the result document, which may include data from the XML source as well as from the XSL

2. In the BPEL process, invoke the function doXSLTransform and specify

   ♦ a path to the XSL

   ♦ a variable that holds the XML source, or an XPath expression that resolves to a single element node

   ♦ optionally, pairs of parameter names and values for use by the XSL

   The function doXSLTransform returns a result document. If the function is a source in a copy element of the assign activity, the result document is placed in the appropriate target field.

Our next examples reflect two ways to use doXSLTransform:

- *single transformation*, which is the conversion of an XML source to a result document by one invocation of the function

- *iterative construction*, which is the building of an increasingly large result document by repeated invocations of the function

Single Transformation

Figure 8.3 illustrates the use of doXSLTransform for a single transformation.

As shown in the figure, a BPEL process can receive data from a partner service, use that data to invoke doXSLTransform in an assign activity, and use the result document when invoking a second partner service.

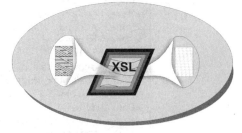

Figure 8.3: doXSLTransform, single transformation

Listing 8.15 shows the XML source for a single transformation.

```
<Insured CustomerID="5">
    <CarPolicy PolicyType="Auto">
        <Vehicle Category="Sedan">
            <Make>Honda</Make>
            <Model>Accord</Model>
        </Vehicle>
        <Vehicle Category="Sport" Domestic="True">
            <Make>Ford</Make>
            <Model>Mustang</Model>
        </Vehicle>
    </CarPolicy>
    <CarPolicy PolicyType="Antique">
        <Vehicle Category="Sport">
            <Make>Triumph</Make>
            <Model>Spitfire</Model>
        </Vehicle>
        <Vehicle Category="Coupe" Domestic="True">
            <Make>Buick</Make>
            <Model>Skylark</Model>
        </Vehicle>
        <Vehicle Category="Sport">
            <Make>Porsche</Make>
```

Listing 8.15: XML source for a single transformation (part 1 of 2)

```
            <Model>Speedster</Model>
        </Vehicle>
    </CarPolicy>
</Insured>
```

Listing 8.15: XML source for a single transformation (part 2 of 2)

Listing 8.16 shows the result document.

```
<VehicleList>
<OneVehicle>
<Make>Honda</Make>
<Model>Accord</Model>
</OneVehicle>
<OneVehicle>
<Make>Ford</Make>
<Model>Mustang</Model>
</OneVehicle>
<OneVehicle>
<Make>Triumph</Make>
<Model>Spitfire</Model>
</OneVehicle>
<OneVehicle>
<Make>Buick</Make>
<Model>Skylark</Model>
</OneVehicle>
<OneVehicle>
<Make>Porsche</Make>
<Model>Speedster</Model>
</OneVehicle>
</VehicleList>
```

Listing 8.16: Result document for a single transformation

Listing 8.17 shows an outline of the BPEL process.

```
<process>
   .
   .
   <variables>
      <variable name="CarPolicies"  element="InsuredElement" />
      <variable name="Vehicles"     element="VehiclesElement" />
   </variables>
   <sequence>
      <invoke ... outputVariable="CarPolicies" />
```

Listing 8.17: BPEL process outline for single transformation (part 1 of 2)

```
        <assign>
            <copy>
                <from>
                    bpel:doXslTransform
                        ("urn:stylesheets:Insured2Vehicles.xsl",
                        $CarPolicies)
                </from>
                <to variable="Vehicles" />
            </copy>
        </assign>
        <invoke ... inputVariable="Vehicles" />
    </sequence>
    .
    .
    .
</process>
```

Listing 8.17: BPEL process outline for single transformation (part 2 of 2)

Last (and though a review of XSLT is out of scope), Listing 8.18 shows the XSL, which selects the CarPolicy nodes and, for each, writes a Make and Model node to the result document.

```
<?xml version="1.0" encoding="ISO-8859-1" ?>
<xsl:stylesheet version="1.0"
    xmlns:xsl="http://www.w3.org/1999/XSL/Transform">

    <xsl:output method="xml"
                version="1.0"
                encoding="ISO-8859-1"
                omit-xml-declaration="yes"
                indent="yes" />

    <xsl:template match="/">
        <VehicleList>
            <xsl:apply-templates select="Insured/CarPolicy"/>
        </VehicleList>
    </xsl:template>

    <xsl:template match="CarPolicy">
        <xsl:for-each select="Vehicle">
            <OneVehicle>
                <xsl:copy-of select="Make">
                <xsl:copy-of select="Model">
            </OneVehicle>
        </xsl:for-each>
    </xsl:template>
</xsl:stylesheet>
```

Listing 8.18: XSL to process the CarPolicy nodes

Iterative Construction

Figure 8.4 illustrates the use of doXSLTransform for iterative construction.

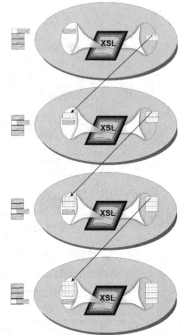

As shown in the figure, a BPEL process loops through the following sequence:

1. Receive data from a partner service.

2. Invoke the function doXSLTransform in an assign activity to add new data to the data received in previous iterations.

In this case:

- The source document (in variable AllVehicles) is different at each iteration, and the invocation of doXSLTransform is as follows.

Figure 8.4: doXSLTransfer, iterative construction

```
bpel:doXslTransform
    ("urn:stylesheets:AddNewVehicle.xsl", $AllVehicles,
    "NewVehicle", $OneVehicle)
```

- As shown, doXSLTransform submits a parameter (called NewVehicle) to the XSL. The content of that parameter is the data most recently provided by the partner service.

On completing the loop, the BPEL process invokes a second partner service with the content that was collected during the loop.

Outline of the BPEL Process

Listing 8.19 shows an outline of the BPEL process.

```
<process>
    .
    .
    <variables>
        <variable name="OneEntry"     element="OneVehicleElement" />
        <variable name="AllVehicles" element="VehicleListElement"
            <from>
                <literal>
                    <VehicleList>
                        <OneVehicle/>
                    </VehicleList>
                </literal>
            </from>
        </variable>
    </variables>

...<while>
        <condition> ... </condition>
        <sequence>
            <invoke ... outputVariable="OneEntry" />
            <assign>
                <copy>
                    <from>
                        bpel:doXslTransform
                        ("urn:stylesheets:AddNewVehicle.xsl",
                            $AllVehicles, "NewVehicle", $OneEntry)
                    </from>
                    <to variable="AllVehicles" />
                </copy>
            </assign>
        </sequence>
    </while>
    <invoke ... inputVariable="AllVehicles" />
    .
    .
</process>
```

Listing 8.19: BPEL process outline for iterative construction

Effect of the BPEL Process

The declaration of AllVehicles initializes the variable as follows.

```
<VehicleList>
<OneVehicle/>
</VehicleList>
```

We'll assume that each iteration provides details on only one vehicle and that successive iterations result in the following content.

```
<VehicleList>
<OneVehicle/>
<OneVehicle>
<Make>Honda</Make>
<Model>Accord</Model>
</OneVehicle>
<OneVehicle>
<Make>Ford</Make>
<Model>Mustang</Model>
</OneVehicle>
<OneVehicle>
<Make>Triumph</Make>
<Model>Spitfire</Model>
</OneVehicle>
</VehicleList>
```

Listing 8.20 shows the XSL, which selects the OneVehicle nodes, copies them to the (growing) result document, and adds the OneVehicle node that was provided in the current iteration of the while loop.

```
<?xml version="1.0" encoding="ISO-8859-1" ?>
<xsl:stylesheet version="1.0"
    xmlns:xsl="http://www.w3.org/1999/XSL/Transform">

    <xsl:param name="NewVehicle"/>

    <xsl:output method="xml"
                version="1.0"
                encoding="ISO-8859-1"
                omit-xml-declaration="yes"
                indent="yes" />

    <xsl:template match="/">
        <VehicleList>
            <xsl:apply-templates select="descendant::OneVehicle"/>
        </VehicleList>
    </xsl:template>

    <xsl:template match="OneVehicle">
        <xsl:copy-of select="." />
        <xsl:if test="position()=last()">
            <xsl:copy-of select="$NewVehicle">
        </xsl:if>
    </xsl:template>
</xsl:stylesheet>
```

Listing 8.20: XSL to select the OneVehicle nodes

CHAPTER 9

Introduction to SCA

*S*ervice Component Architecture (SCA) is a proposed standard for composing and deploying service-oriented applications. When SCA-compliant products are in place at development and run time, you write code in the implementation language of your choice, but with an important difference: you focus on business logic. SCA lets you avoid writing many of the technology-specific details that would otherwise be necessary before you can invoke other code.

With the ease of invoking a local method or function, you do tasks such as the following:

- Invoke a Web service.

- Invoke an *Enterprise JavaBean stateless session bean (EJB SLSB)*, which is a kind of binary-exchange service that is written for the Java EE platform.

- Invoke a traditional application by way of an *adapter*, which is software that allows a data exchange between logical units that were not designed to interact.

- Access a *message queue*, which is a data collection that is administered by messaging software such as WebSphere MQ. The messaging software stores or forwards the data, acting as an intermediary between your service and (for example) a help-desk application. The interaction between your service and the help-desk application is usually asynchronous, with your service continuing to run rather than waiting for a response. The message queue also can forward data to your service — for example, after receiving a callback message from the help-desk application.

At this writing, access of a message queue is possible only by way of a facility called Java Message Service (JMS). Additional technologies are in plan.

SCA also releases you from having to write logic that distinguishes one requester from the next during conversational processing.

SCA does more than make development easier. The technology allows for significant change in service behavior over time without requiring updates and recompilation. By setting values outside the code, your company can initialize variables, choose transport protocols and endpoints for in-code invocations, and specify Quality of Service (QoS) capabilities. In this way, SCA helps your company to retain software but be responsive to change.

Last, SCA makes reuse easier by providing a simple way to compose services from other services. A business analyst can do the assembly, replacing one service with another if the interfaces are alike or assigning an intermediary between services that are otherwise not compatible. A replacement service also can be assembled from other services, to any level of complexity.

SCA supports several implementation languages, including BPEL, C++, Java, and PHP, with more expected. A given SCA runtime may or may not support a given language or runtime technology.

If you are writing code in Java (or, later, in other languages), you can implement your service's argument and return definitions with Service Data Objects (SDO) Version 2, another open-standards technology. We describe SDO in Chapter 10.

Although companies have implemented early versions of SCA and SDO, the situation of interest to this book is that eighteen companies are in the Open Service Oriented Architecture (OSOA) collaboration, which is creating a set of SCA and SDO proposals for a major standards body to adopt. Our descriptions in this chapter are based primarily on early 2007 drafts of the following OSOA documents: *SCA Assembly Model Specification*; *SCA Policy Framework*; *SCA Client and Implementation Model Specification for WS-BPEL*; and *SCA Client and Implementation Model Specification for Java.* The current, publicly available specifications are at the following Web site: *http://www.osoa.org.*

Under the auspices of the Apache Software Foundation, the Tuscany incubator project is developing open-source implementations of SCA and SDO. For details and code, see the following Web sites: *http://incubator.apache.org/tuscany* and *http://www.apache.org.*

Project Phases

The designers of SCA envision three project phases: Development, Assembly, and Deployment.

Development

After you've written an implementation, you set SCA values that configure the runtime behavior. The configured implementation is called a *component.*

The details of a component are stored in an SCA definition like the one shown in Listing 9.1.

```
<component name="ProcessQuoteComponent" requires="confidentiality">
    <implementation.bpel name="ProcessQuoteImplementation" />
    <service name="ProcessQuote">
        <interface.partnerLinkType
           type="ProcessQuotePLT"
           serviceRole="ProcessQuoteRole" />
        <binding.sca/>
    </service>
    <property name="availableDiscount" many="true">Auto Club</property>
    <reference name="calculateOne"
               target="CalculateOneComponent" />
    <reference name="calculateTwo"
               target="CalculateTwoComponent" />
</component>
```

Listing 9.1: Sample SCA component definition

A component provides access to operations. It also has *properties* (each of which assigns an initial value to an implementation variable) and depends on the resolution of *references* (each of which identifies a set of operations that are external to the implementation).

Assembly

At assembly time, the actor is an *SCA assembler*. Although you, as the developer, often act as an assembler, the role may be fulfilled by a business analyst or by another developer.

The SCA assembler composes a logical unit called a *composite*, which solves a business problem and is made up primarily of one or more components. Some composites are deployed in a single operating-system process, while others are distributed across different processes or across different physical machines on a network.

The details of a composite are stored in an SCA definition that includes component definitions. Listing 9.2 shows an outline.

```
<composite name="myComposite" local="false">

    <service> </service>
    <property> </property>
    <reference> </reference>
    <wire> </wire>

    <component>
        <implementation/>
        <service/>
        <property/>
        <reference/>
    </component>

    <component>
        <implementation/>
        <service/>
        <property/>
        <reference/>
    </component>

</composite>
```

Listing 9.2: SCA composite outline

An SCA assembler assembles a composite from components; assembles deployable units from existing composites; creates higher-level assemblies from the deployable units; and creates even higher-level assemblies from the existing assemblies, to any level of hierarchy.

Deployment

At deployment time, an SCA deployer

- assembles higher-level assemblies from existing assemblies.

- overrides configuration values that were established at lower levels of assembly.

- completes the work of connecting one logical unit to another, to the extent that the SCA assembler has not already handled the issue. Specifically, the deployer decides which service endpoint to access in response to a method or function invocation and identifies which transport protocol to use when accessing the endpoint.

- sets Quality of Service values that affect whether requesters can or will access your service — in particular, by setting requirements. One requirement, for example, might be for requesters to use a particular kind of encryption. The developer or assembler may have restricted the deployer's options in an earlier phase.

A Different Perspective

Use of SCA assumes that you're viewing SOA more as a business analyst than as a developer. Given this different and in some ways broader perspective, we'll revisit our use of the words *service* and *implementation*.

Service

We began Chapter 2 by saying that a service *includes* three aspects: an implementation, elementary access details, and a contract. The definition is true but is unnecessarily complex when you're focusing on business concerns.

Figure 9.1: Perspectives on services

As suggested by the right side of Figure 9.1, you can view a service as a set of operations:

- You can make different sets of operations available to different sets of requesters. A subset of operations might be available only to requesters who have a particular access level.

- You can make the same set of operations available to different requesters under different circumstances. A subset of requesters might pay a special fee for a faster response time.

Implementation

We earlier said that an implementation is a logical unit written in a computer language such as BPEL or Java. We need to extend this definition for you to make full use of the SCA technology; and again, the change focuses on the business use of services.

Figure 9.2: A composite includes components

Figure 9.2 conforms to our original usage: a component is based on an implementation that is written in a specific language such as BPEL or Java. The component is a building block that is used to create a composite. The services *exposed* (that is, made available) by a component are available to other components in the same composite and may be exposed to requesters external to the composite.

Figure 9.3: A component can configure a composite

As shown in Figure 9.3, a composite can itself be used as a building block in a higher-level assembly. In this case, the lower-level composite is part of the internal processing in the higher-level composite. At least some of the services exposed by the lower-level composite are made available to other components in the higher-level composite, and the higher-level composite may make some of the exposed services available to other requesters.

How do you use a composite as a building block? You assign the composite as the implementation of a component. The configuration values of the component affect the runtime behavior of the composite.

Is there fog in your microscope? The relationships can be confusing at first, and you need to distinguish carefully between two words that sound alike: *component* and *composite*.

For now, note three points. First, an implementation is a logical unit written in one or more computer languages. Second, a composite can have two kinds of relationships with a component. The composite is an enclosure in one case, an implementation in another. Last, services are sets of operations that are provided by an implementation, which can be a simple logical unit or an assembled one.

SCA Domain

An *SCA Domain* is a collection of composites that are under one group's administrative control. The notion of a Domain is quite variable and might include all the composites available throughout a company and across different platforms, or might be a subset of composites such as those provided by an accounting department or by an accounts-receivable group.

SCA Bindings and the Enterprise Service Bus

A *binding* is a set of details on how to structure and transport a message. When used in relation to WSDL, the word "binding" identifies only a transport protocol or the software that invokes a transport protocol. When used in relation to SCA, however, the word identifies not only those details but also the location of the accessed queue, application, or service implementation. The word is also used informally to refer to a type of access software, as in the phrase "use the JMS binding to access a queue."

Your SCA-compliant products may have bindings for the following software, among others:

- HTTP, which allows a connection to a Web service

- Java EE Connector Architecture (JCA), which allows a connection to an adapter from a service that runs on the Java EE platform

- Java Remote Method Invocation over Internet Inter-ORB Protocol (JMI/IIOP), which allows a connection (for example) to an Enterprise Java Bean running on a Java application server

- Java Messaging Service (JMS), which allows access to a message queue

To guide data transfer to a service that is external to the SCA Domain, you must specify an explicit binding. No default is available. To guide data transfer within the Domain, however, the assembler usually chooses the *SCA binding*, which causes the SCA runtime to decide how to fulfill the transfer. The assembler can specify that setting explicitly or by default.

When the SCA binding is in effect, the SCA runtime might always select the same fixed binding such as HTTP or might select a protocol that is appropriate for a specific case. For example, the runtime might select a secure protocol when two components are transferring financially sensitive data. Use of SCA binding is recommended because the selection is simple for the assembler and gives maximum flexibility to the SCA runtime. For details on configuring the SCA runtime, see your product documentation.

You can specify a binding other than SCA binding for data transfers within the SCA Domain. You might want to select a different binding, for example, if you are transferring financially sensitive data but your runtime product does not provide a component-specific way to configure the behavior caused by SCA binding.

At run time, services can send and receive messages on an *Enterprise Service Bus (ESB)*, which is software that accesses HTTP, JCA, and so on. SCA can interact with an ESB or can operate in its absence.

Policies and Support for Conversations

SCA provides a way for a company to specify *policies*, which are identifiers that define a quality of service. For example, an *interaction policy* such as *confidentiality* specifies a requirement that a service makes on a requester or specifies a capability that a requester can offer. An *implementation policy* such as *logging* specifies another kind of runtime option — specifically, an option controlled by the technology that runs an implementation.

A more important distinction is that SCA divides policy specification into two major levels of detail. An *intent* is a high-level, general identifier such as *confidentiality*. A *policy set* is a lower-level description that makes one or more intents meaningful to a runtime technology.

SCA allows you as the developer to specify intents and to leave the policy sets for the deployer to assign. This division of labor has two benefits. First, it relieves you of a technical burden so you can focus on the business issues; second, it permits maximum flexibility because policy sets are assigned later, allowing for reuse of your component and composite definitions.

You may have reason to specify policy sets at development or assembly time. You might have a detailed understanding of runtime platforms, for example, or might need to use a particular runtime configuration. Nevertheless, we discourage the use of policy sets before deployment time and recommend that you communicate with your SCA deployer instead of creating restrictions in your SCA definitions, however appropriate those restrictions are. We'll say no more about policy sets except to direct the interested reader to the OSOA documents *SCA Policy Framework* and the *SCA Assembly Model Specification*.

Although every SCA installation will support a number of core intents, your company can add to them and is likely to name a policy administrator to handle the special issues involved.

A core intent of particular interest is *conversational*. By specifying that intent, you indicate that each operation in a given service is not separate from the rest but is part of a conversation, as described in Chapter 2. When the requester invokes the second or later operation in a sequence, the SCA runtime selects the appropriate conversation.

In most cases, a BPEL developer won't specify the conversational intent because the correlation-set mechanism is more powerful. Correlation sets maintain data integrity while the BPEL process is interacting with one or more partner services. When the focus is on data exchange with one partner service, however, the conversational intent has the following benefit regardless of the implementation language: you can avoid writing code to store and retrieve the data that helps maintain a conversation. SCA even provides an extension to WSDL so you can embed the conversational intent in a WSDL portType or interface.

Components

Figure 9.4 illustrates a *component*. Listing 9.3 shows the previously described component element within a composite element.

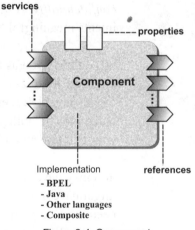

Figure 9.4: Component

```
<composite name="QuoteComposite">
    .
    .
    .
    <component name="ProcessQuoteComponent" requires="confidentiality">
        <implementation.bpel name="ProcessQuoteImplementation" />
        <service name="ProcessQuote">
            <interface.partnerLinkType
                type="ProcessQuotePLT"
                serviceRole="ProcessQuoteRole" />
            <binding.sca/>
        </service>
        <property name="availableDiscount" many="true">Auto Club</property>
        <reference name="calculateOne"
                   target="CalculateOneComponent" />
        <reference name="calculateTwo"
                   target="CalculateTwoComponent" />
    </component>
    <component name="CalculateOneComponent">
        .
        .
        .
    </component>
    <component name="CalculateTwoComponent">
        .
        .
        .
    </component>
</composite>
```

Listing 9.3: ProcessQuoteComponent within a composite element

Let's review several aspects of the definition, starting with the requires attribute, which identifies a list of policy intents, although only one intent is specified in the example.

An interaction intent such as *confidentiality* applies to descendant elements that provide binding details; in this case, those elements (of type service and reference) specify the SCA binding explicitly or by default. In contrast, an implementation intent such as *logging* applies to the subordinate implementation element, which identifies which business logic to run when the component is invoked. The presence of a policy intent at a relatively high-level element in any SCA definition makes the intent available to every subordinate element where the intent applies.

A *component service* identifies a set of operations provided by the implementation. The operations can be made available to other components in the same composite and to software that is outside the composite. Included in this example are the details necessary to access the service: an interface description and a binding (in this case, the SCA binding).

```
<service name="ProcessQuote">
    <interface.partnerLinkType
        type="ProcessQuotePLT"
        serviceRole="ProcessQuoteRole" />
    <binding.sca/>
</service>
```

A *component property* defines a relationship with a variable in the implementation. Specifically, a property has a name and, optionally, an XSD element or data type. (In this example, the data type is identified in the implementation.)

```
<property name="availableDiscount" many="true">Auto Club</property>
```

The property lets you set the initial value of the corresponding implementation variable. In most cases, the property name is the same as the variable name. You can also assign that value from a file or from a property that resides in an enclosing composite.

If the variable in the code accepts a list of values, SCA allows multiple property elements with the same name. As suggested in the following example (from an application at Highlight Insurance), the ProcessQuoteComponent implementation has a variable that holds a list of discounts (for Automobile Club membership, employee status, and so on); and the logic of that code decides which of the discounts will apply to a given applicant.

```
<component name="ProcessQuoteComponent">
    .
    .
    <property name="availableDiscount">
        <value>Auto Club</value>
        <value>Employee</value>
    </property>
</component>
```

The available discounts often vary. By setting the values in property elements of a component definition instead of in the code, the company avoids having to update the code each time a change is required to the discount list.

A *component reference* is a set of operations that are external to the implementation. The ultimate effect of assigning a value to the reference is that you specify the binding detail needed to invoke an operation at a specific endpoint.

The set of operations can be in another component in the same composite. In this case, the SCA assembler assigns the name of a component as the value of the target attribute.

```
<reference name="calculateOne"
           target="CalculateOneComponent" />
```

Alternatively, the set of operations can be in software that is outside the composite. In this case, the SCA assembler or deployer *promotes* the component reference; that is, he or she identifies the component reference in a *composite reference*, which (as shown later) is another definition in the same composite.

An implementation may be coded to handle a *multi-valued reference*, which is a reference that provides a list of target services. Your implementation might use a multi-valued reference, for example, to retrieve prices for the same kind of product from several vendors:

```
<reference name="vendors"
           target="VendorReference01 VendorReference02"/>
</reference>
```

By setting values in a component reference instead of in the code, the company avoids updating the code whenever a change is required in the vendor list.

The next sections further describe properties, services, and references of a component. We focus on the relationship (or *mapping*) of a given kind of configurable value and a construct in the implementation. In brief:

- A service is one of the sets of operations that the code makes available to a requester.

- A property is mapped to a variable that is used in data manipulation.

- A reference is mapped to a variable that provides access to a set of operations external to the component.

We include details for BPEL and Java. A BPEL process that uses SCA properties and multi-valued references requires an extension element and special syntax. SCA can handle a traditionally coded process, however, if you don't need those SCA capabilities. The extension element is as follows.

```
<process>
    <extensions>
        <extension
            namespace="http://www.osoa.org/xmlns/sca/bpel/1.0"
            mustUnderstand="yes"/>
    </extensions>
</process>
```

The mustUnderstand attribute indicates that the BPEL engine must be able to process the SCA detail.

We include Java-specific details because an early goal for Service Component Architecture was to map SCA constructs to that language. If you are unfamiliar with Java, you can skim or skip the details.

When you realize that the code written for an SCA runtime can include details that are specific to SCA, you may ask, "Why are there SCA-specific details in code? Is there a requirement that the business logic be deployed only when an SCA runtime is in use?"

The SCA details in the code help an SCA runtime apply configuration values. In many cases, however, the SCA-specific details are optional or can be specified in a separate file, and the presence of those details does not stop you from deploying the same code outside an SCA runtime.

Defining Services in Implementation Code

An SCA service is a service-interface description. Here are examples:

- In relation to a BPEL process (and for reasons we'll describe), the name of a service is the name of a partner link — specifically, a partner link that defines a conversation initiated by the partner service. The partner link may be assigned to a receive activity, to an onMessage event in a pick activity, or to an OnEvent event in an event handler.

- In relation to a Java class, a service is a Java interface being implemented by the class; or, if the Java class is not explicitly implementing a Java interface, a service is the set of all public methods in the class. In most cases, you identify a service by including, in the Java code, the SCA-specific annotation @Service.

If your implementation has only one service, you have no decision to make in relation to services. If your implementation has multiple services, however, you can select which services to expose; that is, you can select which sets of operations can be accessed. Even a component without a service can do useful work — for example, by acting as a timer that submits a message a few seconds after a composite is invoked.

Let's consider the relationship of a BPEL partner link to a port type. Here are excerpts from a process.

```
<process>
    <partnerLinks>
        <partnerLink name="ProcessQuote"
                     myRole="ProcessQuoteRole"
                     partnerLinkType="ProcessQuotePLT" />
    </partnerLinks>


    <sequence>
        <receive createInstance="yes"
                 partnerLink="ProcessQuote"
                 operation="placeQuote"
                 variable="quoteRequest">
        </receive>
        .
        .
        .
    </sequence>
</process>
```

As described in Chapter 7, a partner link is based on a partner link type and indicates which role is enacted by the BPEL process, which role is enacted by the partner service, or both.

The presence of the attribute myRole in the partner link ProcessQuote means that the BPEL process is making operations available to the partner service. Here's the related partner link type, which is outside the process.

```
<partnerLinkType name="ProcessQuotePLT">
   <role name="ProcessQuoteRole">
      <portType name="ProcessQuotePT" />
   </role>
</partnerLinkType>
```

The portType element in that partner link type identifies the operations that can be accessed by way of the partner link.

Here's what our declarations tell us:

• An SCA service ProcessQuote is named for the partner link referenced in the receive activity.

• The port type ProcessQuotePT describes the operations provided by the SCA service.

Mapping of Properties to Implementation Code

A property in a component is mapped to a data area in an implementation. A property that provides a list of values is mapped to an array or to a similar, language-specific collection variable.

Here are language-specific details:

• In relation to a BPEL process, an SCA property is mapped to a BPEL variable that has an SCA-specific property attribute set to *yes*. Here's an example.

```
<process name="ProcessQuote">
   .
   .
   <variable name="availableDiscount"
             type="xsd:string"
             sca:property="yes"/>
</process>
```

- In relation to a Java class, a property is mapped to a Java object or primitive variable. In most cases, you identify the variable by including the SCA-specific @Property annotation in the Java code. Here's an example.

```
@Property
public String availableDiscount;
```

Mapping of References to Implementation Code

A reference in a component is mapped to a variable that provides access to external operations. A reference that provides a list of endpoint references is mapped to an array or to a similar, language-specific collection variable.

Here are language-specific details:

- In relation to a BPEL process, the mapping depends on whether the reference contains a single endpoint reference or a list. A single-valued reference is mapped to a partner link — specifically, to a partner link whose first runtime use is to send data from the process. The most common example is a partner link used in an invoke activity.

  As shown later, a multi-valued reference is mapped to a variable that holds multiple entries. Each run of a forEach activity, for example, can copy an endpoint reference from the variable to a partner link and then use the partner link in an invoke activity. The activity might elicit a price from one or another vendor.

  Assignment of an endpoint reference always applies to the partner role of a partner link; in other words, the assignment is used when accessing operations that are external to the component.

- In relation to a Java class, a reference is mapped to a Java interface whose methods are invoked. In most cases, you identify a reference by including, in the Java code, the SCA-specific annotation @Reference.

Let's look more closely at how SCA supports multi-valued references in BPEL. Our example is from the OSOA document *SCA Client and Implementation Model Specification for WS-BPEL*.

First of all, the support relies on serviceReferenceList, an XSD element declaration provided by SCA.

```
<xsd:element name="serviceReferenceList">
    <xsd:complexType>
        <xsd:sequence>
            <xsd:element ref="sref:service-ref"
                         minOccurs="0" maxOccurs="unbounded"/>
        </xsd:sequence>
    </xsd:complexType>
</xsd:element>
```

The referenced type (sref:service-ref) is provided with BPEL and conforms to whatever data is required to describe a particular kind of endpoint reference. The important point is that a series of endpoint references is made available to a BPEL variable

```
<variable name="vendors" element="sca:serviceReferenceList">
    <sca:multiReference partnerLinkType="vendorPT"
                        partnerRole="vendor" />
</variable>
```

That BPEL variable is based on sca:serviceReferenceList, includes the SCA extension element sca:multiReference, and is referenced in a partnerLink element, in the
SCA-provided attribute sca.multiRefFrom.

```
<forEach counterName="idx" ...>
    <startCounterValue>1</startCounterValue>
    <finalCounterValue>
        count($vendors/sref:service-ref)
    </finalCounterValue>
    .
    .
    <scope>
    .
    .
        <partnerLink name="vendorLink"
                     partnerLinkType="vendorPT"
                     myRole="quoteRequester"
                     partnerRole="vendor"
                     sca:multiRefFrom="vendors" />
        .
        .
        <assign>
            <copy>
                <from>$vendors/sref:service-ref[$idx]</from>
```

Listing 9.4: forEach activity outline (part 1 of 2)

```
                 <to partnerLink="vendorLink" />
            </copy>
        </assign>
            .
            .
        </scope>
    </forEach>
```

Listing 9.4: forEach activity outline (part 2 of 2)

Listing 9.4 shows an outline of a forEach activity that uses a list of endpoint references.

Component Types

The *component type* is a characteristic of the implementation, describing the configurable aspects of the implementation, with details that are independent of the specific values that will be set at configuration time. The component type has several purposes:

- The SCA assembler uses the component type to identify what services are exposed and what properties and references are available.

- The SCA runtime uses the component type first, to verify that the assembler tried to access only the exposed services and tried to set only the available references and properties; and second, to assign the values that the integrator set for properties and references.

- Last, if your company develops its services from the top down (first designing a component, then writing the related implementation code), project managers can use an XML-based *componentType file* for design validation. First, the designer sends the developer a componentType file. Later, if the SCA runtime has access to the component and to the original componentType file and does not issue an error, your company knows that the developer fulfilled at least some of the designer's intent; specifically, the company has ensured that the interfaces and variables in the code do not conflict with those in the component type.

Our review of component-type details suggests a general characteristic of SCA. You can specify details in the implementation and can change, supplement, or restrict those details at a higher level.

Three kinds of details are involved. First, the details for each component service include the name and interface and may include a list of policy intents and a list of valid bindings. Second, the details for each component property include the name and type; an indicator of whether a property value is required; an indicator of whether multiple property values are valid; and optionally, a default value (for a single-valued property) or one or more default values (for a multi-valued property). Last, the details for each component reference include the name and interface; may include a list of policy intents and a list of valid bindings; and indicate whether a reference value is required and whether multiple reference values are valid.

The SCA runtime tries to determine the component type by inspecting the implementation code. If the SCA runtime cannot determine all details, you must supply additional information in a componentType file. If that file has details that contradict the implementation code, an error occurs at run time.

ComponentType File

We'll give you a sense of the content of a componentType file by showing you an excerpt (Listing 9.5), which we've formatted for easy reading.

```
<componentType>
    <service name="ProcessQuote" requires="confidentiality">

        <!- in relation to a BPEL process, the preferred form
             of interface declaration refers to the partner link
             type, not to the partner link and not (as in the
             later references) to the WSDL port type  ->
        <interface.partnerLinkType
            type="ProcessQuotePLT"
            serviceRole="ProcessQuoteRole" />
    </service>

    <!- includes a default value ->
    <property name="availableDiscount" type="xsd:string"
            many="true" required="false">Auto Club</property>

    <reference name="calculateOne" multiplicity="1..1">
        <interface.wsdl
            interface=
                "http://com/highlight/ProcessQuote#
                wsdl.interface(calculateOne)" />
    </reference>
```

Listing 9.5: componentType file excerpt (part 1 of 2)

```
    <reference name="calculateTwo" multiplicity="1..n">
        <interface.wsdl
            interface=
                "http://com/highlight/ProcessQuote#
                wsdl.interface(calculateTwo)" />
    </reference>
</componentType>
```

Listing 9.5: componentType file excerpt (part 2 of 2)

Additional Details on Properties and References

The details in this section are useful for both elementary and advanced uses. First, consider two attributes of the property element in a componentType file:

- many indicates whether a list of values is acceptable. The default value is *false*.

- required indicates that a property value is needed from the component definition in the composite file or, as described later, from a higher-level composite.

  Use of a default value (in this case, *Auto Club*) is not appropriate when the property value is required. The value of required in this example, however, is *false*, which is the default.

Second, consider the multiplicity attribute of the reference element. That attribute indicates whether the reference is required and whether the reference provides a single value or a list. The valid values are as follows:

- *1..1* (the default) means the reference is required and can provide only one value.

- *1..n* means that the reference is required and can provide multiple values. For example, the component might request price quotes from multiple vendors, with a runtime failure if no vendor is specified.

- *0..1* means that the reference is optional and can provide only one value. For example, the component might send log data to a standard destination if one is available.

- *0..n* means that the reference is optional and can provide multiple values. For example, the component might send data to zero-to-many subscribers.

Composites

Figure 9.5 illustrates a *composite*, which is an assembled, logical unit that solves a business problem. The definition of the composite is in a single composite file in most cases but can be distributed across a set of such files.

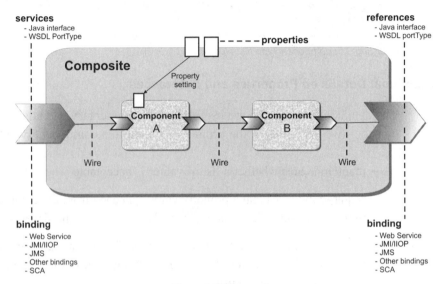

Figure 9.5: Composite

A composite can be invoked as a peer, whether from an independent composite in the same SCA system or from outside the SCA system altogether; or (as described later) a composite can be included as an implementation in a higher-level composite. In either case, a company benefits from having an inventory of composites that were previously tested and deployed.

Listing 9.6 shows an outline of a composite definition.

```
<composite xmlns="http://www.osoa.org/xmlns/sca/1.0"
           targetNamespace="http://www.ibm.com/HighlightInsurance"
           name="myComposite"
           requires="confidentiality"
           local="false">

    <service> </service>
    <property> </property>
    <reference> </reference>
    <wire> </wire>
```

Listing 9.6: Composite definition outline (part 1 of 2)

```
<component>
    <implementation/>
    <service/>
    <property/>
    <reference/>
</component>

<component>
    <implementation/>
    <service/>
    <property/>
    <reference/>
</component>

</composite>
```

Listing 9.6: Composite definition outline (part 2 of 2)

Here are two of the attributes in the composite element:

- targetNameSpace specifies the namespace for names (such as the composite and component names) being assigned in the composite definition.

- local indicates whether all components in the composite definition are required to run in the same operating-system process. The default value is *false*, which means that the composite can include components whose implementations are written in different languages and may even run on different machines.

Introduction to Composite Service

The excerpt shown in Listing 9.7 includes a *composite service*.

```
<composite xmlns="http://www.osoa.org/xmlns/sca/1.0"
        targetNamespace="http://www.ibm.com/HighlightInsurance"
        name="QuoteComposite"
        requires="confidentiality">

    <service name="ProcessQuote"
          promote="ProcessQuoteComponent/ProcessQuote">
        <binding.ws
          port="http://www.highlight.com/ProcessQuote#
                wsdl.endpoint(ProcessQuote/ProcessQuoteSOAP)" />
    </service>
```

Listing 9.7: Excerpt showing a composite service (part 1 of 2)

```
      .
      .
    <component name="ProcessQuoteComponent">
        .
        .
        <service name="ProcessQuote">
            <interface.partnerLinkType
                type="ProcessQuotePLT"
                serviceRole="ProcessQuoteRole" />
        </service>
        .
        .
    </component>
</composite>
```

Listing 9.7: Excerpt showing a composite service (part 2 of 2)

A composite service such as ProcessQuote makes a component service (also called ProcessQuote in this case) available to a requester. We say that the composite service *promotes* the component service. Here's the meaning:

- The SCA runtime uses the endpoint details in the composite service to oversee the connection. If the composite service lacks a binding element, the SCA runtime takes the endpoint details from the component service or (if necessary) from the component type. In most cases (as in the example), endpoint details are only in the composite service.

- Similarly, the SCA runtime reviews the binding element (among others) to determine the required interaction policies such as confidentiality. Again, the definitions in the composite service take precedence, but details in the component service and component type may be used.

- Last, the SCA runtime uses the interface details in the composite service, if those details are present there. The hierarchy of component service and component type applies here as well.

You can use multiple composite services to promote the same component service — for example, to present the same set of operations with a different quality of service.

When you define a composite service, you must identify the promoted service by giving a value to the promote attribute. To set the value of the promote attribute, specify the component name followed by a virgule (/) and the component-service name, as in the following example value:

```
ProcessQuoteService/ProcessQuoteComponent
```

If the component includes only one service, you can specify the component name alone.

Introduction to Composite Property

The excerpt shown in Listing 9.8 includes a *composite property*.

```
<composite name="QuoteComposite">

    <property name="theDiscount"
              type="xsd:string"
              many="true"
              mustSupply="false">
        Auto Club
    </property>

    <component name="policyQuote">
    .

    .
        <property name=availableDiscount source="$theDiscount"/>
    .

    .
    </component>
</composite>
```

Listing 9.8: Composite property

In this case, a composite property (theDiscount) sets the property of a component inside the composite. The source attribute of the component property (in this case, the attribute in property availableDiscount) indicates that the component-property value comes from a composite property.

Here are some of the attributes in the composite-level property element:

- type (or element) specifies the XSD type (or element).
- many indicates whether a list of values is acceptable.

- mustSupply indicates whether an assembler must supply a value for this property when embedding the composite in a higher-level composite. We say more about this issue later. The default value for the mustSupply attribute is *false*, which is appropriate if the composite is invoked directly rather than as an implementation.

A set of same-named composite properties is possible, as shown in Listing 9.9.

```
<composite name="QuoteComposite">

    <property name="theDiscount"
              type="xsd:string"
              many="true">
        <value>Auto Club</value>
        <value>Employee</value>
    </property>

    <component name="policyQuote">
    .
    .
        <property name=availableDiscount source="$theDiscount"/>
    .
    .
    </component>
</composite>
```

Listing 9.9: Same-named composite properties

For details on setting values for properties, see the OSOA document *SCA Assembly Model Specification*.

Introduction to Composite Reference

The excerpt shown in Listing 9.10 includes a *composite reference*.

```
<composite name="QuoteComposite">
    .
    .

    <reference name="MainframeQuoteMgr"
               multiplicity="1..n"
               promote=
                    "ConvertQuoteComponent/ProcessQuoteReference">
        <binding.ws
```

Listing 9.10: Composite reference (part 1 of 2)

```
            port="http://www.highlight.com/QuoteManagement#
                  wsdl.endpoint(QuoteManagement/QuoteManSOAP)" />
    </reference>

    <component name="ConvertQuoteComponent">
        .
        .

        <reference name="ProcessQuoteReference"
                   target="ProcessQuoteComponent/ProcessQuote" />
    </component>

    <component name="ProcessQuoteComponent">
        .
        .

        <service name="ProcessQuote">
            <interface.partnerLinkType
                type="ProcessQuotePLT"
                serviceRole="ProcessQuoteRole" />
        </service>
    </component>
</composite>
```

Listing 9.10: Composite reference (part 2 of 2)

A composite reference provides access to the logic that resides in other composites or in code that is external to an SCA system. We say that the composite reference *promotes* a component reference. Here's the meaning:

- The SCA runtime takes the endpoint details in the composite reference and provides them to the component implementation. If the composite reference lacks a binding element, the SCA runtime takes the endpoint details from the component reference or (if necessary) from the component type. In most cases (as in the example), endpoint details are only in the composite reference.

- Similarly, the SCA runtime reviews the binding element (among others) to guide the runtime use of interaction policies such as confidentiality. Again, the definitions in the composite reference take precedence, but details in the component reference and component type may be used.

- Interface and multiplicity details in the composite reference are used for validation, if those details are present there. The hierarchy of component reference and component type applies here as well.

In the current example, the composite reference MainframeQuoteMgr promotes the component reference ProcessQuoteReference. The example also shows that for a multi-valued reference, the component can access not only logic that is outside the composite but also logic in another component. In this case, reference ProcessQuoteReference also refers to the only service in ProcessQuoteComponent.

When you define a composite reference, you must identify the promoted reference by giving a value to the promote attribute. To set the value of the promote attribute, specify the component name followed by a virgule and the component-reference name, as in the following example value:

```
ConvertQuoteComponent/ProcessQuoteReference
```

If the component includes only one reference, you can specify the component name alone.

Wires

Each *wire* provides the detail needed to connect a component reference to a component service within a composite. (Figure 9.2 illustrates wires by lines.) The wire is not itself a binding, which is provided by the composite service or reference. The default binding is the SCA binding, as described earlier.

You can set a wire by setting the target attribute of the component reference, as shown in Listing 9.11.

```
<composite name="QuoteComposite">
    .
    .
    .

    <component name="ConvertQuoteComponent">
        .
        .

        <reference name="ProcessQuoteReference"
                   target="ProcessQuoteComponent/ProcessQuote" />
    </component>

    <component name="ProcessQuoteComponent">
        .
        .
```

Listing 9.11: Setting a wire (part 1 of 2)

```
        <service name="ProcessQuote">
            <interface.partnerLinkType
                type="ProcessQuotePLT"
                serviceRole="ProcessQuoteRole" />
        </service>
    </component>

</composite>
```

Listing 9.11: Setting a wire (part 2 of 2)

An alternative technique is most appropriate when an SCA assembler wants to isolate the wire declarations into a separate file for separate maintenance. Let's leave the multiple-file issue for later and show the wiring syntax, which involves a wire element (Listing 9.12). The source attribute of that element identifies a component reference, and the target attribute identifies a component service.

```
<composite>
    .
    .
    .
    <component name="ConvertQuoteComponent">
        .
        .
        <reference name="ProcessQuoteReference"/>
    </component>

    <component name="ProcessQuoteComponent">
        .
        .
        <service name="ProcessQuote">
            <interface.partnerLinkType
                type="ProcessQuotePLT"
                serviceRole="ProcessQuoteRole" />
        </service>
    </component>

    <wire source="ConvertQuoteComponent/ProcessQuoteReference"
        target="ProcessQuoteComponent/ProcessQuote" />

</composite>
```

Listing 9.12: Alternative technique for setting a wire

The syntax for specifying a source or target is equivalent to a syntax described earlier:

- For a source, specify the component name followed by a virgule and the component-reference name, as in the example value ConvertQuoteComponent/ProcessQuoteReference. If the component includes only one reference, you can specify the component name alone.

- For a target, specify the component name followed by a virgule and the component-service name, as in the example value ProcessQuoteComponent/ProcessQuote. If the component includes only one service, you can specify the component name alone.

Instead of setting a wire explicitly (by either of the two techniques described earlier), you can request the SCA runtime to wire component references to component services automatically. This SCA capability, called *autowire*, is available only for component references that otherwise have no target. Specifically, the component reference must lack a target attribute and must not be promoted by any composite reference.

In Listing 9.13, the autowire attribute in the component element causes the SCA runtime to wire the reference ProcessQuoteReference to the service ProcessQuote.

```
<composite>
    .
    .
    <component name="ConvertQuoteComponent"
              autowire="true">
        .
        .
        <reference name="ProcessQuoteReference"/>
    </component>
    <component name="ProcessQuoteComponent">
        .
        .
        <service name="ProcessQuote">
            .
            .
        </service>
    </component>
</composite>
```

Listing 9.13: Autowire example

When the SCA autowire capability is in effect, the SCA runtime creates a missing wire by judging the compatibility of the component reference in relation to each of the available component services. The most important compatibility rules concern the interface that was specified for the component reference and for each component service. The SCA runtime also considers policy and multiplicity characteristics.

To enable the autowire capability, add the autowire attribute to any of three kinds of elements — composite, component, or component reference — and set that attribute to *true*. (The default is *false*.) The setting in a component reference is determined by the attribute value in the reference element or (if no setting is there) by the attribute value in the nearest enclosing component or composite element.

Higher- and Lower-Level Composites

Figure 9.6 illustrates the relationship that is forged when a component in one composite uses a second composite as the component implementation. The two composites are in a hierarchical relationship but are not embedding one another in a single XML definition.

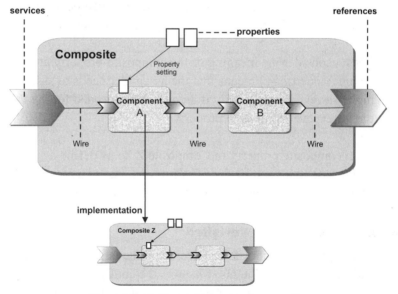

Figure 9.6: Higher- and lower-level composites

To understand the relationships that apply in this case, keep this illustration in mind as we reconsider the meaning of composite services, properties, and references.

Composite Services, Revisited

When a component (like Component A) uses a composite (like Composite Z) as an implementation, the service of interest is a composite service in Composite Z, and that composite service helps define the component type of the implementation.

The assembler can wire a composite service (in the higher-level composite) to the component (here, Component A) that provides access to the functionality of Composite Z. In that case, the assembler provides the business logic available in Composite Z. The assembler can use a binding different from the one specified for the composite service in Composite Z and can supplement the list of policy intents that were specified for the composite service in Composite Z.

Composite Properties, Revisited

The component that uses Composite Z as an implementation can set values for any of the composite properties that are defined in Composite Z. The component sets the composite property by setting a same-named component property in the higher-level composite. The basis of the value can be a literal, a composite property in the higher-level composite, or the content of a file.

Let's reconsider the meaning of the composite-property attribute mustSupply. The default value (*false*) means that the assembler needs to assign a related value in the higher-level composite only if an override is needed for the value that was set in the lower-level composite property.

Each composite property in Composite Z helps define a component type for use by the assembler and by the SCA runtime, just as a component property helps define the component type of a BPEL or Java implementation.

Composite References, Revisited

A higher-level composite can decide on the target and binding of a reference and can supplement the intents, whatever the configuration of the lower-level composite. The component sets the composite reference in Composite Z by setting a same-named component reference in the higher-level composite.

Composite Inclusion

SCA provides a way for developers to work independently on subsets of a single composite. For example, your company asks developer 1 to define one component, asks developer 2 to define a second and third, and asks developer 3 to define a composite service and a set of wires. Although each developer works in a separately named composite, the SCA runtime merges the definitions at deployment time. The benefit is ease of development because the different personnel are not dependent on access to the most recent version of a shared definition.

Composite inclusion relies on include elements such as the ones shown in Listing 9.14.

```
<composite xmlns="http://www.osoa.org/xmlns/sca/1.0"
           targetNamespace="http://www.ibm.com/HighlightInsurance"
           xmlns:highlight="http://www.ibm.com/HighlightInsurance"
           name="QuoteComposite"
           requires="confidentiality">

    <include name="highlight:QuoteComposite01" />
    <include name="highlight:QuoteComposite02" />
    <include name="highlight:QuoteComposite03" />

</composite>
```

Listing 9.14: include elements for composite inclusion

The SCA runtime removes each include element and substitutes the text from the named composite definition. The SCA runtime does not retain the composite element start and end tags from any of the included definitions. Policy intents specified in those tags are present at run time only if those intents were also specified in elements that are retained — for example, in the composite element of the including definition.

The combined text integrates well at deployment time only if the division of labor is carefully planned.

Constraining Type

To help with top-down design, a designer can create a *constraining type*, which is a separately maintained definition that specifies requirements. Specifically, the constraining type defines what services, properties, references, and intents are required for each composite, component, or implementation being constrained. A given composite, component, or implementation may have additional capabilities, but those are not visible to a higher-level definition when the constraining type is in effect. For details and an example, see the OSOA document *SCA Assembly Model Specification.*

10

Introduction to SDO

The computer industry created a variety of solutions (languages, data-storage systems, transfer protocols) to fulfill similar needs. It is now developing technologies to mask the complexity of what's been created. The issue is being addressed because complexity is expensive, increasing the costs of training, development, and testing; and because complexity is confusing, reducing the quality of work.

Like SCA, *Service Data Objects (SDO)* is a response to complexity and is a proposed standard that is likely to gain the approval of a major standards organization. SDO, however, is a technology for representing *data* in a consistent way, even if the data comes from different kinds of sources.

When you work with SDO, you write code

- to create one or more structures called *Data Objects*, each of which includes business data organized into a collection of named properties.

- to get or set the data for each property, whether the property holds a data item such as a customer ID or a reference to another Data Object. Properties that hold data items are based on data types such as *Boolean* or *Integer*.

In fulfilling SDO-related tasks, you use the same syntax (the same *application programming interface*, or *API*) regardless of whether

- the data comes from a relational database, an XML file, a message queue, or some other source; or

- the data is created in the code, in accordance with a description such as an XML Schema definition.

In relation to SOA, SDO allows for changes in the messages passed between services but does not require that those changes affect the service interface. In other words, the kind of interface is *document* rather than *remote procedure call*. If your company adds new functionality to the service, changes to the requester can occur over time (in many cases) rather than in urgent response to the upgrade.

SDO supports Java, C++, and PHP and is expected to support C, COBOL, and other languages.

Although companies have implemented early versions of SDO, the situation of interest to this book is that eighteen companies are in the Open Service Oriented Architecture (OSOA) collaboration, which is creating a set of SDO proposals for a major standards body to adopt. Our description in this chapter is based primarily on the OSOA document *Service Data Objects for Java Specification Version 2.1.0.* The current, publicly available proposals are at the following Web site: *http://www.osoa.org*.

Under the auspices of the Apache Software Foundation, the Tuscany incubator project is developing an open-source implementation of SCA and SDO. For details and code, see the following Web sites: *http://incubator.apache.org/tuscany* and *http://www.apache.org*.

Data Graph

In most cases, the details of your business require that different Data Objects be related to one another in either of two ways:

- in a containment relationship, much as our XML CarPolicy elements contained Vehicle elements; or

- in a non-containment relationship, with one Data Object referencing another.

The SDO structure that organizes Data Objects is called a *data graph*. A data graph is primarily a tree that has, at its root, a single Data Object. The Objects in a data graph may have different properties and even be from different types of data sources.

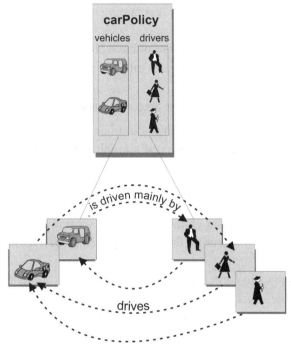

Figure 10.1: Data graph

As shown in Figure 10.1, a graph can be more complex than a tree structure. The solid lines show containing relationships. An Object of type CarPolicy includes

- a property named *vehicles*, which references an array of Objects that are each of type Vehicle

- a property named *drivers*, which references an array of Objects that are each of type Driver

The dashed lines show a series of referencing relationships:

- Each Object of type Vehicle includes a property that references the primary driver.

- Each Object of type Driver includes a property that references a vehicle.

- The references can form a cycle, with a vehicle referencing a driver and a driver referencing a vehicle. A cycle is possible only for a referencing relationship, not for a containing one.

In most cases, the root does not have business data but is a generic Object that unites the subordinate Objects into a hierarchy, as illustrated in a later example.

Relationship to the Data in a Data Source

You can create a data graph to do processing that is internal to your code. In many cases, however, the meaning of a graph depends on how data is organized in a particular type of data source.

For SQL data, a Data Object represents a row of data in most cases, with each property of the Data Object's type representing a column and with the data graph as a whole representing the rows returned from a database query.

A column can contain a *foreign key*, which is a value that references a row in a second table. A table of employees, for example, usually has a column that contains a department ID, and each of those IDs is also in a column in a table of departments.

In keeping with how a foreign-key relationship is usually reflected in a data graph, each selected row in the employee table is represented by an Employee Object; each selected row in the department table is represented by a Department Object; and each Employee Object refers to a Department Object.

For XML data (including a Web-service message), a Data Object represents an element in most cases, including

- the attributes of that element
- child elements that have no subordinate elements

Each property of the Data Object represents an attribute or element. If an XML element includes a child element that itself has subordinate elements, the child element is usually represented by a second Data Object that is referenced from the first.

Change-Tracking

SDO allows for *change-tracking*, which has two main purposes:

- to allow for a reversal of changes to Data Objects

- to submit changes to a data source in light of changes that were made to the Data Objects when your code was disconnected from the data source

You can enable change-tracking by setting a property in a data graph or Data Object. A data graph enabled in this way retains details on additions and deletions of Data Objects. A data graph or Object enabled in this way retains details on the changes made to the data that is internal to a single Object.

Inverse Integrity

As you alter Data Objects in a data graph, the SDO runtime can retain the integrity of your data by making related changes to other Objects in the graph. For example, your company transfers an employee from one department (Sales) to another (Marketing). To begin that transfer, a service retrieves data from a relational database into a data graph, which now includes details on the employee (as stored in the Employee table) and on each of the two departments (as stored in the Department table).

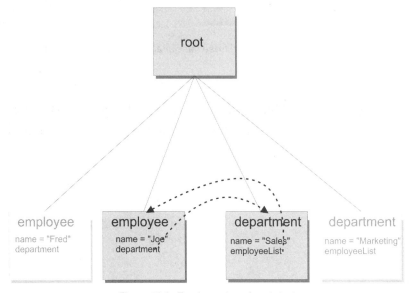

Figure 10.2: Employee transfer at start

As shown in Figure 10.2, one Data Object

- contains data that is specific to the employee

- references a Data Object that contains data on the Sales department

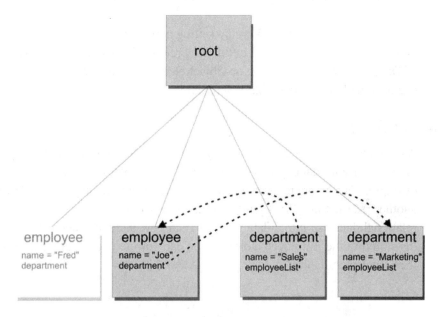

Figure 10.3: Employee transfer after the service's change

As shown in Figure 10.3, the service changes the Data Object so that the reference is not to the Sales department but to Marketing.

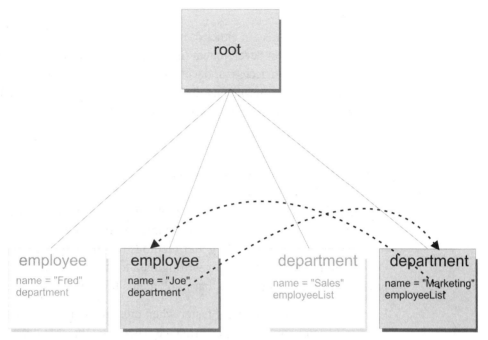

Figure 10.4: Employee transfer after the SDO runtime reacts

As shown in Figure 10.4, the SDO runtime ensures *inverse integrity*, which means that the Data Object that holds data on the Marketing department automatically references the new employee, while the Data Object that holds data on the Sales department does not. Your logic is simpler than would be the case without SDO.

Your service updates the relational database by submitting the changed data graph. Your update (like your original reading of data) is usually by way of a Data Access Service, as described later.

Terminology

We are obliged to tell you the following detail. A data graph (as expressed in two words) is a general phrase. A DataGraph, in contrast, is a separate object whose use was required in earlier versions of SDO. This separate object is still available as an option for creating and accessing data graphs but is no longer central to using or understanding the technology.

Object Definition

You can define a Data Object in either of two ways. *Static definition* means that the Data Object is structured at development time rather than at run time. This alternative is available only if you can access, at development time, the data definition of interest to you. *Dynamic definition* means that the Data Object is structured at run time — for example, in response to configuration settings or user input.

Static Definition

Static definition has the following benefits.

- Your task is easy. You create and submit a data description that (in many cases) is in the form of an XML Schema definition. SDO then generates interface classes that identify getter methods (for reading data from the Data Object) and setter methods (for writing data to the Data Object); also, the product generates a class file that implements those interfaces.

- In most cases, your code runs faster when creating and processing the Data Object, as compared to the performance when the Object is defined dynamically.

- The variables in your access statements are strongly typed, protecting against runtime errors that occur if your code assigns data incompatible with the data type.

Static definition is available only in SDO for Java but is expected to be available in other languages.

Even when you use static definition, you can use XPath-like syntax from the dynamic API to retrieve the value of a property. Furthermore, if you categorize an Object as *open*, you can add properties at run time and use the dynamic API to access them.

Dynamic Definition and Access

When you define a Data Object dynamically, you reference data-type descriptions at run time. This kind of access keeps you from having to maintain any generated interface and implementation files, so you don't need to deploy and maintain them.

Dynamic access is often required or preferable because it increases corporate agility, as in the following cases:

- Your code queries a database, but characteristics of the database query cannot be known at development time; they are specified by user input or in a configuration file.

  For example, a Web application at Highlight Insurance lets executives review data on active insurance policies. A service invoked by the application returns only the kinds of data requested by the manager, and the data is ordered in accordance with the manager's request. The service provides the needed flexibility by creating a query only at run time, and the result of that query is stored in a Data Object whose specific type is known only at run time.

- You are developing a service to validate details that are embedded in different kinds of input. For example, a service might check the validity of address data in any of the company's insurance policies (for car insurance, homeowner's insurance, and so on). To support the different kinds of policies that may be added over the years, your service might search the input for a field of a pre-specified *address* type, rather than relying on the static structure of a specific kind of policy.

Dynamic access is possible because, when you use SDO, you can access not only the business data, but the *metadata*, which is a description of the data. An example of metadata is an XML Schema definition.

SDO Annotations

SDO annotations are extensions to XML Schema definitions (XSDs). The annotations guide the conversion of XSDs to Data Objects and are necessary when the default conversion is not appropriate or when SDO requires information that is not otherwise found in an XSD.

SDO annotations are now available for Java code and are expected to be available for all languages.

The SDO annotations are in boldface in the XSD shown in Listing 10.1, which is based on an example in the SDO Java specification.

```
<schema targetNamespace="http://www.example.com/IPO"
        xmlns:ipo="http://www.example.com/IPO"
        xmlns="http://www.w3.org/2001/XMLSchema"
        xmlns:sdo="commonj.sdo"
        xmlns:sdoXML="commonj.sdo/XML"
        xmlns:sdoJava="commonj.sdo/java"
        sdoJava:package="com.example.myPackage">

   <complexType name="PurchaseOrderType" >
      <sequence>
         <element name="shipmentID" type="string"/>
         .
         .
         .
      </sequence>
      <attribute name="orderDate" type="date"
         sdo:dataType="ipo:MyGregorianDate"/>
   </complexType>

   <simpleType name="MyGregorianDate"
      sdoJava:instanceClass="java.xml.datatype.GregorianCalendar"/>
</schema>
```

Listing 10.1: XSD featuring SDO annotations

As a result of those annotations:

- The SDO-generated Java classes are assigned to the package com.example.myPackage.

- The orderDate property contains a Data Object that is defined by the simple type MyGregorianDate.

- Each Data Object that is defined by simple type MyGregorianDate is based on the Java class java.xml.datatype.GregorianCalendar.

For details on SDO annotations, see Chapter 9 of *Service Data Objects for Java Specification Version 2.1.0.*

Data Access Service

The relationship of a data graph and a data source (for example, a relational database) is made easier by a specialized Data Access Service (DAS). Chapter 2 described the general idea of a data-access service, but in this case we're referring specifically to a service that works with SDO data graphs.

The nature of an interaction between a DAS and a data source is called *optimistic concurrency*. In response to your request for data, the Data Access Service connects to the data source, retrieves data without locking the source, converts the data into a data graph, disconnects from the source, and returns the data graph to your code. Your code can use the data without interacting again with the Data Access Service; or your code can modify and return the data to the Data Access Service, which uses the change-tracking facility mentioned earlier.

In response to a request to update data, the Data Access Service accepts the data graph that you send, connects to the data source, creates a lock, compares the locked data and the expected data, stores the data (if appropriate), releases the lock, and disconnects from the Data Access Service.

Optimistic concurrency increases the number of users that can be supported and is especially appropriate if multiple users only rarely overwrite the same data. This kind of disconnected processing also reduces your service's dependency on network connections and on the availability of data-storage systems.

The SDO change-tracking facility gives Data Access Services the information necessary to throw a fault when overwriting would occur. The service that invoked the DAS would respond to the situation, usually by repeating the transaction — in other words, by

1. reading and processing the changed data

2. submitting another request to revise the stored content

A Data Access Service may be coded by an individual or provided by a vendor. Commercial Data Access Services are available, and a set of open standards is in development.

We expect that by early 2008, open standards will guide the details of interaction between your code and any SDO-related Data Access Service. Data Access Services will use a combination of SQL and XQuery to interact with XML documents stored in a relational database, and you'll be able to use a single query to access data not just from columns in specific rows but from XML elements in those columns. In addition, you'll be able to configure a Data Access Service so that you can query a database, not only by writing code into your service implementation (as is now possible) but also by simply using the name of a command that is defined in a configuration file. In this way, the trend in SDO reflects the general SOA trend toward easier coding and toward deferring decisions from development time.

SDO Code Details

At this time (March 2007), the most advanced SDO specification is *Service Data Objects for Java Specification Version 2.1.0*. The rest of this chapter gives details from that document and from the Apache Tuscany project. We also provide Java examples, and they reveal aspects of SDO that are likely to be true in any language. For example, you'll always register Data Object types to the SDO runtime.

If you're unfamiliar with Java, we can offer a pair of tutorials. They even introduce you to Eclipse, which is an open-source development environment that supports a variety of languages:

- *http://www.ibm.com/developerworks/edu/j-dw-java-intjava-i.html*

- *http://www.ibm.com/developerworks/edu/j-dw-java-intermed-i.html*

If you wish to avoid the code detail, we suggest you skip to Appendix A, which is of more general interest.

Helper Interfaces

Implementations of SDO for Java provide the following interfaces:

- CopyHelper has methods for copying one Data Object to another in either of two ways:
  - A *deep copy* reproduces not only the Data Object but every Data Object contained in the Object being copied.
  - A *shallow copy* reproduces only the Data Object.
- DataFactory has methods for creating Data Objects.
- DataHelper has methods for converting data from one type to another.

- EqualityHelper has methods for comparing one Data Object to another or for comparing one data graph to another.

- TypeHelper has methods to create a new type, to create a Data Object from a type, to identify the type of a Object, or to list Object properties that were specified at run time.

- XMLHelper has methods to serialize a Data Object to an XML source (as shown earlier) or to de-serialize XML source to a Data Object.

- XSDHelper has methods to retrieve data descriptions from XML Schema Definitions and to create new XSDs from types and from Data Object properties.

In addition, a HelperContext interface gives you access to a set of instances of other Helper classes. Those Helper instances in turn provide access to data that is specific to a set of Data Object types. You might create Data Object types by using an XSDHelper instance from one HelperContext, for example, and use a DataFactory instance from the same HelperContext instance to create Data Objects based on those types. You can't create Data Objects based on registered types, however, if you try to use a DataFactory instance retrieved from a HelperContext instance other than the HelperContext instance used to create the types.

The SDO HelperProvider class gives you access to a globally scoped HelperContext instance, as shown in a later example.

Example Code

This section shows snippets of the XML Schema definitions that describe an insurance quote. Also shown is Java code for defining Data Objects that reflect the XML Schema. We'll start with a few general points:

- The preferred way to create Data Objects statically is to use Java factory classes.

- The only way to create Data Objects dynamically is to use such classes.

- When you work with the Apache Tuscany implementation of SDO, one option is to use the factory classes that are specific to Tuscany.

Type Definition of an Insurance Quote

Listing 10.2 shows the XSD that holds the complex type Quote. An Object of this type might be passed from one service to another.

```xml
<xsd:schema xmlns:xsd="http://www.w3.org/2001/XMLSchema"
       xmlns:Q1="http://com/highlight"
       targetNamespace="http://com/highlight">
  <xsd:include schemaLocation="CustomerQuoteInformation.xsd"/>
  <xsd:complexType name="Quote">
    <xsd:sequence>
      <xsd:element name="quoteID" type="xsd:string"
             minOccurs="0" />
      <xsd:element name="dateOfQuote" type="xsd:dateTime"
             minOccurs="0" />
      <xsd:element name="customerInformation"
                type="Q1:CustomerQuoteInformation"
             minOccurs="0" />
    </xsd:sequence>
  </xsd:complexType>
</xsd:schema>
```

Listing 10.2: XSD for the complex type Quote

Listing 10.3 shows the XSD that holds the complex type CustomerQuoteInformation.

```xml
<xsd:schema xmlns:xsd="http://www.w3.org/2001/XMLSchema"
       xmlns:Q1="http://com/highlight"
       targetNamespace="http://com/highlight">
  <xsd:include schemaLocation="Auto.xsd"/>
  <xsd:include schemaLocation="NameAddress.xsd"/>
  <xsd:complexType name="CustomerQuoteInformation">
   <xsd:sequence>
     <xsd:element name="applicant" type="Q1:NameAddress"
            minOccurs="0"/>
     <xsd:element name="dependents" type="Q1:NameAddress"
           minOccurs="0" maxOccurs="unbounded" />
     <xsd:element name="auto" type="Q1:Auto"
           minOccurs="0" maxOccurs="unbounded" />
   </xsd:sequence>
  </xsd:complexType>
</xsd:schema>
```

Listing 10.3: XSD for the complex type CustomerQuoteInformation

Listing 10.4 shows the XSD that holds the complex type NameAddress.

```
<xsd:schema xmlns:xsd="http://www.w3.org/2001/XMLSchema"
            targetNamespace="http://com/highlight">
    <xsd:complexType name="NameAddress">
        <xsd:sequence>
            <xsd:element name="first" type="xsd:string" />
            <xsd:element name="last" type="xsd:string" />
        </xsd:sequence>
    </xsd:complexType>
</xsd:schema>
```

Listing 10.4: XSD for the complex type NameAddress

Listing 10.5 shows the XSD that holds the complex type Auto.

```
<xsd:schema xmlns:xsd="http://www.w3.org/2001/XMLSchema"
            targetNamespace="http://com/highlight">
    <xsd:complexType name="Auto">
        <xsd:sequence>
            <xsd:element name="VIN" type="xsd:string" />
            <xsd:element name="licensePlate" type="xsd:string" />
            <xsd:element name="model" type="xsd:string" />
            <xsd:element name="year" type="xsd:int" />
        </xsd:sequence>
    </xsd:complexType>
</xsd:schema>
```

Listing 10.5: XSD for the complex type Auto

Static Definition

When you review our sample code for defining Data Objects statically, be aware of naming conventions from the Apache Tuscany project. First, each generated method that gets or sets properties has a name like quote.getQuoteID() in accordance with the following rules:

- The method name begins with the characters *get* (for getting a value) or *set* (for setting a value).

- Append the init-capped property name (use getQuoteID instead of getquoteID, for example).

Second, the name of a generated factory class (in this case, HighlightFactory) is derived from the last qualifier (in this case, highlight) in the target namespace of the XML Schema.

```
<xsd:schema xmlns:bo="http://com/highlight"
            xmlns:xsd="http://www.w3.org/2001/XMLSchema"
            targetNamespace="http://com/highlight">
```

Listing 10.6 shows the Java code.

```java
import java.util.Date;

import commonj.sdo.DataObject;
import commonj.sdo.helper.DataHelper;
import commonj.sdo.helper.XMLHelper;
import commonj.sdo.helper.HelperContext;
import commonj.sdo.impl.HelperProvider;

import com.highlight.CustomerQuoteInformation;
import com.highlight.HighlightFactory;
import com.highlight.NameAddress;
import com.highlight.Quote;
import com.highlight.impl.HighlightFactoryImpl;

public class StaticDataAPI
{
    private HelperContext scope = HelperProvider.getDefaultContext();

    public static void main(String[] args) throws Exception
    {
        HighlightFactory.register(scope);
        Quote quote = HighlightFactory.INSTANCE.createQuote();
        quote.setQuoteID("0001");
        quote.setDateOfQuote(DataHelper.INSTANCE.toDateTime(new Date()));

        CustomerQuoteInformation customerInfo =
            HighlightFactory.INSTANCE.createCustomerQuoteInformation();
        quote.setCustomerInformation(customerInfo);

        NameAddress applicantNameAddr =
            HighlightFactory.INSTANCE.createNameAddress();
        applicantNameAddr.setFirst("John");

        applicantNameAddr.setLast("Doe");
```

Listing 10.6: Java code to define Data Objects statically (part 1 of 2)

```
      customerInfo.setApplicant(applicantNameAddr);

      XMLHelper.INSTANCE.save((DataObject)quote,
         HighlightFactoryImpl.NAMESPACE_URI, "quote", System.out);
   }
}
```

Listing 10.6: Java code to define Data Objects statically (part 2 of 2)

The example

- imports the Java Date class, a set of SDO classes, and a set of application-specific, generated interface classes.

- creates a HelperContext instance, which is how we expect the Apache Tuscany project to register SDO-generated types to the SDO runtime.

- creates quote, which is a Data Object of type Quote. The code uses the Tuscany-generated factory class.

- sets the properties quoteID and dateOfQuote. (SDO uses an Object property of type string to handle an XSD element of type dateTime.)

- creates customerInfo, which is a Data Object of type CustomerQuoteInformation, and references that Object from quote.

- creates applicantNameAddr, which is a Data Object of type NameAddress; sets the properties first and last; and references that Object from customerInfo.

- uses the SDO XMLHelper class to *serialize* (create text from) the quote object and to write that text to the standard output. The arguments are as follows:

    - the Data Object being serialized.

    - the namespace of the root element in the output XML. (That namespace came from the XML Schema definition.)

    - the name of the root element.

    - the output destination.

Here is the serialized XML, formatted for easy reading.

```xml
<?xml version="1.0" encoding="ASCII"?>
<highlight:quote
    xmlns:xsi="http://www.w3.org/2001/XMLSchema-instance"
    xmlns:highlight="http://com/highlight"
    xsi:type="highlight:Quote">
    <quoteID>0001</quoteID>
    <dateOfQuote>2006-11-29T18:35:26.464 EST</dateOfQuote>
    <customerInformation>
        <applicant>
            <first>John</first>
            <last>Doe</last>
        </applicant>
    </customerInformation>
</highlight:quote>
```

Dynamic Definition

Listing 10.7 shows Java code that defines Data Objects dynamically.

```java
import java.io.InputStream;
import java.net.URL;
import java.util.Date;

import commonj.sdo.DataObject;
import commonj.sdo.Type;
import commonj.sdo.helper.DataHelper;
import commonj.sdo.helper.HelperContext;

public class DynamicDataAPI
{
    public static void main(String[] args) throws Exception {

        URL url = DynamicDataAPI.class.getResource
        ("/xsd-includes/http.com.highlight.xsd");
        InputStream inputStream = url.openStream();

        HelperContext hc = SDOUtil.createHelperContext();
        hc.getXSDHelper().define(inputStream, url.toString());

        inputStream.close();

        Type quoteType =
        hc.getTypeHelper.getType("http://com/highlight", "Quote");

        DataObject quote = hc.getDataFactory.create(quoteType);
```

Listing 10.7: Java code to define Data Objects dynamically (Part 1 of 2)

```
quote.set("quoteID", "0001");
quote.set("dateOfQuote", DataHelper.INSTANCE.toDateTime(new Date()));

DataObject customerInfo =
        quote.createDataObject("customerInformation");

DataObject applicantNameAddr =
    customerInfo.createDataObject("applicant");
applicantNameAddr.set("first", "John");
applicantNameAddr.set("last", "Doe");

hc.getXMLHelper.save
    (quote, quote.getType().getURI(), "quote", System.out);

System.out.println("Dear " + quote.getString("applicant/first"));
}

private static HelperContext methodToGetHelperContext() {
    return /* application logic goes here */;
}
}
```

Listing 10.7: Java code to define Data Objects dynamically (Part 2 of 2)

The example

- imports a set of standard Java classes and SDO classes, but no application-specific interface or implementation classes.

- accesses a HelperContext instance, which registers all the retrieved Object types. The SDO specification does not specify the details for creating the HelperContext instance, and the Apache Tuscany project uses SDOUtil.createHelperContext().

- isolates the Quote type from the TypeHelper class.

- creates quote, which is a Data Object of type Quote.

- sets the properties quoteID and dateOfQuote, referring to the properties by name.

- creates the Object customerInfo in relation to the quote Object. The type for customerInfo is identified by the name customerInformation, which is the name of an element in the XML Schema complex type called Quote.

```
<xsd:sequence>
    <xsd:element name="quoteID" type="xsd:string"
                 minOccurs="0" />
    <xsd:element name="dateOfQuote" type="xsd:dateTime"
                 minOccurs="0" />
    <xsd:element name="customerInformation"
                 type="Q1:CustomerQuoteInformation"
                 minOccurs="0" />
</xsd:sequence>
```

The created object is based on the complex type CustomerQuoteInformation.

- similarly, creates the Object applicantNameAddr in relation to the customerInfo Object. The type for applicantNameAddr is identified by the name applicant, which is the name of an element in CustomerQuoteInformation.

```
<xsd:sequence>
    <xsd:element name="applicant" type="Q1:NameAddress"
                 minOccurs="0"/>
    <xsd:element name="dependents" type="Q1:NameAddress"
                 minOccurs="0" maxOccurs="unbounded"/>
    <xsd:element name="auto" type="Q1:Auto"
                 minOccurs="0" maxOccurs="unbounded"/>
</xsd:sequence>
```

The created object is based on the complex type NameAddress.

- sets the properties first and last, referring to the properties by name.

- uses the SDO XMLHelper class to serialize the quote object and to write that text to the standard output. In this case, the namespace is provided by quote.getType().getURI(), which is a dynamic API call that gets the type of the Object as well as the namespace of the type.

Advanced SDO Capabilities in Java

For a Java example that demonstrates more advanced capabilities, see Kelvin Goodson and Geoffrey Winn's two-part article called "SOA and Web Services – What Is SDO?" in *Java Developer's Journal*. Part 1 is in volume 11, issue 12: *http://java.sys-con.com/read/313547.htm*.

Guide to a Subset of the Proposed SOA Standards (WS-*)

A variety of standards are being developed to provide the runtime Quality-of-Service (QoS) support that applications often need when they interact with Web services. The industry refers to this group of specifications by the abbreviation *WS-** (sometimes called *WS splat*). In many cases, the standards affect the composition of SOAP header blocks or runtime configuration files.

Standards are written for multiple purposes. To communicate, in a shorthand way, how a given SOA runtime product uses a set of standards, the vendor may indicate that the product adheres to one or more *profiles*. A profile lists the supported standards and describes *profile requirements*. Each requirement is a rule indicating how some aspect of a given standard applies to any product that is in conformance with the profile. One requirement might state that the product must always use a specific, optional feature of the standard. A second requirement (sometimes called a *restriction*) might state that the product must never use a specific, optional feature of the standard. The purpose of profiles is to make the technology more consistent for a given use and to promote Web service interoperability.

A particularly important profile is the Web Services Interoperability Organization (WS-I) Basic Profile, which clarifies the use of Web Services Description Language (WSDL) and SOAP. For details on that profile and on the sponsoring organization, see the following Web site: *http://www.ws-i.org*.

This appendix lists more than a dozen WS-* specifications in an order that highlights the most widely accepted ones. People may have different opinions on our choices, and the situation will change, but here's our list of greatest hits:

- WS-Addressing

- WS-Policy

- WS-ReliableMessaging

- WS-Security family of specifications

- WS-MetadataExchange

- WS-AtomicTransaction

- WS-BusinessActivity

- WS-Coordination

- Web Services Unified Management (WS-UM), which relies on

  - Web Services Distributed Management (WSDM)

  - WS-Management

- WS-EventNotification, which relies on

  - WS-Notification, including WS-BaseNotification, WS-BrokeredNotification, and WS-Topics

  - WS-Eventing

- Web Services Resource Transfer (WS-RT), which relies primarily on WS-Transfer

- WS-ResourceFramework

- WS-Enumeration

- Web Services for Remote Portlets

- WS-Agreement (which is little used, but quite interesting)

WS-Addressing

Document: *Web Services Addressing (WS-Addressing)*

Purpose: To define a type of endpoint reference that can be included (for example) in a SOAP message header. The endpoint reference allows an SOA runtime

- to direct data to a particular service location or service operation
- to specify that the returned message is destined for a location other than that of the requester

WS-Addressing is the most basic WS-* specification and allows support of advanced message-exchange patterns.

Sponsor: World Wide Web Consortium (W3C)

Link: *http://www.w3.org/2002/ws/addr*

WS-Policy

Document: *Web Services Policy 1.5 – Framework* and
Web Services Policy 1.5 – Attachment

Purpose: To define a way to express Quality-of-Service requirements and capabilities, as needed at design time or run time.

The following example (from a previous version of *Web Services Policy Framework*) expresses a security requirement for requesters of a service.

```
<wsp:Policy
    xmlns:sp="http://schemas.xmlsoap.org/ws/2005/07/securitypolicy"
    xmlns:wsp="http://schemas.xmlsoap.org/ws/2004/09/policy" >
    <wsp:ExactlyOne>
        <sp:Basic256Rsa15 />
        <sp:TripleDesRsa15 />
    </wsp:ExactlyOne>
</wsp:Policy>
```

The ExactlyOne element indicates that a requester must use one of two security algorithms (Basic256Rsa15 or TripleDesRsa15).

As suggested by the example, WS-Policy provides an XML vocabulary and a way to embed that vocabulary in WSDL, UDDI, and other XML-based definitions. However, WS-Policy does not define the meaning of each *policy assertion*, which is content (such as Basic256Rsa15) that expresses a requirement or capability. A policy assertion is defined in one or another *domain*, which is an area of concern such as security, reliability, or transaction control. Many policy assertions are defined in other WS-* specifications.

The main purposes of the WS-Policy vocabulary and the embedded policy assertions are as follows:

- To express what behavior a service expects or prefers from a service requester, beyond the data that fulfills a service interface. A service might require a particular kind of authentication or encryption, for example.

- To express what capability is provided by a service, beyond the data that is returned to a requester. A service might guarantee availability during certain hours of the day, for example.

For further details, see *Web Services Policy 1.5 – Primer*.

Sponsor: W3C

Link: *http://www.w3.org/2002/ws/policy/#drafts*

WS-ReliableMessaging

Document:*Web Services Reliable Messaging Protocol (WS-ReliableMessaging)* and related specifications

Purpose: To specify ways to ensure that messages are delivered without duplication and in the order in which they were sent. This specification is based on work by IBM Corporation and others and is different from WS-Reliability.

Sponsor: Organization for the Advancement of Structured Information Standards (OASIS)

Link: *http://www.oasis-open.org/committees/tc_home.php?wg_abbrev=ws-rx#technical*

WS-Security, WS-Trust, and Others

Document:*Web Services Security* and other specifications

Purpose: To define standards for handling security-related tasks during a message transmission. Among the tasks:

- To invoke *encryption software*, which is used

  - to prevent information from being understood by persons who intercept the message without authorization.

  - to guarantee that the message cannot be *repudiated*, which means that the originator cannot honestly claim (a) that the data was changed in transit, (b) that the data came from a different originator, or (c) that the data was never delivered.

- To retrieve an *encryption key*, which is a value used in the process of encrypting or decrypting data. The source of a key may be a *certificate authority*, which is software whose administrators ensure that a given encryption key is from a given user.

- To ensure that the requester submits authentication details only once, even when the transmitted message will be handled by multiple services.

Sponsor: OASIS, with other specifications sponsored by various corporations

Links: Several OASIS specifications are available:
http://www.oasis-open.org/committees/tc_home.php?wg_abbrev=wss

For Web Services Trust Language (WS-Trust):
http://www.oasis-open.org/committees/tc_home.php?wg_abbrev=ws-sx

For Web Services Secure Conversation Language (WS-SecureConversation):
http://www.oasis-open.org/committees/tc_home.php?wg_abbrev=ws-sx

For Web Services Security Policy Language (WS-SecurityPolicy):
http://www.oasis-open.org/committees/tc_home.php?wg_abbrev=ws-sx

For Web Services Federation Language (WS-Federation):
http://www.ibm.com/developerworks/library/specification/ws-fed

A number of security technologies are useful during message transmission and in other contexts. Among those technologies:

XML Encryption, which is sponsored by W3C:
http://www.w3.org/TR/xmlenc-core

XML Signature, which is sponsored by W3C:
http://www.w3.org/TR/xmldsig-core

Security Assertion Markup Language (SAML), which is sponsored by OASIS:
http://xml.coverpages.org/saml.html

Extensible Access Control Markup Language (XACML), which is sponsored by OASIS:
http://www.oasis-open.org/committees/tc_home.php?wg_abbrev=xacml

Key Management Specification (XKMS), which is sponsored by W3C:
http://www.w3.org/TR/xkms2

WS-MetadataExchange

Document: *Web Services Metadata Exchange (WS-MetadataExchange)*

Purpose: To specify how a requester is to retrieve metadata (data about data) that pertains to a service. The retrieval of metadata precedes the requester's invocation of the service itself and allows the invocation to occur with less likelihood of error. The retrieved data is from WDSL definitions, XML Schema definitions, and WS-Policy statements.

Sponsor: Several corporations

Link: *http://schemas.xmlsoap.org/ws/2004/09/mex*

WS-AtomicTransaction

Document: *Web Services Atomic Transaction (WS-AtomicTransaction)*

Purpose: To handle a two-phase commit process, including the following steps:

1. Services register with a coordinating service, as described in relation to WS-Coordination.

2. Each registered service attempts to update a database. Even if an update is successful, changes are not committed.

3. In response to a poll conducted by the coordinating service, one of two outcomes occurs:

    ◆ Each registered service responds to the coordinating service and indicates that the changes were successful, in which case the coordinating service issues a commit directive to all resource managers that were involved in the transaction.

    ◆ Alternatively, if any service fails to respond or if any response indicates a failure, the coordinating service issues a rollback directive to all the resource managers.

WS-AtomicTransaction also can be used to ensure the integrity of data in memory.

Sponsor: OASIS

Link: *http://www.oasis-open.org/committees/tc_home.php?wg_abbrev=ws-tx#technical*

WS-BusinessActivity

Document:*Web Services Business Activity Framework (WS-BusinessActivity)*

Purpose: To handle a relatively complex business interaction. In many cases, the interaction occurs over a relatively long period of time (days rather than seconds); includes manual steps (such as product manufacture); and requires that failure be followed by a compensating service rather than by a database rollback. WS-BusinessActivity extends WS-Coordination and defines a set of processing states so that (for example) a requester responds appropriately when a service notifies the requester that the service has completed all work.

Sponsor: OASIS

Link: *http://www.oasis-open.org/committees/tc_home.php?wg_abbrev=ws-tx#technical*

WS-Coordination

Document:*Web Services Coordination (WS-Coordination)*

Purpose: To specify how multiple services work together. When WS-Coordination is in effect, a requester interacts with a *coordinator* (or *coordination service*), which is composed of the following:

> • *An activation service:* On invocation, an activation service returns a *context*. A context is data (such as an ID) that must be available to any service that participates in a *coordination protocol*, which is a particular activity such as a database transaction. The requester receives the context from the activation service and uses the context to invite other services to register for (and then participate in) the coordination protocol.

> • *A registration service:* A registration service allows a service that holds a context to register for a particular activity. One effect of the registration is to provide the access details for one or more coordination-protocol services, as described next.

> • *Coordination-protocol services:* The coordination-protocol services provide the functionality that is being coordinated. That functionality might define a transaction from an initial database change, through other database changes, up to and including a subsequent commit, rollback, or compensation.

The specifics of the coordination protocol are usually defined in another standard such as WS-AtomicTransaction, WS-Business Activity, or WS-BPEL. The addresses passed between services conform to the rules describe in WS-Addressing.

Sponsor: OASIS

Link: *http://www.oasis-open.org/committees/tc_home.php?wg_abbrev=ws-tx#technical*

WS-Unified Management (WS-UM)

The Web Services-Unified Management (WS-UM) specification is in development and is expected to extend aspects of several standards, including those described next: Web Services Distributed Management (WSDM) and WS-Management.

Web Services Distributed Management (WSDM)

Document:*Web Services Distributed Management* (several specifications)

Purpose: To specify how one Web service can communicate with a second Web service that in turn accesses a resource such as a printer or storage disk. The first service might receive status information (to determine whether a printer is low on toner, for example) or might control the device remotely (as by shutting off an overheating storage disk).

A Web service can itself be treated as a resource. If a Web service (a resource) processes customer orders, for example, another service might seek information on the number of orders that were handled in recent hours.

Sponsor: Submitted to OASIS

Link: A primer is available, along with the specifications:
http://www.oasis-open.org/committees/tc_home.php?wg_abbrev=wsdm

WS-Management

Document:*Web Services for Management (WS-Management)*

Purpose: To provide rules for exchanging information on resources — from handheld devices to personal computers to large-scale data servers — so that they can be monitored and accessed remotely.

Sponsor: Distributed Management Task Force, Inc. (DMTF)

Link: *http://www.dmtf.org/standards/wbem/wsman*

WS-EventNotification

The WS-EventNotification specification is in development and is expected to extend aspects of several standards, including those described next: WS-Notification and WS-Eventing.

WS-Notification

Document:*Web Services Base Notification* and related specifications

Purpose: To specify how an SOA runtime product handles a *publish-and-subscribe* pattern between a requester (which acts as a subscriber, asking to be notified of an event) and a service (which sends the requested detail when the event occurs, either directly or by way of a separate software unit called a *notification broker*). An event could be (for example) a printer failure or the addition of an entry in an online forum.

WS-Notification provides support for large-scale or complicated applications.

Sponsor: OASIS

Link: Specifications for WS-BaseNotification, WS-BrokeredNotification, and WS-Topics are available:
http://www.oasis-open.org/committees/tc_home.php?wg_abbrev=wsn

WS-Eventing

Document: *Web Services Eventing (WS-Eventing)*

Purpose: To specify how an SOA runtime product handles a *publish-and-subscribe* pattern between a requester (which acts as a subscriber, asking to be notified of an event) and a service (which sends the requested detail when the event occurs).

WS-Eventing is a relatively simple publish-and-subscribe specification.

Sponsor: Several corporations

Link: *http://www.ibm.com/developerworks/library/specification/ws-eventing*

Web Services Resource Transfer (WS-RT)

Document: *Web Services Resource Transfer (WS-RT) and WS-Transfer*

Purpose: To specify a set of rules for accessing, creating, and deleting fragments of named data, so long as the named data (called a *resource*) has an XML representation. The resource can be a Web page, an SOA-registry entry, or other data that is available at an endpoint or can be produced by a Web service.

Sponsor: A group of several corporations has submitted the proposed WS-Transfer standard to the W3C and is working on WS-RT, which will follow.

Links: For WS-RT:
http://schemas.xmlsoap.org/ws/2006/08/resourceTransfer/

For WS-Transfer:
http://www.w3.org/Submission/WS-Transfer

WS-ResourceFramework

Document:*Web Services Resource Framework* and related specifications

Purpose: To specify how an SOA runtime product handles *state information*, which is a set of values that reflect the current status of a client-service conversation, as is needed (for example) when a client adds one product after another to an online shopping cart and later enters credit-card details for payment.

Sponsor: OASIS

Link: A primer is available, along with specifications for WS-Resource, WS-ResourceProperties, WS-ResourceLifetime, WS-ServiceGroup, and WS-BaseFaults:
http://www.oasis-open.org/committees/tc_home.php?wg_abbrev=wsrf

WS-Enumeration

Document:*Web Services Enumeration (WS-Enumeration)*

Purpose: To help guide the processing necessary to transfer large quantities of data from one Web service to another.

Sponsor: Several corporations, which have submitted the proposed standard to the W3C.

Link: *http://www.w3.org/Submission/WS-Enumeration*

Web Services for Remote Portlets

Document:*Web Services for Remote Portlets Specification*

Purpose: To guide the interaction between portals and remote portlets, as described in Chapter 1.

Sponsor: OASIS

Link: A primer is available, along with the specification:
http://www.oasis-open.org/committees/tc_home.php?wg_abbrev=wsrp

WS-Agreement

Document: *Web Services Agreement Specification (WS-Agreement)*

Purpose: To specify a runtime mechanism by which

- a service advertises the capabilities that can be the basis of an agreement

- a requester comes to an agreement with the service for a specified duration

- the agreement is monitored for compliance

The agreement might measure the expected number of requests and the allowed response time for each request in accordance with the network resources available at the time of agreement. The service (acting as a requester of other services) also might use the WS-Agreement mechanism to update agreements with other services in response to changing requester demand, much as a manufacturer updates agreements with suppliers in response to changing consumer demand.

WS-Agreement has not been widely adopted but is likely to become important.

Sponsor: Open Grid Forum (OGF)

Link: At this writing, the most recent draft is *http://www.ogf.org/Public_Comment_Docs/Documents/Oct-2005/ WS-AgreementSpecificationDraft050920.pdf*

You may find a more recent draft by searching for WS-Agreement at *http://www.ogf.org*.

Setup for XPath Practice

If you wish to try out XPath, do as follows:

1. Ensure that your machine has Java installed:

    a. Select **Start > Run**.

    b. Type **cmd** and press **Enter**.

    c. At the command prompt, type the following string and press **Enter**:

    ```
    C:\ java -version
    ```

    d. If the command is unrecognized, continue with the next step; otherwise, continue with step 3.

2. To download and install the Java J2SE Runtime Environment (JRE) 5.0, go to the following Web site and follow the directions there: *http://java.sun.com/javase/downloads/index.jsp*.

3. As of this writing, you can get the required Xalan files (xalan-j_2_7_0-bin-2jars.zip) from the site *http://www.axint.net/apache/xml/xalan-j*. If that site is unavailable, go to the download site for the Apache Xalan project, *http://xml.apache.org/xalan-j/downloads.html*. From there, follow directions to download Xalan.

4. After downloading the files, unzip them to a directory (for example, C:\Xalan).

5. Set up the system variable CLASSPATH on your machine. On Windows XP, for example:

   a. At the desktop, double-click **My Computer** and select **Control Pane**

   b. Select **System.**

   c. Select the **Advanced** tab and from there, **Environment Variables**.

   d. Under **System Variables**, click **New**; name a variable **CLASSPATH**, and, without line breaks, type a **Variable value** such as the following (substituting the directory names from your download, if appropriate):

```
.;C:\Xalan\xalan-j_2_7_0\xalan.jar;
C:\Xalan\xalan-j_2_7_0\serializer.jar;
C:\Xalan\xalan-j_2_7_0\xml-apis.jar;
C:\Xalan\xalan-j_2_7_0\xercesImpl.jar;
C:\Xalan\xalan-j_2_7_0\xalansamples.jar;
C:\Xalan\xalan-j_2_7_0\xalanservlet.jar;
C:\Xalan\xalan-j_2_7_0\\JavaSDK\jdk\lib;
```

6. In a working directory (for example, C:\AAA), create insured.xml, as shown here, and make sure that the first line starts at the first position of the file:

```
<?xml version="1.0" encoding="ISO-8859-1"?>
<!- CarPolicy applicant ->
<Insured CustomerID="5">
   <CarPolicy PolicyType="Auto">
      <Vehicle Category="Sedan">
         <Make>Honda</Make>
         <Model>Accord</Model>
      </Vehicle>
      <Vehicle Category="Sport" Domestic="True">
         <Make>Ford</Make>
         <Model>Mustang</Model>
      </Vehicle>
   </CarPolicy>
   <CarPolicy PolicyType="Antique">
      <Vehicle Category="Sport">
         <Make>Triumph</Make>
         <Model>Spitfire</Model>
      </Vehicle>
      <Vehicle Category="Coupe" Domestic="True">
         <Make>Buick</Make>
         <Model>Skylark</Model>
      </Vehicle>
      <Vehicle Category="Sport">
         <Make>Porsche</Make>
         <Model>Speedster</Model>
      </Vehicle>
   </CarPolicy>
</Insured>
```

7. In the same working directory, create test.xsl, which is an Extensible Stylesheet Transformation (XSLT) style sheet, as shown here:

```
<?xml version="1.0" encoding="ISO-8859-1"?>
<xsl:stylesheet
  xmlns:xsl="http://www.w3.org/1999/XSL/Transform"
  version="1.0">
  <xsl:template match="/">
    <html>
      <head>
        <title>Testing XPath 1.0</title>
      </head>
      <body>
        <p>
        <xsl:value-of select=
"/Insured/CarPolicy/Vehicle[@Category='Coupe']/Make"/>
        </p>
      </body>
    </html>
  </xsl:template>
</xsl:stylesheet>
```

The XPath expression that you will change is in the middle of the file, in quotation marks. You need not change anything else in that file.

8. To open a command window:

   a. Select **Start** > **Run.**

   b. Type **cmd** and press **Enter**.

   At the command prompt, type the following string *on one line*, making whatever changes are needed to correspond with your directory and file names:

```
java org.apache.xalan.xslt.Process
-IN C:\AAA\insured.xml
-XSL C:\AAA\test.xsl
-OUT C:\AAA\test.html
```

If you exclude the line that begins with -OUT, the output goes to the command window.

Press **Enter**. If you included the line that begins with -OUT, inspect the last listed file by opening it in a browser. If you excluded the line with -OUT, you will view HTML tags and will need to locate the data that resides in between the paragraph (<p> </p>) tags, which are inside the body (<body> </body>) tags.

If you are using the files insured.xml and test.xsl as shown earlier, the output displays the string *Buick* for reasons described in Chapter 6.

Revise the XSL and XML files as you wish, testing the effect of different XPath expressions in relation to different XML source.

To rerun the command at the command prompt, click **F3** or the **Up Arrow** and then press **Enter**.

If you are using a browser to review the output, you can click the browser's **Refresh** button to see the last result.

Reference Guide to BPEL 2.0

This appendix describes the Business Process Execution Language (BPEL) 2.0 syntax for

- durations and deadlines

- basic activities

- structured activities

- functions

- additional constructs in the BPEL process

- BPEL extensions to Web Services Definition Language (WSDL)

This appendix uses grammar from the BPEL 2.0 specification (*Web Services Business Process Execution Language Version 2.0*), which is available at the following Web site: *http://www.oasis-open.org/committees/documents.php? wg_abbrev=wsbpel*. Here are some of the symbols and phrases that we reproduced from there:

- *?* means 0 or 1 time. The element or attribute that precedes the symbol is optional and can appear only once.

- *** means 0 or more times. The element or attribute that precedes the symbol is optional and can be repeated.

- *+* means 1 or more times. The element or attribute that precedes the symbol is required and can be repeated.

- Unless otherwise stated in this introduction, an element or attribute that is not followed by one of the aforementioned three symbols (*?* * +) is required and can appear only once.

- | means that the preceding and following characters are alternatives; for example, *yes* | *no* means a choice: *yes* or *no*.

- Various strings mean what they say, though you may need to add spaces or remove hyphens. For example:

    - *activity* is a BPEL activity.

    - *anyURI* is a universal resource identifier (URI); for example, you use a URI to specify the query language in an assign activity.

    - *BPELVariableName* is an XML identifier that is valid for a BPEL variable name; the identifier has no colon, period, or reverse virgule (\).

    - *BPELVariableNames* is a list of BPEL variables names with no intervening commas or other punctuation.

    - *standard-elements* refers to the BPEL elements sources and targets, as described in relation to concurrency (Chapter 7). Those elements are optional.

    - *standard-attributes* refers to the optional attributes name and suppressJoinFailure, as described in Chapter 8. Those attributes are optional.

- Parentheses isolate characters from other characters. In the next example, the for and until elements are alternatives, and a BPEL activity is required.

```
(
    <for expressionLanguage="anyURI"?>duration-expr</for>
    |
    <until expressionLanguage="anyURI"?>deadline-expr</until>
)
activity
```

A function name is followed by a single pair of parentheses, typed as is.

- expr is short for expression:

  - *bool-expr* resolves to *true* or *false*.

  - *duration-expr* resolves to a duration (described later).

  - *deadline-expr* resolves to a deadline (described later).

- *QName* is an XML qualified name, which is an identifier that can include an initial prefix and colon.

- *QName-list* is a list of XML qualified names with no intervening commas or other punctuation.

- *NCName* is an XML identifier that has no colon. (The *NC* came from the phrase *no colon.*)

Most examples do not include namespaces, but the distinction between *QName* and *NCName* gives you additional detail. The name of a port type, for example, is a *QName*, which means that the name can include a namespace prefix. The name of an operation, however, is an *NCName*, which means that the name cannot include a namespace prefix. In this case, BPEL relies on the namespace in a given WSDL definition being identical for the two names.

Durations and Deadlines

The details in this section are usually sufficient for expressing durations and deadlines in a BPEL process. If you need further details, see *XML Schema Part 2: Datatypes Second Edition* at the following Web site: *http://www.w3.org/TR/xmlschema-2.*

For durations:

- A positive duration begins with the letter *P*.

- A calendar-duration subset (for years, months, or days) is composed of integers followed by a capital *Y*, *M*, or *D*:

  - 14Y means 14 years.

  - 9M means 9 months.

  - 5D means 5 days.

- The calendar-duration subsets must be in sequence from the largest to smallest unit of time:

  - P2Y9M5D means 2 years, 9 months, and 5 days.

  - P9M5D means 9 months and 5 days.

  - P5D means 5 days.

  You can skip values but cannot change the order:

  - P1Y5D means 1 year and 5 days.

  - P5D1Y is not valid because years must precede days.

- A clock-duration value begins with a capital *T*, and each subset (for hours, minutes, or seconds) is composed of integers followed by a capital *H*, *M*, or *S*:

  - PT6H means 6 hours.

  - PT9M5S means 9 minutes and 5 seconds.

  - PT5.23S means 5.23 seconds.

- The clock-duration subsets must be in sequence from the largest to smallest unit of time:

  - PT2H9M5S means 2 hours, 9 minutes, and 5 seconds.

  - PT9M5S means 9 minutes and 5 seconds.

  - PT5S means 5 seconds.

  You can skip values but cannot change the order:

  - PT1H5S means 1 hour and 5 seconds.

  - PT5S1M is not valid because minutes must precede seconds.

- You can combine the date and time durations. P4Y2DT5M1S, for example, means 4 years, 2 days, 5 minutes, and 1 second.

- Durations must conform to the XSD data type xsd:duration.

For deadlines:

- You must fulfill either of two formats in full:

    ◆ CCYY-MM-DD

    ◆ CCYY-MM-DDThh:mm:ss

- You can add an optional time zone to either format:

    ◆ the literal *Z* (for Coordinated Universal Time, which is nearly identical to Greenwich Mean Time); or

    ◆ (+ | -) hh:mm, which is an offset from Coordinated Universal Time. The offset is negative from west of the meridian to the international date line and is otherwise positive.

- Include literal hyphens and (for the second format) literal colons and the capital letter *T*.

- Substitute digits for the other characters:

    ◆ CCYY stands for a four-digit year ("C" is for *century*).

    ◆ MM stands for a two-digit month.

    ◆ DD stands for a two-digit day.

    ◆ hh stands for a two-digit hour (0–23).

    ◆ mm stands for a two-digit minute.

    ◆ ss stands for a two-digit second.

- 2109-02-06T09:15:03 refers to 9:15:03 AM on 6 February 2109. The time zone is unspecified.

- 2109-02-06T14:15:03-05:00 refers to 2:15:03 PM Eastern Standard Time on 6 February 2109.

- Deadlines must conform to the XSD data type xsd:date or xsd:dateTime.

Basic Activities

Basic activities (such as receive and invoke) do discrete tasks.

assign

The assign activity copies sources to targets and was described in Chapter 8. As shown later, a *from-spec* describes a source; a *to-spec* describes a target.

```
<assign validate="yes|no"? standard-attributes>
   standard-elements
   <copy keepSrcElementName="yes|no"?
         ignoreMissingFromData="yes|no"?>
      from-spec
      to-spec
   </copy>+
</assign>
```

The from-spec is any of the next from elements.

```
<from variable="BPELVariableName" part="NCName"?>
   <query queryLanguage="anyURI"?>?
      queryContent
   </query>
</from>

|

<from partnerLink="NCName" endpointReference="myRole|partnerRole" />

|

<from variable="BPELVariableName" property="QName" />

|

<from expressionLanguage="anyURI"?>expression</from>

|

<from><literal>literal value</literal></from><from
```

The to-spec is any of the next to elements.

```
<to variable="BPELVariableName" part="NCName"?>
   <query queryLanguage="anyURI"?>?
      queryContent
   </query>
</to>

|

<to partnerLink="NCName" />

|

<to variable="BPELVariableName" property="QName" />

|

<to expressionLanguage="anyURI"?>expression</to>
```

Here's an example.

```
<assign name="DefaultQuoteAssignment">
   <copy>
      <from variable="quoteRequest" part="placeQuoteParameters">
         <query>/quoteInformation</query>
      </from>
      <to variable="highlightQuote" part="placeQuoteResult">
         <query>/quote/customerInformation</query>
      </to>
   </copy>

   <copy>
      <from variable="mvRecord" property="licenseNumber"/>
      <to variable="vehicleLicense"/>
   </copy>

   <copy>
      <from><literal>false</literal></from>
      <to variable="highlightQuote" part="placeQuoteResult">
         <query>/quote/quoteProvided</query>
      </to>
   </copy>

   <copy>
      <from>$input.msgPart/descendant::Make[.="Ford"]</from>
      <to variable="output"/>
   </copy>
</assign>
```

A BPEL engine may extend the assign activity. For details, see your product documentation.

compensate

The compensate activity is available only in a fault handler, a compensation handler, or a termination handler. The activity invokes the compensation handler for each nested scope that completed successfully. We describe this activity in Chapter 7.

```
<compensate standard-attributes>
    standard-elements
</compensate>
```

Here's an example.

```
<scope name="Primary">
    <faultHandlers>
        <catch faultName="QuoteCancelled">
            <compensate/>
        </catch>
    </faultHandlers>

    <eventHandlers>
        <onEvent>
            .
            .
            <scope>
                <if>
                    <condition>$status="cancelled"</condition>
                    <throw faultName="QuoteCancelled" />
                </if>
            </scope>
        </onEvent>
    </eventHandlers>

    <sequence>
        <scope name="StoreQuote">
            <compensationHandler>
                <!- remove the stored quote ->
            </compensationHandler>

            <sequence>
                <!- store the quote ->
            </sequence>
        </scope>

        <scope name="InformCustomer">
            <compensationHandler>
                <!- withdraw the quote by email ->
```

```
            </compensationHandler>

            <sequence>
                <!- confirm the quote by email ->
            </sequence>
        </scope>
    </sequence>
</scope>
```

compensateScope

The compensateScope activity is available only in a fault handler, a compensation handler, or a termination handler. The activity invokes the compensation handler for a specific scope. We describe this activity in Chapter 7.

```
<compensateScope target="NCName" standard-attributes>
    standard-elements
</compensateScope>
```

Here's an example.

```
<scope name="Primary">
    <faultHandlers>
        <catch faultName="QuoteProblem">
            <compensateScope target="StoreQuote"/>
        </catch>
    </faultHandlers>

    <eventHandlers>
        <onEvent>
            .
            .
            <scope>
                <if>
                    <condition>$status="problem"</condition>
                    <throw faultName="QuoteProblem" />
                </if>
            </scope>
        </onEvent>
    </eventHandlers>

    <scope name="StoreQuote">
        <compensationHandler>
            <!- remove the stored quote ->
```

```
            </compensationHandler>

            <sequence>
                <!- store the quote ->
            </sequence>
        </scope>
    </scope>
```

empty

The empty activity is used as a placeholder for other activities or as the source or target of links.

```
<empty standard-attributes>
    standard-elements
</empty>
```

Here's an example.

```
<if>
    <condition>$numberOfDrivers &gt; 5</condition>
    <empty>
        <sources> <source linkName="manyDrivers"/> </sources>
    </empty>
</if>
```

exit

The exit activity ends all processing immediately, without invoking a fault handler or termination handler and without responding in any way to partner services.

```
<exit standard-attributes>
    standard-elements
</exit>
```

Here's an example.

```
<if>
    <condition>$numberOfDrivers &gt; 10</condition>
    <exit/>
</if>
```

extensionActivity

The purpose of an extension activity is specific to a BPEL engine. If an extension activity is not recognized by a BPEL engine, the activity is treated as empty.

```
<extensionActivity>
   <anyElementQName standard-attributes>
      standard-elements
   </anyElementQName>
</extensionActivity>
```

Here's an example of an activity that writes a message to a log.

```
<sequence>
   <extensionActivity>
      <writeToLog>
         <message>Received a new task</message>
         <variable>otherInfo</variable>
         <severity>2</severity>
      </writeToLog>
   </extensionActivity>
</sequence>
```

invoke

The invoke activity invokes a service synchronously or asynchronously and can include fault handlers and a compensation handler. We describe this activity in Chapter 8.

The attribute inputVariable and element toParts refer to the data that the BPEL process sends to the partner service. The attribute outputVariable and element fromParts refer to the data returned in a synchronous invocation.

```
<invoke partnerLink="NCName"
   portType="QName"?
   operation="NCName"
   inputVariable="BPELVariableName"?
   outputVariable="BPELVariableName"?
   standard-attributes>
   standard-elements
   <correlations>?
      <correlation set="NCName" initiate="yes|join|no"?
                  pattern="request|response|request-response"? />+
```

```
      </correlations>
      <catch faultName="QName"?
         faultVariable="BPELVariableName"?
         faultMessageType="QName"?
         faultElement="QName"?>*
         activity
      </catch>
      <catchAll>?
         activity
      </catchAll>
      <compensationHandler>?
         activity
      </compensationHandler>
      <toParts>?
         <toPart part="NCName" fromVariable="BPELVariableName" />+
      </toParts>
      <fromParts>?
         <fromPart part="NCName" toVariable="BPELVariableName" />+
      </fromParts>
   </invoke>
```

Here's an example.

```
<invoke name="RecalculateQuote"
        partnerLink="QuoteManagementPL"
        portType="QuoteManagementPT"
        operation="buildQuote"
        inputVariable="customerQuoteInfo"/>
```

receive

The receive activity waits for a message that matches the detail in the related WSDL operation. We describe this activity in Chapter 8.

```
<receive partnerLink="NCName"
    portType="QName"?
    operation="NCName"
    variable="BPELVariableName"?
    createInstance="yes|no"?
    messageExchange="NCName"?
    standard-attributes>
    standard-elements
    <correlations>?
       <correlation set="NCName" initiate="yes|join|no"? />+
    </correlations>
    <fromParts>?
       <fromPart part="NCName" toVariable="BPELVariableName" />+
    </fromParts>
</receive>
```

Here's an example.

```
<receive name="UnderwritingApprovalResponse"
         partnerLink="UnderwriterPL"
         portType="UnderwriterPT"
         operation="policyEvaluation"
         variable="underwriterResponse">
</receive>
```

reply

The reply activity responds to a message received by one of the following kinds of *inbound message activities (IMAs):*

- receive activity
- onMessage handler (within the pick activity)
- onEvent handler

We describe this activity in Chapter 8.

```
<reply partnerLink="NCName"
    portType="QName"?
    operation="NCName"
    variable="BPELVariableName"?
    faultName="QName"?
    messageExchange="NCName"?
    standard-attributes>
    standard-elements
    <correlations>?
        <correlation set="NCName" initiate="yes|join|no"? />+
    </correlations>
    <toParts>?
        <toPart part="NCName" fromVariable="BPELVariableName" />+
    </toParts>
</reply>
```

Here's an example.

```
<reply name="StatusReply"
       partnerLink="ProcessPolicy"
       portType="NewPolicySystem"
       operation="status"
       variable="statusResponse" />
```

rethrow

The rethrow activity is available only in a fault handler. The activity forwards a fault to the parent scope. If any data was provided in the original fault, the same (unchanged) data is forwarded, too. We describe this activity in Chapter 7.

```
<rethrow standard-attributes>
    standard-elements
</rethrow>
```

Here's an example.

```
<faultHandlers>
    <catchAll>
        <compensate />
        <rethrow name="invalid" />
    </catchAll>
</faultHandlers>
```

throw

The throw activity throws a fault to the parent scope, with or without data. The purpose is to identify a business error. We describe this activity in Chapter 7.

```
<throw faultName="QName"
       faultVariable="BPELVariableName"?
       standard-attributes>
    standard-elements
</throw>
```

Here's an example.

```
<eventHandlers>
    <onEvent messageType="abandonRequestMsg"
             partnerLink="ProcessPolicyPL"
             portType="ProcessPolicyPT"
             operation="abandon"
             variable="abandonVar">
        <throw faultName=" cancelPurchase"
            name="CancelPurchase" />
    </onEvent>
</eventHandlers>
```

validate

The validate activity verifies that the data contained in one or more variables is consistent with the data types used to declare those variables. A data type may be expressed as an XML Schema simple type, complex type, or element; or as a WSDL **message** definition.

```
<validate variables="BPELVariableNames" standard-attributes>
    standard-elements
</validate>
```

Here's an example.

```
<validate variables="applicantInfo spouseInfo"/>
```

wait

The wait activity causes a delay for a specified period or until a specified date and time. We describe this activity in Chapter 8.

```
<wait standard-attributes>
    standard-elements
    (
        <for expressionLanguage="anyURI"?>duration-expr</for>
        |
        <until expressionLanguage="anyURI"?>deadline-expr</until>
    )
</wait>
```

Here's an example.

```
<sequence>
    <!- wait until 6:00 PM Pacific Standard Time
        on 25 December 2010                        ->
    <wait>
        <until>'2010-12-25T18:00-08:00'</until>
    </wait>
    <invoke ... />
</sequence>

<sequence>
    <!- wait for 1 year, 2 months, and 1 hour ->
    <wait>
        <for>'P1Y2MT1H'</for>
    </wait>
    <invoke ... />
</sequence>
```

Structured Activities

Structured activities (such as if and while) specify an order or condition that affects the circumstance for running a set of other, embedded activities. The embedded activities may be basic, structured, or both.

flow

The flow activity embeds activities that run concurrently. We describe this activity in Chapter 7.

```
<flow standard-attributes>
    standard-elements
    <links>?
        <link name="NCName" />+
    </links>
    activity+
</flow>
```

Here's an example.

```
<flow>
    <links> <link name="ApplicantLink" />
            <link name="SpouseLink" />   </links>

    <sequence ... name="Calculate credit report for spouse">
        <sources> <source linkName="SpouseLink" /> </sources>
        .
        .
    </sequence>
    <reply partnerLink="CreditCheck"
            operation="checkFamilyCredit"
            variable="resultSpouse"
            messageExchange="spouse">
        <targets> <target linkName="SpouseLink" /> </targets>
    </reply>

    <sequence ... name="Calculate credit report for applicant">
        <sources> <source linkName="ApplicantLink" /> </sources>
        .
        .
    </sequence>
    <reply partnerLink="CreditAndAccountPL"
            operation="creditCheck"
            variable="resultApplicant"
            messageExchange="applicant">
        <targets>
```

```
            <target linkName="ApplicantLink" />
        </targets>
    </reply>
</flow>
```

forEach

The forEach activity issues the embedded activities as a group, either sequentially or concurrently. We describe this activity in Chapter 8.

```
<forEach counterName="BPELVariableName" parallel="yes|no"
    standard-attributes>
    standard-elements
    <startCounterValue expressionLanguage="anyURI"?>
        unsigned-integer-expression
    </startCounterValue>
    <finalCounterValue expressionLanguage="anyURI"?>
        unsigned-integer-expression
    </finalCounterValue>
    <completionCondition>?
        <branches expressionLanguage="anyURI"?
            successfulBranchesOnly="yes|no"?>?
            unsigned-integer-expression
        </branches>
    </completionCondition>
    <scope>...</scope>
</forEach>
```

Here's an example.

```
<forEach counterName="loopIndex" parallel="yes">
    <startCounterValue>1</startCounterValue>
    <finalCounterValue>
        <query>count(/CustomerQuoteInformation/vehicle)</query>
    </finalCounterValue>
    <scope>
        <assign>
            <copy>
                <from variable="inputRecord">
                    <query>
                        (/CustomerQuoteInformation/vehicle)[loopIndex]
                    </query>
                </from>
                <to variable="currentVehicle"/>
            </copy>
        </assign>
        <invoke name="CheckVehicleWithDMV"
                partnerLink="dmvPL"
```

```
                    portType="dmvPT">
                    operation="retrieveLicenseStatus"
                    inputVariable="currentVehicle"
                    outputVariable="receiveDetail"
          </invoke>
       </scope>
    </forEach>
```

if

The if activity runs an activity if a Boolean expression evaluates to true. The activity may include one or more embedded elseif activities, each with its own Boolean expression, and may include a single embedded else activity.

```
<if standard-attributes>
    standard-elements
    <condition expressionLanguage="anyURI"?>bool-expr</condition>
        activity
    <elseif>*
        <condition expressionLanguage="anyURI"?>bool-expr</condition>
        activity
    </elseif>
    <else>?
        activity
    </else>
</if>
```

Here's an example.

```
<if>
    <condition>
        bpel:getVariableProperty('mvStatusVariable',
                                   'AutoStatus') = 'OWN'
    </condition>
        .
        .
        .
    <elseif>
        <condition>
            bpel:getVariableProperty('mvStatusVariable',
                                       'AutoStatus') = 'INCOMPLETE'
        </condition>
        <throw faultName="IncompleteFault" />
    </elseif>
    <else>
        <throw faultName="StatusFault" />
    </else>
</if>
```

pick

The pick activity waits for one of potentially several events to occur, often including a timeout and always including receipt of an inbound message. We describe this activity in Chapter 8.

```
<pick createInstance="yes|no"? standard-attributes>
    standard-elements
    <onMessage partnerLink="NCName"
        portType="QName"?
        operation="NCName"
        variable="BPELVariableName"?
        messageExchange="NCName"?>+
        <correlations>?
            <correlation set="NCName" initiate="yes|join|no"? />+
        </correlations>
        <fromParts>?
            <fromPart part="NCName" toVariable="BPELVariableName" />+
        </fromParts>
        activity
    </onMessage>
    <onAlarm>*
    (
        <for expressionLanguage="anyURI"?>duration-expr</for>
        |
        <until expressionLanguage="anyURI"?>deadline-expr</until>
    )
        activity
    </onAlarm>
</pick>
```

Here's an example.

```
<pick name="CustomerResponseToQuote">
    <onMessage operation="requestMore"
                partnerLink="ProcessQuotePL"
                portType="ProcessQuotePT"
                variable="furtherConsiderationReq">
        <correlations>
            <correlation initiate="no" set="applicantEMailAddr" />
        </correlations>
        <sequence name="customerWantsUnderwriterToContactPostReview">
            <assign name="copyQuoteForReview">
                <copy>
                    .
                    .
                </copy>
            </assign>
```

```
                <invoke name="underwriterFollowupAndCall"
                        partnerLink="UnderwriterPL"
                        portType=" UnderwriterPT"
                        operation="retrieveAndFollowUp"
                        inputVariable="underwriterReview"/>
        </sequence>
    </onMessage>
    <onAlarm>
        <for>'PT5M'</for>
        <invoke .../>
    </onAlarm>
</pick>
```

repeatUntil

The repeatUntil activity defines a loop that always runs at least once and iterates
until the Boolean expression at the bottom of the loop evaluates to *true*.

```
<repeatUntil standard-attributes>
    standard-elements
    activity
    <condition expressionLanguage="anyURI"?>
        bool-expr
    </condition>
</repeatUntil>
```

Here's an example.

```
<repeatUntil>
    <invoke name="GetUnderwriterWorkLoad"
            partnerLink="UnderwriterPL"
            operation="getWorkLoad"
            outputVariable="underwriterStatus" />
    <condition>
        $underwriterStatus.result &gt; 100
    </condition>
</repeatUntil>
```

scope

A scope activity is a unit of logic that can be compensated without interfering with the
behavior of activities and handlers in other scopes. We describe scopes in Chapter 7.

```
<scope isolated="yes|no"? exitOnStandardFault="yes|no"?
  standard-attributes>
  standard-elements
  <partnerLinks>? ... </partnerLinks>
  <messageExchanges>? ... </messageExchanges>
  <variables>? ... </variables>
  <correlationSets>? ... </correlationSets>
  <faultHandlers>? ... </faultHandlers>
  <compensationHandler>? ... </compensationHandler>
  <terminationHandler>? ... </terminationHandler>
  <eventHandlers>? ... </eventHandlers>
  activity
</scope>
```

Two attributes are available:

- If you set the isolated attribute of two concurrently running scope activities to *yes*, you ensure that there is no difference in the common data available to the two scopes whether the first scope runs before the second or the second runs before the first. The default value is *no*.

- If you set the exitOnStandardFault attribute to *yes*, a BPEL standard fault exits the scope without causing invocation of a fault or termination handler. The only standard fault that is unaffected by this attribute is the concurrency-related fault *bpel:joinFailure*. The default value is *no*.

Here's an example.

```
<scope name="Primary">
  <faultHandlers>
    <catch faultName="QuoteCancelled">
      <compensate/>
    </catch>
  </faultHandlers>

  <scope name="StoreQuote">
    <compensationHandler>
      <!-- remove the stored quote -->
    </compensationHandler>

    <sequence>
      <!-- store the quote -->

    </sequence>
  </scope>
```

```
<scope name="InformCustomer">
    <compensationHandler>
        <!-- withdraw the quote by email -->
    </compensationHandler>

    <sequence>
        <!-- confirm the quote by email -->
    </sequence>
</scope>

<eventHandlers>
    <onEvent>
        .
        .
        <scope>
            <if>
                <condition>$status="cancelled"</condition>
                <throw faultName="QuoteCancelled" />
            </if>
        </scope>
    </onEvent>
</eventHandlers>
</scope>
```

sequence

The sequence activity embeds activities that run sequentially.

```
<sequence standard-attributes>
    standard-elements
    activity+
</sequence>
```

Here's an example.

```
<sequence>
    <!- wait for 1 year ->
    <wait>
        <for>'P1Y'</for>
    </wait>
    <invoke name="ContactCustomer"
            partnerLink="PrintShopPL"
            portType="PrintShopPT"
            operation="sendFormLetterByEmail"
            inputVariable="customerDetail"/>
</sequence>
```

while

The while activity defines a loop that iterates while a Boolean expression at the top of the loop evaluates to *true*. If the Boolean expression evaluates to *false* initially, the activity does not run at all.

```
<while standard-attributes>
    standard-elements
    <condition expressionLanguage="anyURI"?>bool-expr</condition>
    activity
</while>
```

Here's an example.

```
<while>
    <condition>$numberOfDrivers &lt; 5</condition>
    <invoke ... />
</while>
```

Functions

BPEL 2.0 provides two XPath extension functions, each in a specific namespace:

- namespace URI: "http://docs.oasis-open.org/wsbpel/2.0/process/executable"
- usual prefix: bpel

doXSLTransform

The function doXSLTransform lets you transform data from an XML source, as described in Chapter 8.

```
object bpel:doXslTransform(string, node-set,(string, object)*)
```

The parameters are

- a path to the XSL
- a variable that holds the XML source; or an XPath expression that resolves to an element node, which may contain descendants
- optionally, pairs of parameter names and values for use by the XSL

The function returns a result document.

Here's an example.

```
bpel:doXslTransform
    ("urn:stylesheets:AddNewVehicle.xsl", $AllVehicles,
     "NewVehicle", $OneVehicle)
```

getVariableProperty

The function getVariableProperty returns the value of a property. The value may be of a simple or complex type. We describe getVariableProperty in Chapter 7.

```
object bpel:getVariableProperty(string, string)
```

The two parameters must be quoted strings. The first is a variable name, and the second is a property alias.

Here's an example.

```
theAddress = bpel:getVariableProperty
                ("quoteRequest", "emailAddr")
```

Additional Constructs in the BPEL Process

The next sections outline the following, additional constructs:

- compensation handlers
- correlation sets
- event handlers
- fault handlers
- imports
- message exchanges
- partner links
- process
- termination handlers
- variables

Compensation Handlers

A compensation handler is an activity (usually a structured activity) that

- compensates for a change made successfully by the scope

- runs after being invoked by a parent scope

We describe compensation in Chapter 7.

```
<compensationHandler>
    activity
</compensationHandler>
```

Here's an example.

```
<compensationHandler name="RemoveQuote">
    <sequence>
        <invoke name="RemoveQuote"
                partnerLink="QuoteManagementPL"
                portType="QuoteManagementPT"
                operation="releaseQuote"
                inputVariable="quoteDetail" />
    </sequence>
</compensationHandler>
```

Correlation Sets

A correlation set is a list of properties whose values are expected to remain constant throughout a process or throughout a specific scope. We describe correlation sets and their purpose in Chapter 7.

```
<correlationSets>?
    <correlationSet name="NCName" properties="QName-list" />+
</correlationSets>
```

Here's an example.

```
<correlationSets>
    <correlationSet name="Order"
                    properties="customerID orderID" />
</correlationSets>
```

Event Handlers

An event handler is a set of activities that run concurrently with the primary activity of the same scope or, outside a scope, with the primary activity of the process. We describe event handlers in Chapter 8.

```
<eventHandlers>?
    <onEvent partnerLink="NCName"
            portType="QName"?
            operation="NCName"
            ( messageType="QName" | element="QName" )?
            variable="BPELVariableName"?
            messageExchange="NCName"?>*
        <correlations>?
            <correlation set="NCName" initiate="yes|join|no"? />+
        </correlations>
        <fromParts>?
            <fromPart part="NCName" toVariable="BPELVariableName" />+
        </fromParts>
        <scope ...>...</scope>
    </onEvent>
    <onAlarm>*
        (
        <for expressionLanguage="anyURI"?>duration-expr</for>
        |
        <until expressionLanguage="anyURI"?>deadline-expr</until>
        )?
        <repeatEvery expressionLanguage="anyURI"?>?
            duration-expr
        </repeatEvery>
        <scope>...</scope>
    </onAlarm>
</eventHandlers>
```

Here's an example.

```
<process>
    <eventHandlers>
        <onEvent partnerLink="ProcessPolicyPL"
                portType="ProcessPolicyPT"
                operation="status"
                messageType="statusRequestMsg"
                variable="statusRequest">
            <correlations>
                <correlation initiate="no" set="quoteID" />
            </correlations>
            <sequence name="provideCallerTheCurrentStatus">
                <assign name="Assign" validate="no">
```

```
                <copy>
                    <from variable="currentStatus" />
                    <to    variable="statResponse"
                           part="statResult" />
                </copy>
            </assign>
            <reply name="StatusReply"
                    partnerLink="ProcessPolicyPL"
                    portType="ProcessPolicyPT"
                    operation="status"
                    variable="statusResponse" />
        </sequence>
    </onEvent>

    <!- the event fires at 9AM Eastern Standard Time
        on 24 December 2010 ->
    <onAlarm>
        <until>'2010-12-24T09:00-05:00'</until>
        <scope>
            <invoke .../>
        </scope>
    </onAlarm>

    <!- the event fires every 3 hours ->
    <onAlarm>
        <repeatEvery>'PT3H'</repeatEvery>
        <scope>
            <invoke .../>
        </scope>
    </onAlarm>

    <!- the event fires after 5 minutes
        and every day thereafter ->
    <onAlarm>
        <for>'PT5M'</for>
        <repeatEvery>'P1D'</repeatEvery>
        <scope>
            <invoke .../>
        </scope>
    </onAlarm>
    </eventHandlers>
</process>
```

Fault Handlers

A fault handler responds to a runtime error. We describe fault handling in Chapter 7.

```
<faultHandlers>?
    <!- Note: There must be at least one faultHandler ->
    <catch faultName="QName"?
        faultVariable="BPELVariableName"?
        ( faultMessageType="QName" | faultElement="QName" )? >*
        activity
    </catch>
    <catchAll>?
        activity
    </catchAll>
</faultHandlers>
```

Here's an example.

```
<faultHandlers>
    <catch faultName=" cannotCompleteRequest"
        faultVariable="DMVFault"
        faultMessageType="DMVFaultType">
        <reply partnerLink="dmvPL"
        portType ="DMVPT"
        operation="sendDMVRecord"
        variable="DMVFault"
        faultName="cannotCompleteRequest" />
    </catch>
</faultHandlers>
```

Imports

An import element includes a WSDL or XML Schema definition in a BPEL process.

```
<import namespace="anyURI"?
    location="anyURI"?
    importType="anyURI" />*
```

The namespace attribute specifies the namespace of interest; the location attribute indicates where the file resides; and the importType attribute specifies a URI that tells the technology type and version.

Here are two commonplace values for importType:

- For WSDL 1.1: "http://schemas.xmlsoap.org/wsdl/"

- For XSD (XML 1.0): "http://www.w3.org/2001/XMLSchema"

Here's an example.

```
<import namespace="http://www.dmv.org/"
       location="dmv/MotorVehicleRecordsService"
       importType="http://schemas.xmlsoap.org/wsdl/" />
```

Message Exchanges

Message exchanges help you to pair a reply activity with an inbound message activity in unusual cases, as described in Chapter 7.

```
<messageExchanges>?
  <messageExchange name="NCName" />+
</messageExchanges>
```

Here's an example.

```
<messageExchanges>
  <messageExchange name="applicant" />
  <messageExchange name="spouse" />
</messageExchanges>
```

Partner Links

Each partner link identifies the relationship between the BPEL process and a partner service, including the role played by one, the other, or both. We describe partner links in Chapter 7, starting with a review of partner link types.

```
<partnerLinks>?
  <!- Note: At least one role must be specified. ->
  <partnerLink name="NCName"
     partnerLinkType="QName"
     myRole="NCName"?
     partnerRole="NCName"?
     initializePartnerRole="yes|no"?>+
  </partnerLink>
</partnerLinks>
```

Here's an example.

```
<partnerLinks>
   <partnerLink name="ProcessQuotePL"
                partnerLinkType="ProcessQuotePLT"
                myRole="ProcessQuoteRole" />

   <partnerLink name="riskAnalysisPL"
                partnerLinkType="PartnerPLT"
                partnerRole="evaluateRisk" />
   <partnerLink name="QuoteManagementPL"
                partnerLinkType="PartnerLinkPLT"
                partnerRole="storeQuote" />
</partnerLinks>
```

Process

The process element is the topmost definition of a BPEL process. We describe the overall structure in Chapter 7.

```
<process name="NCName" targetNamespace="anyURI"
         queryLanguage="anyURI"?
         expressionLanguage="anyURI"?
         suppressJoinFailure="yes|no"?
         exitOnStandardFault="yes|no"?
         xmlns=
         "http://docs.oasis-open.org/wsbpel/2.0/process/executable">
</process>
```

Here's an example.

```
<process name="ProcessQuote">

   <!- omitted namespaces, as well as
        imports of WSDL and XSD definitions ->
   <partnerLinks>
      <partnerLink name="ProcessQuotePL"
         partnerLinkType="ProcessQuotePLT" myRole="ProcessQuoteRole" />
      <partnerLink name="QuoteManagementPL"
         partnerLinkType="PartnerLinkPLT" partnerRole="partnerRole" />
   </partnerLinks>

   <variables>
      <variable name="quoteRequest"
                messageType="placeQuoteRequestMsg" />
      <variable name="highlightQuote"
                messageType="placeQuoteResponseMsg" />
```

```
      <variable name="buildQuoteReq"

              messageType="buildQuoteRequestMsg" />
      <variable name="newHighlightQuote"
              messageType="buildQuoteResponseMsg" />
  </variables>


<sequence>
    <receive name="processQuoteRequest" createInstance="yes"
            operation="placeQuote" partnerLink="ProcessQuotePL"
            portType="ProcessQuotePT" variable="quoteRequest" />

    <assign name="AssignQuoteReq">
       <copy>
          <from variable="quoteRequest" part="placeQuoteParameters">
             <query>/quoteInformation</query>
          </from>
          <to variable="buildQuoteReq" part="buildQuoteParameters">
             <query>/customerQuoteInfo</query>
          </to>
       </copy>
    </assign>

    <invoke name="CalculateQuote" inputVariable="buildQuoteReq"
            operation="buildQuote" outputVariable="newHighlightQuote"
            partnerLink="QuoteManagement" portType="QuoteManagement" />

    <assign name="AssignQuoteRes">
       <copy>
          <from variable="newHighlightQuote" part="buildQuoteResult">
             <query>/quote</query>
          </from>
          <to variable="highlightQuote" part="placeQuoteResult" >
             <query>/quote</query>
          </to>
       </copy>
    </assign>

    <reply name="processQuoteResponse"
          operation="placeQuote" partnerLink="ProcessQuotePL"
          portType="ProcessQuotePT" variable="highlightQuote" />
  </sequence>
</process>
```

Termination Handlers

A termination handler is an activity (usually a structured activity) that is issued when a running scope is being forced to terminate. We describe termination in Chapter 7.

```
<compensationHandler>
    activity
</compensationHandler>
```

The default termination handler in each scope is as follows.

```
<terminationHandler>
    <compensate/>
</terminationHandler>
```

The effect of the default is to run the compensation handlers of all nested scopes.

Variables

Variables are named data areas. As described in Chapter 7, each is based on a WSDL message definition (called a *message type*) or on an XML Schema element or type. To assign an initial value, include a from-spec, which is described later.

```
<variables>
    <variable name="BPELVariableName"
        messageType="QName"?
        type="QName"?
        element="QName"?>+

        from-spec?
    </variable>
</variables>
```

The from-spec is any of the next from elements, which are also the source for assign activities.

```
<from variable="BPELVariableName" part="NCName"?>
    <query queryLanguage="anyURI"?>?
        queryContent
    </query>
</from>

|

<from partnerLink="NCName" endpointReference="myRole|partnerRole" />

|

<from variable="BPELVariableName" property="QName" />

|

<from expressionLanguage="anyURI"?>expression</from>

|

<from><literal>literal value</literal></from>
```

Here are examples.

```
<variables>
    <variable name="quoteRequest"
            messageType="placeQuoteRequestMsg" />

    <variable name="theAddress" type="xsd:string">
        <from variable="quoteRequest"
            property="emailAddr" >
    </variable>

    <variable name="theAddress02" type="xsd:string">
        <from variable="quoteRequest"
            part="placeQuoteParameters" >
            <query>

                /quoteInformation/applicantEmailAddr
            </query>
        </from>
    </variable>

    <variable name="currentStatus"type="xsd:string"
        <from>
            <literal>approved</literal>
        </from>

    </variable>

    <variable name="myRequestID"element="placeQuote"/>
</variables>
```

BPEL Extensions to WSDL

BPEL provides three extensions to WSDL definitions: *partner link types, properties,* and *property aliases.* Each extension element is in a BPEL-specific namespace.

- For partner link types:

  ◆ Namespace URI: "http://docs.oasis-open.org/wsbpel/2.0/plnktype"

  ◆ Usual prefix: plink

- For properties and property aliases:

  ◆ Namespace URI: "http://docs.oasis-open.org/wsbpel/2.0/varprop"

  ◆ Usual prefix: vprop

Our examples do not show namespace URIs.

Partner Link Types

A partner link type specifies the roles that are enacted during a runtime conversation between the BPEL process and a partner service. We describe partner link types in Chapter 7.

```
<wsdl:definitions name="NCName" targetNamespace="anyURI" ...>

<plnk:partnerLinkType name="NCName">
     <plnk:role name="NCName" portType="QName" />
     <plnk:role name="NCName" portType="QName" />?
  </plnk:partnerLinkType>

</wsdl:definitions>
```

Here's an example.

```
<wsdl:definitions name="properties">

  <plnk:partnerLinkType name="ProcessQuotePLT">
     <plnk:role name="ProcessQuoteRole"
                 portType="ProcessQuote" />
  </plnk:partnerLinkType>
```

```
    <plnk:partnerLinkType name="PartnerPLT">
        <plnk:role name="partnerRole"
                    portType="RiskAnalysis" />
    </plnk:partnerLinkType>

</wsdl:definitions>
```

Property

A property creates a name that refers to an XML Schema type. Creating a property of a given name is a prerequisite to creating a property alias. We describe properties in Chapter 7.

```
<wsdl:definitions name="NCName" targetNamespace="anyURI" ...>

    <vprop:property name="NCName" type="QName"? element="QName"? />

</wsdl:definitions>
```

Here's an example.

```
<wsdl:definitions name="properties">

    <vprop:property name="quote" type="xsd:string" />

</wsdl:definitions>
```

Property Alias

A property alias allows your BPEL process associate a property name with a field in a BPEL variable. We describe property aliases in Chapter 7.

```
<wsdl:definitions name="NCName" targetNamespace="anyURI" ...>

    <vprop:propertyAlias propertyName="QName"
            messageType="QName"?
            part="NCName"?
            type="QName"?
            element="QName"?>
        <vprop:query queryLanguage="anyURI"?>?

            queryContent
        </vprop:query>
    </vprop:propertyAlias>

</wsdl:definitions>
```

Here's an example.

```
<wsdl:definitions name="properties">

    <vprop:propertyAlias messageType="NewPolicyRequestMsg"
                         part="NewPolicyParameters"
                         propertyName="tns:quote">
      <vprop:query>/quote/quoteID</bpws:query>
    </vprop:propertyAlias>

    <vprop:propertyAlias messageType="statusRequestMsg"
                         part="statusParameters"
                         propertyName="tns:quote">
      <vprop:query>/quote/quoteID</bpws:query>
    </vprop:propertyAlias>

</wsdl:definitions>
```

Index